A Woman's Way
to Wisdom

A Woman's Way to Wisdom

through an understanding of her sexuality & relationships

Pamela J. Ball

quantum

LONDON • NEW YORK • TORONTO • SYDNEY

quantum

An imprint of W. Foulsham & Co. Ltd
The Publishing House, Bennetts Close, Cippenham,
Slough, Berkshire, SL1 5AP, England

ISBN 0-572-02767-2

Printed in Great Britain by St Edmunsbury Press, Bury St Edmunds, Suffolk.

CONTENTS

PREFACE

'Believe nothing because it is written in books.
Believe nothing because wise men say it is so.
Believe nothing because it is religious doctrine.
Believe it only because you yourself know it to be true'.

Buddha (c.563-483 BC) [Siddharta Gautama]

When I was first asked to write this book it was suggested that it should be a book which set out my ideas on how to make the best of the potential there is in being a woman – a subject close to my heart. I little thought that, in order to do the subject justice, the writing would be such a fascinating journey. There is so much material left by others who have gone before me that it truly needs to be an encyclopaedia. In my own search for womanhood over the years I have travelled down many pathways to gain some coherence, so it has been a joy to put together a hopefully simplified guide to the labyrinth.

In this task I have been ably assisted, first of all by my team; Fiona, who lost her dissatisfaction with feminism and carefully vetted and edited every word I wrote, and Andrew who, finally understanding the real reason for having undertaken Women's Studies at university, manfully researched most of our sources. Behind them stand many friends and colleagues who have supported, encouraged and kept the show on the road. The biggest debt of all goes to Sue Gardner from the Fawcett Library who knew, without fail, the source material we were looking for, no matter which part of the book we presented to her. Her interest was a huge help. Lastly, we must acknowledge the work of Tessa Rose, my editor-in-chief, who deconstructed and reconstructed the book in its entirety.

Finally this book is dedicated to all those women from the past, the present and the future who dare to be the best they can be.

Introduction

*'To be a woman is something so strange,
so confusing and so complicated
that only a woman could put up with it and,
what is worse, feel happy about it.'*

Any book which presumes to study, or for that matter to understand, woman in all her glory has to look at the status of women in the here and now. Historically, it has not been easy for women to be themselves because, whether we like it or not, for many centuries we have lived in a patriarchal society. However strongly a woman may feel about herself, man's fear – and sometimes her own passivity – has resulted in her acceptance of many misconceptions. There have always been women who have sensed within themselves a deep and abiding awareness of and a passionate commitment to being themselves. In the first section we highlight certain of these women whose efforts to maintain their integrity in this way often ran counter to the prevailing climate of opinion.

In some ways woman has been her own worst enemy. Saddled with the soubriquet of harlot and whore from the beginning of time purely and simply because her sexuality and drive were not understood, it was difficult for her to overcome such beliefs without becoming strident and shrewish in the process. Partly because she herself had not understood her own drives it was difficult for her to give the necessary rational explanations for some of her actions. She could only react to the injustice that she perceived, rather than responding in a mature and focused manner.

The more she was treated as a 'second-class citizen', the more uncomfortable she became. This would result in what today would be called regressive and childlike behaviour but which was eventually to be labelled neurotic. Inevitably, the more her natural urges were suppressed, the more her wild side sought self-expression. In each epoch the suppression forced upon her simply highlighted the blocks to progress she experienced within herself. The more she suffered efforts to control her, the more she reacted.

The concept of the Triple Goddess – understood so well as a fertility symbol by our ancestors – clarifies the three most important ages of woman, the maid, the mother and the crone. These give us a framework for understanding how the feminine and that most mysterious aspect – sexuality – develop. It also gives the opportunity to consider which stage of life we ourselves have reached. These stages are not linear – that is, they do not necessarily progress from one to the other. Aspects of each of the themes of femininity can appear within one another: thus the young woman – the maid – can show evidence of the mother that she can become. She also may show the latent older, wiser woman and her connection with the essential feminine in Sophia, the principle of wisdom. The mother will retain many of the qualities of the young woman she was, and she will also cherish the potential of the person she will become. The crone on the other hand still has opportunities to develop into the wise woman, applying the experience that she has gained in being both maid and mother.

In this book the reader has the opportunity to explore and experiment with each of these aspects, and through them it is hoped she will develop her own magic and mystery. This experimentation means living life with awareness and being conscious that we can choose to change at any moment. Choosing to change means discovering those things that interest you and finding out exactly what needs to be incorporated into your life to enhance it. This is truly the process of self-discovery.

Women have a legacy of achievement and also a legacy of under-achievement, doubt or sinfulness due largely to the way they are viewed by society. Much of a woman's sense of self is also predicated by feelings that are largely to do with hormonal changes. Whenever there are distinct phases to be accommodated, there are also transitions. These are always periods of challenge – puberty, pregnancy, menopause and that most final transition of all, death, have traditionally been perceived as times of trial. As medical science, psychological knowledge and spiritual awareness continue to make great leaps forward, these 'trials' offer opportunities for growth. The stages of transition between child/maid, maid/mother, mother/crone and crone/wise woman can be extremely confusing times when spiritual and sexual aspects get mixed up. They are the rites of passage between the stages of maid, mother and crone, not the stages themselves.

We start the journey through them as though entering at one end of an airlock, taking our early influences with us. As we move through the airlock at our own pace we begin to experience other sensations, ideas and thoughts. These may produce confusion in us as they come up against those old beliefs. The new influences will increasingly begin to have an effect on our thinking until finally we reach the other side of the airlock and emerge from it with a new state of awareness and being. Once we reach the other side, life will never be as it was before. Our ability to deal with the life we must live will depend on the use we make of these times of transition, and the insights that the experiences give us. Any woman who has the vision to confront the issues that arise during these periods of her life is well on the way to developing very necessary self-confidence and emotional maturity. By creating the confidence to be herself she is developing her emotional maturity, and with these two aspects firmly in place she can afford to take risks.

Perhaps one of the most risky aspects of life is that of relationship. Frequently, right from childhood, we are searching for and forming relationships. These relationships often reflect those parts of the personality that we are unable – or rather have not been able until now – to access. Once this is understood, we can then appreciate the idea that gender issues are a great deal to do with the hidden masculine or feminine – the animus/anima. Self-awareness and honesty require that all of us come to know those hidden parts. We must also acknowledge and learn to harness the darker side of ourselves in what has become known as the Dragon and the Witch. The journey of exploration that we have to undertake in order to discover them is fraught with both risks and revelations.

As women we need to understand how to relate to the masculine. More importantly, though, we need to understand how the masculine relates to us. There is, of course, no denying that men are intrinsically different from women and it is the way in which women handle the differences that allows them to express their own story and to find the hidden magic within. Eventually the myths and stories that are created of the conflict between men and women, masculine and feminine, logic and intuition will become unnecessary and redundant.

In the future, men and women may learn to co-operate and collaborate, instead of continually struggling with the polarities and highlighting the imbalance, as has happened until recently. The more we take responsibility for ourselves, the closer we move towards our own spiritual centre. The closer we are to our own centre the more likely it is that we shall take responsibility for our own spiritual progress. Relationships are no longer sought to supply something hidden or lacking in the personality but can be undertaken in a spirit of independence. Two people who have taken the time and made the effort to understand themselves and each other can be mutually supportive in finding their own spiritual centres and exploring the dynamic of a relationship that is full of meaning.

The changes that are made when a wider viewpoint is adopted enable you to explore the way that childhood has affected how you think or feel. Within the framework of this book you are encouraged to explore some of the issues that may be left over from your childhood. By tracing how a child grows up you gain an understanding and appreciation of how difficulties can arise in the relationship with parents or family members. Childhood perception, unless we have the courage to reassess what we have learnt, can colour many aspects of adult life. If we are to create a present that is acceptable, we need to have the right perspective on what has gone before.

Old ideas and concepts do need to be reconsidered at regular intervals if we are to integrate the experiences that we have as we mature. Maturity and responsibility mean that rather than simply dealing with the present, the individual can look to the future – perhaps the best future for the world in which we all exist. Each of us can take the opportunity to create our own future. It is perhaps because the future is not fixed that we can think at this stage of combining the past with all its rich information and the present with its many experiences to create a sustainable future for ourselves. By being prepared to try some of the suggestions contained in the workbook section, you may be able to confront some of the issues that are unique in your own life.

One way in which we can help ourselves to make necessary changes is to use two of the oldest images there are – that of the labyrinth and the spiral. The seven stages of spiritual and psychological growth that lead to wisdom have been represented since time immemorial by the spiral and the seven circuits of the labyrinth. Once we have an understanding of how this works, we can use the knowledge gained from understanding the concepts of the labyrinth and spiral to monitor and assess our own progress; and through it take charge of our future. Through these and other ancient concepts, today's woman can find new ways of growth, and make her life an exciting adventure rather than one of drudgery or difficulty.

Several strands of information and guidance are woven into this book. These are an appreciation of how past, present and future apply to woman; the spiritual and physical aspects that make a woman react the way she does; the seven stages of childhood growth and how these affect us; and the seven stages of spiritual and psychological growth which lead us through to wisdom. The three ages or stages of woman's life give us an easy pattern to follow. If we are truly to fulfil our destiny, however, we must push forward and become wise. The women of the 21st century have an unparalleled opportunity of doing this and stepping into the inheritance of Sophia. Today, as in no other century, many more women have freedom to be themselves. Behind them is a multitude of examples from previous generations, of women whose realization of their potential chimed with the times in which they lived.

It is difficult to know which is cause and which is effect, but historically the problems arising in society over the position of woman echo her feelings about herself. Her search for spirituality very early on led her to seek refuge in religious houses, spiritual marriages or alternative communities. Her search for autonomy led to her developing principles which showed determination and bloody-mindedness, while her search for equality led her to confront misconceptions about her abilities and capacity for knowledge. All the while she has had within her grasp an awareness of her own power. Long ago this power was experienced and recognized in a simplistic fashion in the fertility goddesses.

It is up to the women of the 21st century to look closely at that inheritance and then select for themselves the aspects, qualities and perceptions they wish to develop. The beauty of this process is that we can take the best from each era and make it our own, but equally take pride in what is on offer in our own time.

CHAPTER 1

Aspects of the Triple Goddess

'Women never have young minds.
They are born three thousand years old.'

Every woman reacts and responds to an inner calling which enables her to make the best use of her attributes. This response is so basic that it has become a fact of female existence, an entity that has been worshipped in various forms, initially as the Great Mother, a life-giving power that makes us what we are, and subsequently, perhaps in an effort to understand that power more fully, as the so called 'Triple Goddess'.

Representations of her have been found all over the world and from all periods of history. She crops up with such regularity that we have a very clear idea of the importance attached to her. Although she has gone by many different names, in all cultures claiming her she has appeared as the nurturing, caring, all-encompassing mother figure, sometimes married to the Sky God.

First and foremost she was, of course, a fertility goddess and it was in these terms her followers strove to understand her. This led to a perception of the three aspects which nature manifests – Young, Mature and Old – and it was but a short step to recognition that these aspects were echoed in the phases of the moon cycle. Even without sophisticated measuring implements the ancients recognized the subtle energy changes exerted by the moon and acknowledged them in her changing faces. This led very easily to acceptance of one entity having three faces, each one depicting a different aspect of the phases of existence.

Since Mother Earth was feminine the faces would have to be feminine also and so different goddesses and aspects of the feminine were used to depict each phase. Largely it is the Greek goddesses such as Persephone, Demeter and Hecate that spring to mind when we think of this triplicity; the Celts and other cultures also had their triple goddesses, however. This personalization of the phases of life – or rather the cyclical aspects of birth, life and death (the Maid, the Mother and the Crone) – which women recognized within themselves meant that they were able to relate to certain goddesses at various points in their lives and could pray to whichever one was appropriate.

We will now consider the three faces or aspects of the Triple Goddess as she is represented by three ancient icons of the three principal phases of womanhood: Brighid the Maid, the Virgin Mary, and Hecate. Each of them has something to teach us and qualities which we can utilize.

Brighid the Maid

Brighid is one of the best known personifications of a fertility goddess in her role as Maid. Derived from the Gaelic words Breo-Saighit, her name means 'fiery arrow'. As a goddess she is found in many mythologies including those of Ireland, France and Wales and is the goddess of inspiration, smithcraft and healing. Often symbolized by fire, flames and the hearth, she is also symbolized by water (particularly cauldrons), grain, certain creatures (such as a white cow with red ears, and the swan) and also by various talismans such as the spinning wheel. All these representations are those of a fertility goddess.

She is interesting because she holds such a strong following in both the pagan and Christian traditions. Brighid has many different names and has gone through many different phases in her 'existence'. At present her cult appears to be undergoing something of a revitalization. The sacred flame, initially lit at Kildare (meaning 'Church of the Oak') and tended by her maidens, was later adopted by the Christians, whereupon it was tended by nuns. It was extinguished during the time of the dissolution of the monasteries in the reign of Henry VIII but has lately been rekindled in the belief that, as a sacred symbol of life, it must never be extinguished.

The woman who became known by Christians as St Brigid – and Ireland's most famous woman saint – may have begun life as the last high priestess of Brighid. Brigid (also Bridget, Bride, Ffraid) was held sacred for her charity, miracles and generosity. It is said that she held authority over the bishops in Ireland. If she had indeed been a priestess of the pagan goddess previously, she would have recognized the inevitability of change and the need for transition and would have taught her people to adapt accordingly. Very often when Christianity replaced an established faith it attempted to absorb important aspects of that native religion and culture to limit resistance; one example of this is the Spanish Christians' incorporation of local South American gods and goddesses into their belief system.

Brighid is known as the Two-Faced One, and ruled over the transition between winter and spring, or the transformation of the withered woman of winter into the fair maiden of spring. She was also known as the Lady of the Shores and had dominion over the magical spaces between two states of being. So potent is this image that it was suggested that it was she who acted as midwife at the birth of Christ. However this myth originated, it demonstrates very clearly Brighid's function as both mediator and arbitrator between the spiritual and the physical.

In pagan terms, Brighid is both a triple goddess in her own right and one aspect of the greater Triple Goddess. Her domain is multifarious; she supervises creativity, poets, poetry, prophecy and the arts; she oversees blacksmiths, goldsmiths and household crafts, thus balancing masculine and feminine occupations; and she superintends fertility, healers, medicine and spiritual healing. She is also recognized in her aspect of the 'Wild One', an image which her Christian adherents have exchanged for the principle of purity.

As women begin to reclaim their power and recognize the essential energy within, some are prepared to accept Brighid as an icon of femininity. By recognizing their ability to cross between the physical and spiritual realms at will, women can model themselves on figures such as Brighid. Whether you believe in her magical side – as do pagans and neopagans – or in her more spiritual side, contemplation of her story and her personality will put you in touch with the basic awareness we need to reach an understanding of the self and the world beyond.

At the back of the book you will find two different ways of working with the energy which Brighid embodies.

The Virgin Mary, the Mother

In considering the second aspect of the Triple Goddess, that of the mother, we cannot do better than contemplate that icon of femininity beloved of the Catholic Church, the Virgin Mary. The basic prayer, *Hail Mary*, is addressed to the Mother of Christ in much the same way as the pagan goddesses would have been petitioned by their followers. Many scholars believe this was an effort by the Mother Church to accommodate the pagan practices of the people they converted. Others consider that Mary is petitioned because of her special status as the Mother of God. In a religion as outwardly patriarchal as Catholicism, one of the central issues is still that of Mary's place in the hierarchical structure.

Mary as Madonna, Lady of Heaven, Mother of Christ, was

not a goddess – that is, she did not have divine status. However, in Gnostic thought (the knowledge of spiritual mysteries) it is felt that Mary, being human, was 'overshadowed' by, or perhaps had to become intimately at one with, the spiritual aspects of Sophia, who was known as the Consort of God and therefore not mortal. Thus a man who was both divine and human could be born. This is not an easy concept to understand until one remembers that, even in pagan thought, there had to be a uniting of sacred and secular elements to ensure the continuation of fertility and prosperity.

Most of the fertility rites of ancient times highlighted the idea of a union between the spiritual (sacred) and the physical (secular). This mystical union was achieved – often with some difficulty – and symbolized by sexual union, by a High Priestess, earthly representative of the Goddess (Mother Earth), and her priest. So, at the moment of the conception of Christ – apparently without human agency – Mary was a living embodiment of the same Sophia who became known as the Concept of Wisdom.

For the Christian religion, it is worthwhile remembering that 'virgin birth' suggests the total purity of the woman concerned. Ordinary men and women coupled through lust. Sex, therefore, was considered sinful. Mary was, because of the Immaculate Conception and Virgin Birth, without sin, and hence had overcome the problems inherent in her sexuality. Right from the beginning the Church scribes had held Eve responsible for Man's fall from grace, and made the connection between her sexuality and 'wrongdoing'.

This attitude is very different from that associated with the ancient concept of virgin. The term 'Holy Virgins' was applied to the harlot priestesses of Babylonian Ishtar, Phoenician Asherah or the Greek Aphrodite. These women were seen as 'teachers of the soul' and in this sense were true seductresses, leading men back to their own beginnings. The title 'virgin' did not mean virginity as we understand it today; it meant 'unmarried'. The 'Holy Virgins' were expected to dispense the grace of the Mother Goddess and – through love by sexual worship – to heal; to foretell the future; to perform sacred dances; to weep for the dead and to become 'Brides of God'.

As part of their initiation or rite of passage into womanhood, every woman in 5th century (BC) Babylon was expected to go once to the temple of Aphrodite, also known as Ishtar or Inanna, and wait there until a man gave her a silver coin. She was then to go with him and have sex outside the temple. Aphrodite, as goddess of love, is also goddess of prostitutes – brothels often displayed statues and figurines of her. Many of the models who posed for statues of the goddess were prostitutes; that is, women who were free with their sexual favours.

The New Testament story of the penitent whore whom Jesus protected when others would throw stones at her, demonstrates a difference in thinking from that evident in the Old Testament. In pre-Christian times a woman was encouraged to make use of her innate sense of self in a sexual way and was not judged adversely for doing so. Christian compassion and pity have done women no favours, and have not helped her to feel comfortable with her sexuality or that of other women.

The early Christians had other plans for a woman's virginity, considering it to be a valid way of serving God, and even more valid if suffering was also involved. Female suffering was thought to expiate sin, as various examples show. Many of the early women of the church were tortured in ways that were also assaults on their womanhood. Agatha's breasts were cut off. Apollonia's teeth were drawn, Juliana was shattered on a wheel then plunged into a lead bath. Euphemia was tormented. It is said that fasting rid her of the 'curse of Eve', probably a reference to amenorrhoea (lack of menstruation), which would have resulted from the extreme deprivation she suffered.

Thus we have two distinct attitudes to the feminine. One is that the ideal woman must be without sin, and this in Christianity can only refer to Mary as Mother of God, and the other that somehow women are to be feared and are – in whatever way – evil.

We have in the Virgin Mother as adopted by the Christian world the idea of blameless nurturing or a love that is non-judgmental and cannot be measured – that is unconditional. Mary would have been well aware of her position as the Mother of Christ, and would also have recognized within herself a deep calling to the principle of Universal Love.

Later Christian artistic representations of Mary as an icon of motherhood depict her as Queen of Heaven, the Mater Dolorosa weeping for her son and as the Seated Madonna holding her baby, often showing the moon and stars, suggesting acknowledgement of her connection with the Moon goddesses, at least in the mind of the artist. All of these representations of aspects of motherhood are seen also when the Triple Goddess is represented in other religions, showing the universality of the concept of Mother as Goddess and Goddess as Mother.

The concept of the darker more frightening side of the Mother Goddess is well depicted in the Greek goddess, Hera, wife of Zeus and also his sister, who was made extremely jealous by his many affairs. This aspect of vengeful mother is not quite the same as that of the Dark Goddesses seen in the Crone, although certain characteristics are similar.

Hecate the Crone
The similarity between all of the so-called 'Dark Goddesses', or crones, is phenomenal and shows how pervasive this image is. For

our purposes when considering the Crone we concentrate mainly on the Greek goddess Hecate and her story, because it is so well known.

Her name comes initially from 'heq', which means matriarch and harks back to her probable Egyptian origins as keeper of 'mother's words of power' (the hekau). In Egypt the Egyptian midwife goddess was Hequit or Kekat, which gives us a link to Brighid in her role as Christ's midwife.

Hecate was herself one part of the threefold (Triple) Goddess. She was also the Goddess of the Three Ways set to guard three-way crossroads and therefore ultimately the correct decision. The original female trinity ruled Heaven, Earth and the Underworld and it is this Crone aspect as guardian of the Underworld that is given prominence even today. Hecate herself was especially responsible for the rites of magic, divination and meeting with the dead, which is why in modern times she is accepted as queen of the witches. It was believed that dogs were able to see her as she moved about the Earth at the dead of night. At the time of the full moon offerings were left at her shrines.

Hecate had real power, not power that was vested in her by another authority. Just as she acted as midwife into this life, she acted as midwife into the next and therefore ruled death. She does not seem to have judged or challenged men, nor does any man seem to have tried to bring her into submission. In fact, this is a quality shared by many of the 'Dark Goddesses'. None of them had been given power as such – they had either negotiated it or had developed it for themselves.

Each culture has its own version of the Crone aspect, for instance Kali of the Indian pantheon or the many dark Goddesses of the pre-Islamic world such as Ereshkigal of ancient Sumeria, Lilith of ancient Israel and Holle of northern Europe. Kali owed allegiance to no-one, but if one dared to dance with her she would answer one's supplication. She was also capricious and unpredictable. Ereshkigal, Inanna's sister or sister-in-law, was supreme goddess of the underworld and ruled death. When angered, her face grew livid and turned black.

Lilith also ruled death as a natural function of her concern with life from creation to destruction. She judged men and, not troubling to command them, she nevertheless challenged their authority when they attempted to command her. She also used her seductive powers to good effect. She, like Ereshkigal, acknowledged and gave vent to her displeasure without request for forgiveness. Additionally, she was compassionate to those women and children who acknowledged and honoured her.

As Crone, Holle was viewed as the Queen of Winter, and in Germany was called 'The Queen of the Witches'. It is said that she shakes her bed till the feathers fly to make it snow. Like all the dark Goddesses, she would reward diligence with her favours, but would punish laziness. It is interesting that the representation of the Black Madonna at Czestochowa in Poland is beloved of Catholics and of the present Pope, without some of them perhaps realizing or fully giving due regard to where the image may come from.

As one of the models for today's woman, Hecate has been appropriated by the Wiccan religion, whose practices include witchcraft. For many, therefore, she will not seem to be the right representation of the Goddess to address for assistance. Some women may fear her power, others will doubt their own abilities and yet others will fear retribution. If Hecate does not seem appropriate to approach directly, another personification of the Crone might be used. As with Brighid, a simple form of supplication is given later (see page 305).

When we are aware, through understanding, of how powerful and yet destructive our own energy can be, we will begin to appreciate the use of our personal magic as a tool for the Greater Good and learn to turn our negativity into positive action.

We, as modern-day women, recognize that the ancients instinctively gave representation to the phases of the moon through their images of the Triple Goddess and at the same time acknowledged their own fertility rites. There is something mystical and magical in looking at femininity in this way, and it also offers us the opportunity of learning about our own essential phases of existence and our growth to maturity. Geoffrey Chaucer, in his treatise *The Maid, The Mother and the Gudewife*, written in the 14th century, paid due regard to the idea of women's lives being cyclical and having their own rhythm. We would do well to follow that example.

CHAPTER 2

From Maid to Wise Woman

*'All womanhood is hampered today
because the world on which it is
emerging is a world that
tries to worship both virgins and mothers
and in the end despises motherhood
and despoils virgins.'*

Women throughout the ages have been accused of being changeable and capricious, yet when we look at our lives today in a very practical fashion we can still discern a pattern to our growth of awareness. From the instinctive behaviour of the Maid, we move through the knowledge of the Mother to the wisdom of the Crone. Add to these the handling and understanding of the transition stages which we now call Puberty, Pregnancy, the Menopause and Death and a woman's journey to herself has many recognizable themes and milestones. In setting out these themes in the following pages we are walking in the steps of those women of old who, like us, had their own fears to overcome and battles to win. We start this journey with a brief comparison of the practical aspects of the medieval and the modern-day maid.

The Maid
In medieval times a maid or maiden was a young girl who had not yet been exposed to the vicissitudes of life outside the family. She was expected to defer to her more experienced elders (to be submissive), was often likely to have her innocence and purity

protected, was required to remain a virgin and was expected to tame her spirit until such times as a suitable husband was found for her. In the meantime she would carry out whatever tasks were appropriate – whether she was nobly born or otherwise – to assist in the running of the household, hovel or castle and also learn her craft for her future life. Due regard would be paid to the spiritual and instinctive side of life, in that she would experience the natural cycles of life in the births and deaths around her and would be taught of Man's relationship with God.

At this stage in her life a young woman would learn what was appropriate behaviour in her society. She would no doubt spend a considerable amount of time daydreaming about what was to come and even creating fantasies about how life might be in the future. These last two activities were very much private and conducted inside herself and were probably only shared with those of a similar age. One can only assume that she would dream of a knight in shining armour who would whisk her away from the life she knew.

In many respects the teenagers of today are little different from their medieval counterparts. Hopefully, they too start out with awareness that their elders seem to know more than they do, they are innocent of the ways of the world and their minds are not yet polluted by too many negative issues. They, too, will daydream and fantasize about their lives and their eventual partners, although their objects of adulation will be pop and film stars. Such fantasies and dreams of idols are used quite frequently in the transition stage as teenagers grow in maturity and awareness. The pursuit of the unattainable is a necessary part of growing up, and is only a block to progress if it continues too long.

In one important respect the situation of girls in today's more permissive society is very different from that of the past – near and distant – when virginity was a prized possession. Secrecy, confusion and fear are associated with the first sexual experience of most girls, as well as discomfort and disappointment. In today's society a problem will arise if there cannot be openness and clarity about this. The young person does need to know the facts and dangers and how to prevent the avoidable consequences, and ideally these should come from older friends and siblings, sympathetic parents and teachers. Equally, if the young person wants to wait until she feels sexual activity is right, her innocence and integrity should be respected. Chronological age is not necessarily important except from a legal standpoint, but emotional maturity is, and allowing the young person to wait enables her to become a lot wiser and to cope better with the experience.

It can seem as though learning how to handle the first phase of womanhood – being a maid – is all about avoiding disappointment and hurt. In many ways this time should be one of wonder and magic. Dreaming of all the things that 'one day' you will do or be, exploring all the potential that lies dormant, experimenting with new-found knowledge and awareness gives an exciting quality to life which can lead to a lifelong curiosity about things that really matter to you.

This curiosity can extend to the way other people live, their systems of belief, why people think the way they do, how they reached their conclusions and what sorts of beliefs and constructs are appropriate. As well as coming to terms with bodily changes and with her sexuality, every maid needs to learn how to handle her relationship with her own spirituality. This process is as valid today as it was in medieval times.

Almost all religions highlight not only a basic conflict between the masculine and feminine, a subject dealt with elsewhere in this book, but also an apparent conflict between the 'good' and 'evil' in women. This is polarized as light and dark, passive and passionate, virgin and whore, Eve and Lilith, sexuality and spirituality and numerous other opposites. Every woman must learn to reconcile the opposites that co-exist within her, and may very well spend a lifetime doing it.

The young woman will often first experience this dichotomy within herself as a deep yearning that she does not recognize or understand. This yearning seems to belong both within herself and beyond, to be a search for a partner or mate, but at the same time to reflect a need for solitude. It also seems to be a deep welling anger or passion and yet is also a still, quiet space. It is an energy that is uncontrollable yet must be controlled. All of this occurs as she catches glimpses of a seemingly unattainable power above and beyond herself. Convention teaches that such power is dangerous and must be suppressed, or at least managed. She recognizes it as an integral part of herself, alarming not only herself but also others around her. Small wonder, then, that she might try to close down on something which she perceives as negative or divert it into sexual activity and so-called 'wild child' or inappropriate behaviour.

Such wildness, as we shall see, is a facet of all passionate and 'dark' Goddesses, and is only inappropriate when it occurs at the wrong time and in the wrong place, not when it is properly handled. Controlling this aspect will start our maid on the path to her eventual destiny, that of a woman who is secure in her own knowledge, power and spirituality.

Spirituality may be defined as the connection between one's concept of oneself as a physical being and the ultimate power that is available to everybody. Whatever name it is given – and there are many – when this connection is made there is a strong sense of knowing and belonging to something greater than oneself. Women tend to experience this sense of knowing and belonging more strongly than do men, have access to it through their intuition and are able to use it to a greater or lesser degree in their lives.

If our young lady is to be able to develop her own power and spirituality in a way that is appropriate for today's world, then the first thing she must do is to learn to trust her own intuition. For that she must discover and strengthen her connection firstly with her inner self and then with her own concept of the Ultimate.

When, for instance, she discovers a side of her nature which is passionate (about boys, animals, ecology or whatever it might be), she should stop for a moment and let herself feel the energy within. Hopefully, she will not want to suppress this but will be prepared to monitor and channel it in a way that is appropriate for her. As she practises, whether by words or actions, her intuition and awareness will expand. She will gradually become more adept and will be able to speak her truths with conviction. This does not necessarily mean that she must do this stridently and 'with attitude', as the saying goes, but quietly and with dignity, allowing her passion to speak for itself. She may occasionally make mistakes, but she will learn from these.

Dreamscapes

Because she is taking in and uncovering so much information at this time, our maid will often find her sleep taken over by dreams. These will help her to handle the energies within. Dreams of a sexual nature can often be interpreted as trying to achieve a balance between the opposites we have already noted and are a way of allowing the girl to come to terms with herself as both a newly awakened sexual and a spiritual being.

From a sexual point of view, she is learning to understand her own need of companionship, closeness and comfort and how to obtain it from those around her. Many of her dreams will echo the intensity of feeling she has about these people – both male and female – and erotic dreams will often demonstrate how to work with those feelings, without causing harm to anyone else.

From a spiritual viewpoint she is learning just how vast is the energy and power available to her, and how she must handle this vastness. It is not helpful to get caught up in either the sexual or spiritual polarity of being, for a woman must learn to reconcile them and become complete in the process.

The Mother

In today's society there is a tremendous blurring of the roles that a woman undertakes as she moves through life. The phase of maid is traditionally ended by a woman's first pregnancy when the transition to mother begins. Yet, many women today choose not to have children, but to fulfil their mothering role in other ways.

As we shall see in Chapter 10, single women have often been regarded with suspicion, but still will often fulfil the role of mothering through their spiritual awareness, as did Mother Teresa of Calcutta. They may also find fulfilment through careers as carers or through, for instance, voluntary work. Nurturing is such a natural part of a woman's make-up that generally she will find a way of expressing this side of herself. Today, particularly as women become – at least in the Western world – more independent, the need to marry and procreate is not so pressing. The freedoms won are not to be exchanged lightly for the responsibility of a family.

Previously there was quite a clear-cut division between a woman's working life and her life as mother. Nowadays many mothers continue with their careers through choice or economic necessity; there can be considerable conflict as working mothers juggle these two roles. Traditionally, the attributes of the 'good' mother were warmth, patience and a nurturing disposition that manifested in support of the husband in his endeavours and always putting him and the children first. In Western societies until relatively recently it was largely accepted that the woman would sacrifice her own career, possibly returning to work –

usually part time – after her children were grown-up and had left the parental home. This aspect of self-sacrifice was extolled as a virtue and accepted as the norm.

In poorer societies, children were – and in many cases still are – seen as an insurance against the future, and giving birth to large numbers of children was accepted as making basic economic sense, in that those who did not die from disease and deprivation would support their parents later. Birth control measures introduced by social reformers and aid workers often did not take account of this way of thinking.

From the needle-workers of the 19th century to the part-time workers of the 20th, women in particular have been notoriously badly paid. This is largely still true today not only in terms of monetary payment, but also with regard to benefits and privileges such as holiday and sick pay, company cars and pensions.

In the period between the two World Wars and immediately after the end of hostilities in 1945, women who had willingly taken jobs previously performed by men – and thus become aware of their own abilities – were expected to return to the home and accept that they were best suited to the role of wife and mother. This resumption of the status quo caused heartache to many women, seemingly putting paid to hopes they had of attending to their own needs. The choice was clear-cut: career or motherhood. Nowadays the pendulum is swinging towards a position where a woman can at least contemplate having both.

Women still bear the larger share of childcare responsibility and are often forced into finding the middle ground between home, office and children. A woman still, therefore, stands in danger of losing her identity or her sense of self and must take care, while paying due regard to her position as mother, to ensure that other aspects of her character are not smothered and forgotten. Today a good mother is one who while having the best interests of her children at heart also recognizes the need to use the resources she has, which may well be her status, her own financial security and even – if it suits her purpose – former lovers and contacts.

Motherhood

The woman in search of self needs to define for herself what she regards as motherhood. For instance, a mother who considers herself to be perfectly adequate with a certain number of children may have difficulty in adjusting to the additional demands of a new baby, but may relish the thought of that baby growing into a toddler or older child. Conversely a woman who has found that she is an archetypal earth mother, enjoying suckling and nursing her babies, may discover that she has difficulty in dealing with her children when they are less passive.

As mother, she often also has to pay more attention to her principles and beliefs as she becomes aware of her responsibilities towards the new beings she and her partner have created. The values and responses she cherished as a young woman may have to change in the light of her experiences as a mother. For example, state education may have seemed perfectly adequate before she became a mother, but now she discovers it is not fulfilling her children's needs. Does she then ensure that her children receive additional coaching; fulfil those needs at the expense of her own career; campaign for better education; or do all three? There is obviously no right or wrong answer to her dilemma, but she can, and indeed should, do what she feels is most empowering for her. It will depend on her personality, and how far she dare push her own boundaries, as to how much she can do. Many women have found an inner strength they did not know they possessed when they take action on behalf of their children.

Another way in which a woman may be changed by having children is when she finds that pregnancy or motherhood is putting at risk her own health or that of her children. Women with multiple sclerosis, for instance, may find that their condition worsens considerably during and after pregnancy. While some may consider the difficulties worthwhile and develop coping strategies, others may not and may truly suffer as a consequence.

Modern medicine is able to widen the options for such women, who may now be encouraged to make a decision for themselves as to whether they wish to undertake pregnancy in the light of what they feel they and their partners can manage.

The birth of a handicapped child can also have devastating consequences for a mother. Always there will be negative thoughts: 'Was it my fault?' 'Was it something I did/did not do that has caused this?' 'Is my family to blame in some way?' In such a circumstance a mother's natural self-sacrifice is called for and she must find the strength and tenacity to cope. It is often when she learns to call on a power beyond herself that she will find a faith and a spirituality of which she was unaware.

On purely mundane levels the growing family also changes a mother. The sweet little smiling child may well turn into a raging inferno of contradictions and difficulties. In this day and age young people are faced with very different challenges to previous generations, and parents must guide their young people through the minefield of sex, drugs and other dangers in a way that has not had to be done previously.

All too often information and knowledge is difficult to find, and when a mother is trying to help her youngsters through to self-awareness she may well find herself constantly questioning her values and beliefs. Her growing teenage daughter may, for instance, cause her no little concern as she matures into womanhood. Petty jealousies, lack of understanding and recognition of the opportunities that have been lost – or are to come – can sour the relationship for both mother and daughter.

If it is possible to shift the relationship from that of principally mother and daughter to one where friendship and respect for each other as individuals is paramount, the development process that each woman is going through may be helped.

Mothers have many opportunities for learning and reaching beyond their own boundaries, self-imposed or otherwise, within the family. It is all too easy to feel trapped within this framework and to blame others for that entrapment. Often it is only with hindsight that we recognize that we could have been stronger, more tolerant, happier or whatever. The idealized vision of the fecund Earth Mother is very seductive both to men and women, and it is an important one in every woman's makeup. However, it does need to be acknowledged that motherhood seldom attains that idealized state, and certainly not when the woman herself is beset by fears and doubts. It is only by facing these doubts that a mother will be able to find her true self. Perhaps the most important aspect of this learning is that, as so often, there is no right or wrong answer.

Often it is only in the face of adversity or a major trauma possibly involving the family that a woman becomes aware of her ability to make changes in her life as a mother. A miscarriage, post-natal depression or the death of a beloved child may open the door to a void of depression which seems unending and is only alleviated when there is a realization of the vastness of the universe and the smallness of the individual. It may be that not until she loses her own mother will a woman question the validity of her own beliefs. It may even be not until she reaches the menopause and the children have left home – perhaps to have children of their own – that a woman has the opportunity to assess her life as a mother, but assess it she will.

Almost inevitably, she will find herself lacking or inadequate, maybe because she has been accustomed to thinking about herself in these terms. This sense of inadequacy probably stems from the fact that she is not making use of all aspects of her personality and has little to do with her competence as a mother. At this point she *can* firmly grasp with hands and heart the notion that, as mother, she has done the best she can and been the best that she could be and is ready to move on to experience different awarenesses. In doing this she is 'owning' being a mother, and taking responsibility for being the woman she has become. It is important that she acknowledges that she feels a sense of inadequacy but moves through it to where she feels stronger about herself.

After the birth of a child, many women find that their sexuality no longer operates in quite the same way as it did before. This is hardly surprising. Much has been made of the idea of the business tycoon whose libido disappears in proportion to the effort he puts into creating an empire for himself. His energies are concentrated on the job in hand, often to the exclusion of all else. So it is with a mother who has to be aware of her many responsibilities within an ever-changing environment. Having achieved the goal of motherhood, her body needs to recover its equilibrium or natural rhythm and often this will necessitate foregoing sexual activity for a while. Often affection and support may be enough to fulfil her needs at this time, though not of those of her mate and partner. Should there seem to be problems in this area, it might be wise to seek counselling, although only if both partners are willing. Often there are ways of compromising that neither partner may have considered.

One aspect of mothering – or perhaps, more correctly, non-mothering – can occur when a mother is either forced or decides to give up her children. This can come about for many reasons. It may be that being a single mother – either through choice or circumstance – becomes too difficult for her or that her status within the family group changes radically and she feels she must make the sacrifice of letting the child go. It could perhaps be that a disability, handicap or illness – either in herself or another member of the family – renders looking after her child or children impossible, or quite simply that her ability to nurture and care for her family is curtailed in some way.

When, for instance, she is deemed by an external authority to be an unfit mother or when the fight to maintain the family unit becomes too difficult, the decision to let go is not easy. This course of action results in the necessity to grieve, in precisely the same way as if she had lost her child or children through death. Indeed, it can sometimes be even more difficult, because in death there is a finality, whereas when mothers still have some contact with their children each parting can be filled with grief. For both parents this grief can often turn to bitterness and blame as they struggle with their sense of loss and deprivation. Father may be losing a wife, the security of a known way of life or possibly constant contact with his children. Mother may be taking on different responsibilities and have to give up cherished dreams of a stable family life. The children may feel they are losing parents, stability, friends and security.

Dreamscapes

During motherhood the focus of a woman's dreams and aspirations tends to move away from herself and to centre on her children's future – how and what they will be or will be like – and what part she will play in that future. She will often dream of her mother and perhaps come to an understanding of why the latter reacted in the way she did during her own formative years. If great emphasis is placed on the nurturing side of her character in waking life, mother may find herself coming to terms with other aspects of her personality through dreams. She may move towards balancing her personality by beginning to understand the positive and negative sides of herself, or perhaps the archetypes of femininity mentioned elsewhere.

Dreams often perform the function of trying to compensate or instruct. Frequently the first warning of the next stage of growth, that of moving into Mature Woman or Crone, occurs in dreams. The image of Earth Mother or mother figure, which so often occurs in dreams at this time, subtly changes from a symbol of fertility to a figure of wisdom.

The Crone or Hag

In this phase a woman is usually portrayed as wizened, gnarled and old. She fits the stereotype of the wicked witch of fairy tales and was perhaps someone to be both feared and, if at all possible, ignored. The word 'hag' actually means 'blessed', foretelling the Wise Woman she would become, and the negative connotations placed upon it are of recent origin, probably from the time of the reign of James I (1603–25).

Once, the elder woman was accepted within the community and shown the respect she deserved. Certainly, when her husband and protector died, she was to be cared for by her eldest son, although in reality the quality of this care varied. One way of a crone preserving her independence, or rather her integrity, was for her – of her own volition – to enter a nunnery and fulfil her destiny by doing good works. Another way was to relinquish her position as mistress of her household and withdraw to the dower house or the fireside and keep her mouth shut. In cultures where there was no room for superfluous people within the economic structure, a widow would cast herself on her husband's funeral pyre rather than endure the indignities of poverty and disgrace.

Cronehood was thus accepted as a time when a woman was able – and indeed needed – to attend to her own concerns, and could expend energy on learning a new kind of wisdom arising out of experience and knowledge. The wise crone recognized that life would never be the same again. She could explore, for want of a better word, her own personal magic. This often meant that she would enhance her natural healing and nurturing skills through the use of herbalism and associated arts, or would be able to follow a particular line of philosophical or religious thought which might intrigue her. She would often be consulted as a wise woman and act as counsellor to others of her community.

The situation is not so different nowadays. Once a woman has negotiated the transition phase of the menopause, and is prepared to look at what lies ahead, she will find that many fresh options are open to her. When she has no longer to concentrate on her children and their welfare to such a great extent, she has more time to follow her own concerns, or to generate new ones. It is possible for her to learn new skills or brush up on old ones; she can turn her mind to interests that she and her husband can share, or she can follow her own star. If she so wishes she can find herself new employment using the skills of time and team management that she has honed in the service of the family or she can choose a totally different way of working from the one she has used hitherto.

If she has no need to work for financial reasons, she may find the time to do as her ancestors did and pursue her own studies into, for example, philosophy and religious thought. One way or another she will come to a new understanding of what spirituality means to her. Her focus will no doubt move from the narrower confines of the family to a concern for the community in which she lives and often to an even wider appreciation of global concerns.

Her sexuality at this time of her life is also different from earlier. Now that she is no longer concerned with procreation, she can handle the differences in one of two ways. Should she discover that her interest in sex wanes, she can concentrate more on her and her partner's need for love and affection, and find new ways of expressing her sexuality and sensuality. Should she find, on the other hand, that her libido increases, channelling it in other, more creative directions should help. (Some suggestions for creative work are shown on page 61 and in Section 4 of the Workbook.)

Almost every woman will find her own way of handling the different energies that become apparent during this time of life. Certain hitherto unsuspected aspects of her personality may come to the fore, surprising her and requiring a re-think on her part and that of her partner. Indeed her partner may be experiencing problems of his own as business pressures, waning libido or self-doubts rise to the surface. It is perhaps worthwhile instigating a mutually supportive conversation so that understanding can be reached.

Such a conversation might be structured to include the following questions:

- How do I/you feel at this moment?
- What would I/you like to change (if anything) about the present situation?
- What do you think about our relationship and the direction in which it is going?
- What can we do separately and together in the future to create a mutually satisfying relationship?
- Is there anything which I/you feel should be done differently?

Such questions are not easy to ask or to answer. Bravery is required if relevant issues are to be faced and perhaps the habits of a lifetime changed to achieve a different way of being.

At this point there will inevitably be changes in her way of thinking and there is a very real danger of a woman becoming completely selfish as she pursues her own reality. This is actually in keeping with her need for autonomy and her right to decide her own future. The drive towards self-expression cannot be denied and is impossible to ignore. It is unlikely in the present day and age that any woman will be prepared to fade into nothingness and obscurity, as she reclaims those parts of herself which she may have suppressed for years. The ways in which this drive is articulated may be both shocking and amusing. An outrageousness more appropriate to adolescence may become apparent as the woman of mature years experiments with different modes of behaviour.

This is a resurgence of the 'wild woman', the potentially destructive side of woman's nature. Properly managed, this aspect can become a real force for change, both in the woman herself and in her community, as she begins to recognize the sort of life she wishes to bequeath to her descendants. Without control it becomes a destructive influence that destroys for the sake of it and lays waste to anything that displeases her. Two important questions need to be answered before she makes decisions that may distress others: 'Do I understand why I am doing this?' and 'Could this be seen as being for the Greater Good'? (that is, the good of the community or the world in general). By and large, this should allow there to be a balance between selfishness and altruism.

Establishing a balance in her life is probably the most important thing that a woman of mature years can do, both for herself and for those around her. Most of the goddesses associated with this age have dual aspects and every mortal woman experiences within herself a similar duality. On the one hand there is the truly matriarchal, gentle side, which perceives the need within her family or group for wise guidance and clarity, and on the other hand there is the destructive, darker side. Not until a woman has faced and comprehended the true power of this darker side can she attain the wisdom and perception of the truly wise. At this stage of her development she has the choice of a search for understanding or a downhill struggle into cantankerousness and destruction. She must walk a tightrope between these two extremes.

Dreamscapes

As a woman undertakes this particular stage of her journey, her dreams will reflect her changing concerns. She is more likely to dream about her relationships with her family and will often 'know' through dreams when something is not quite right with them. It is as though the antennae she used as a mother have simply extended their range to take account of the physical distance there may be between them.

She will also find herself musing and often dreaming about things she has not been able to do before now or about unexpressed parts of her personality. Often there is a sense of urgency, highlighting her recognition of the passage of the years. Her dreams may also underline her need for autonomy and the integration of the many facets of her – by now – rich personality. All in all she is ready to move into perhaps the last and most fulfilling part of her life as a human being – that of Wise Woman – with a spirit of integrity.

The story of Baba Yaga, from Russian and Hungarian folklore, perhaps best epitomizes the delicate balance of power that needs to be established by every aspiring Crone of today. Used as a threat to young children if they do not behave, Baba Yaga is seen in much the same way as the Wicked Witch of Western fairytales. (Baba Yaga, which translates as 'old woman', is the archetypal hag.) In the form of ogress, she is said to cook and eat children. She will also bring about death if she is displeased or if one of her adult captives fails at a given task. Capricious to the last, she is reputed to live in a hut on top of a large chicken leg that moves from place to place at will! To curry favour with her, one first has to find her and then answer a riddle, the solution to which is a series of magical words. Even if you do manage to speak to her and put your request, she will set difficult tasks that can only be accomplished by the clever or by using magic. Success allows you to continue with your life and receive what you asked for. If you are favoured or you have been especially open and fair, you will receive exceptional rewards, and in some versions of the tale you are allowed the use of magic to which you have earned the right.

Any woman starting out on her journey of enlightenment must face the darker side of herself, and Baba Yaga or the Wicked Witch represents just this. Woman must learn not to be afraid of it but to use her own personal 'magic' (i.e. her creativity and ability to make things happen) responsibly. Responsibility is only learnt in the hard school of experience, and coupled with age and dignity it is this which allows the Crone to be herself and to become Wise Woman in a way not possible previously.

Wise Woman

Unlike other aspects of womanhood, the line between Crone and Wise Woman is almost imperceptible. The transition from one to the other is so subtle that many modern-day writers are unable to distinguish between them – a Crone is a Wise Woman and vice versa. However, the phase of Wise Woman does have a character all its own which is in no way associated with any of the negative connotations of Cronehood. The Wise Woman realizes that, if she chooses, she can make far more use of the energies and powers she has developed over the years. She has to reach beyond a purely physical framework to a more spiritual and esoteric (beyond self) existence.

Up until this point in her life a woman will have been concerned with herself, her family, her community and the world beyond, in that order. Now she is in a position to attend to more 'cosmic' concerns, such as the insights she may receive regarding the continuation of life. She may consider whether that is 'life everlasting' in the religious sense, or recognize that life itself will continue for generations on this earthly plane and that she herself has played a part in that continuation. She may come to the realization that Death visits as a friend and not as an enemy to be conquered. The perception of herself as a small cog in a very large wheel will be accompanied by an appreciation of the larger patterns of life, and how she will need to adjust her thinking to take account of them.

The need to relinquish much of the material she has suppressed and chosen not to handle over the years will be a major part of this adjustment process. Just as in the Crone stage she recognized the wild woman, so now she must come to terms with the destructive side of her being, transforming that energy into wisdom and clarity of perception. Past traumas, her destructive behaviour (and that of others), doubts, guilt and fears must be dealt with and forgiven, otherwise they are likely to come to the fore in dreams, clamouring for attention.

As her sexuality changes yet again, she becomes aware that the true union she has been looking for in her partners is actually occurring within herself – that is, on an inner level – and that the outward expression of her search is no longer of such pressing concern. When such aspects of life are faced bravely, and understood in a much wider context, the energy that is released can be transformed and put to good use – helping others deal with their difficulties, and achieving a true sense of tranquillity and rightness.

Clarity of perception, or clear seeing, becomes a tool in the service of humanity. It enables the Wise Woman to help other individuals to assess the consequences of their actions. Before she can help others, however, she must learn to use this perception on her own behalf to ensure that, insofar as she is able, she does nothing to disturb the delicate balance she has learned to establish as Crone between the various positive and negative aspects of her personality. She must learn to maintain more consistently her own sense of inner peace. Often this can seem like a self-discipline that does not sit well with her newfound sense of personal freedom. Yet in many ways the two are mutually dependent. Without personal freedom – choosing to be the person she knows she can be – she will not find the discipline to enable her to follow her Self (that part of her which works for the Greater Good). Without the discipline and determination to be herself, she cannot search for, or demand, personal freedom.

Personal freedom in the spiritual sense is only gained when it is realized that true freedom consists of working in harmony with all things, both spiritual and physical. This does not mean that everything is always sweetness and light – this would be almost impossible to live with. It does mean recognizing that discord and difficulty arise for a purpose. Where it is possible to make changes in the *status quo* such action is appropriate. Where change is not possible, then taking no action is equally right.

As she learns to discriminate on her own behalf, a woman also learns to discriminate for others. She is then enabled to distinguish between appropriate and inappropriate behaviour and will be able to forecast accurately what someone is likely to do. Guidance for others then comes naturally, particularly if she has learned to trust her intuition. This enables a situation to be explored in the fullest detail to bring about a solution to whatever difficulty there may be. If, as Wise Woman, she recognizes her ability to hold a safe and sacred space so that the other individual does what is right for them, this is her true magic.

Such perspicacity is seen in Hecate's role in the story of Persephone and Demeter. In one version of the legend, Hecate sits and observes the whole scenario while Persephone and Demeter play out their story of mother and daughter. Pluto, the King of the Underworld, then captures Persephone as his bride. It is only when Hecate deems that there has been enough suffering and tells Demeter what has happened, that the situation is resolved. On the face of it, her actions are simply those of a malign old woman, and yet in her wisdom she recognizes that things have to happen in the way they do in order for everyone to learn the required lesson. Persephone must exist separately from her mother, Demeter must allow her daughter freedom, and Pluto must assist in bringing Persephone to a recognition of her own womanhood.

As someone who is able to hold her space sacred (that is, consecrated through meditation or prayer for the energy and power that is woman), Wise Woman is now able to use that space on behalf of all mankind. We can now begin to think of her situation in terms of the Priestess, who has forged a link with all knowledge and is now able to access information hitherto inaccessible to her. She is able to ask questions and to intercede on behalf of others and to accept that, even if she herself does not know it, the answer will be given to her.

Dreamscapes

Her dreams now will tend to be *for* her family and her culture, and give explanations as to how life should be lived. She will often dream of her ancestors, or of customs perhaps long forgotten. Many of her dreams and musings will, if she allows them, be of the archetypes and archetypal patterns belonging to the past, and yet with understanding can be used in the future. Gods and goddesses – and sometimes symbols and patterns that she recognizes but cannot necessarily interpret – become part of her repertoire. She senses within herself a mystical connection with 'all that is'. If she comes this far she will have placed herself at the crossroads between the spiritual and the physical realms and have begun to appreciate the power of the feminine principle, recognized by many as Sophia, the Goddess of Wisdom.

CHAPTER 3

The Mystery and Magic of Women

*'What we truly and earnestly aspire to be, that in some sense
we are. The mere aspiration, by changing the frame of mind,
for the moment realizes itself.'*

– Anna Jameson, author

When we recognize the place of wisdom and the principle of
Sophia in our lives, we must come to terms with the changes in
awareness that are essential to safeguarding and understanding the
true meaning of femininity. To embrace these changes, and to
utilize the gifts that become available, many women return to
basics by exploring ancient religions and systems of belief. Wicca
(the study of witchcraft) and so called neopaganism – an update of
old truths – are genuine attempts to return to an intimate
relationship with 'all that is', but from a feminine rather than a
masculine perspective.

This approach enables a woman to become comfortable with
her own power and also to give due respect to the power of nature
manifested by the Earth on which we depend. If instinctively she
perceives this energy as one of the many forms of the Goddess,
that is because she relates more easily to a personalized image
rather than simply a concept. By drawing on an energy and an
authority that she senses to be both within her and without, she is
attempting to reconcile the inner Self with the outer being.
Through this reconciliation she will become aware of yet a further
manifestation of the Goddess, that of Wisdom, given the name
Sophia (literally, from the Hebrew, 'God Inspiration').

Sophia is the essence of woman's creative, material and spiritual life. As an energy she gives meaning to everything that a woman is. As a concept – a basic tenet by which we live – she offers information and answers that cannot be obtained from elsewhere, and a set of qualities and ideals for women to aspire to. So important is this aspect that Sophia is a powerful archetype for all women, and has relevance on many levels of existence. Whenever a woman's integrity is put to the test, whether negatively or positively, Sophia's wisdom is available. When a woman is reviled, threatened, abandoned or cut off from loved ones, she will find an inner strength, seemingly out of nowhere. When a woman struggles to express her creativity, maintain her self-respect, survive in the face of danger or simply faces adversity with courage, Sophia will empower her. The practice of wisdom builds an alliance with Sophia.

Sophia, in another aspect, is also the goddess of philosophy. Initially this meant a love of wisdom, an understanding of the whole of being. Given its present status as an intellectual pursuit, there is a need for it to become a way of life. The inner fire, the very spark of life and thus the sheer enthusiasm for being, needs to be nurtured if mankind is to survive. Formerly many cults of Goddess worship involved the ritual guardianship of sacred fires, as we have seen with Brighid. As this practice waned so did the passion and fervour those fires represented and, it could be argued, the sense of reverence for life. The search for autonomy and meaning returns to us that sense of reverence.

In the Bible, Solomon, when teaching his son, speaks of the quality of wisdom as being feminine. He suggests that if a man were to fall in love with this attribute within himself, he would find the most rewarding and the most precious things in life. Much thought has been given to whether certain aspects of God were – and indeed still are – feminine. Some believe that Sophia epitomizes the higher more spiritual aspects of Mary, others that she is a representation of the soul. Many have postulated that the Holy Spirit has to be feminine in order to balance the masculinity within the holy Trinity. Gnostics believe that in creating the universe God must have been helped by his Shekinah (feminine counterpart), Sophia. For most of us it may be enough to accept that woman, in developing those multifarious aspects of maid, mother and crone – and, hopefully, wise woman too – must inevitably reach for all that is best in herself. If she does this, she will be given the opportunity to understand the more ephemeral qualities of wisdom, magic and mystery and all that Sophia represents.

Images of Women's Power
We have already touched on woman's magic and power and also on her mysterious aspect. Her magic may be thought of as her ability to make things happen and her mystery as the innate knowledge and wisdom which has been perceived in the personification of Sophia. There are two images which may be used to represent these aspects of a woman's power, both within herself and for others: the labyrinth and the spiral. As tools within meditation and as images that resonate on a subliminal level, both can be used as pathways to that power. The labyrinth is one of the oldest representations of the feminine mystery. Thought by some to be a crude representation of how the brain was perceived, it allows the freedom to follow many paths and yet still arrive triumphant in the 'centre' of oneself. The spiral suggests spiritual aspirations and ideals and a return to the centre of all things.

The labyrinth
As early as four thousand years ago the power of the symbol of the labyrinth was well recognized. It was often traced as a design – particularly on the walls of houses – when it served as a form of

magic device to confuse and prevent the entry of hostile powers and evil spirits. Then, as today, it might be built as a path and either open or enclosed by hedges. As an enclosed structure it usually represented the mystery of the feminine ideal and the hidden aspect of woman. Chartres cathedral, in France, built in 1200AD, has one of the best known medieval representations of an eleven-circuit labyrinth (shown below), and this is said to be based on the classical seven-circuit Cretan labyrinth in which, legend has it, the Minotaur at Knossos was concealed. There are several modern-day constructions of similar designs, such as that at Grace cathedral in San Francisco. In Britain there are now over 125 mazes (multicursal forms) open to the public, compared with 42 in 1980.

Even today such symbols of centrality surface in women's dreams, so archetypal is the image, touching a deeply held understanding. For instance, a garden with a tree growing in the centre is often the symbol of the soul; enclosed or walled gardens represent the feminine protective principle and also virginity.

In Native American, Greek, Celtic, Mayan and Hopi culture they are magical geometric forms that define sacred space; in Hopi culture the labyrinth is the symbol for 'mother earth'. The path of the labyrinth was often traced as a dance, suggesting the journey undertaken by the soul as it seeks to reunite with its own origin, and again creating a sacred space. The various ordeals, trials and initiations into occult and hidden knowledge were seen as rites of passage to an awareness of the true meaning of life. If we choose to follow or adapt these ancient rites, we may draw closer to the centre of our own personal labyrinth and become increasingly aware of the illusions of life. In seeking to understand the meaning of enlightenment, we will find a way of living within our own abilities and self-expression.

As a spiritual journey, the labyrinth both empowers and inhibits. Only those who have sought and equipped themselves with the necessary key or system of knowledge can reach the centre, yet only those who set out upon their journey in a spirit of innocence are likely to succeed. In this respect the labyrinth shares the symbolism of the enchanted forest. The forest, too, is the realm of the psyche and the feminine principle – that is, the art of intuition and realization. It is a place of test and initiation both for men and women. Entering the dark or enchanted forest is a symbol of threshold or a new beginning and is often used as a motif in fairy stories and myths.

This symbol of the new beginning also touches on the idea of death and rebirth – another aspect of the feminine that will arise at some time in a woman's consideration of herself. The concept of travelling to a still centre within herself – there to accrue knowledge and to return reborn to a different life – does not seem strange, because, whether she has given birth to a child or not, she is so intimately connected with the process of regeneration, experienced through her own menstruation. The sense of initiation into a new way of being happens not only spiritually but also psychologically, as hormonal changes bring about a further step in maturity. She also may react to astrological influences and respond to the subtle changes that these bring about.

In the Christian religion the labyrinth was initially seen as the path of ignorance with hell, or illusion, at the centre guarded by the Devil or the personification of evil. Christ, as the pilgrim, then showed the way to the vanquishing of this evil force. It was also used to lure devils, and was a representation of the uncertainty and difficulties that the Christian comes up against in the physical world with its many opportunities for wandering off the true path to the centre. In the going in and coming out, and the concentration needed, there is also the opportunity to forget the temptations of the physical world, of anything other than the path one is following. The labyrinth is not in evidence as a representation in the art of the early Christian catacombs, though this may be because the religion was still in its infancy and its symbolism was not fully developed. Only later would the labyrinth become the positive representation we know today, although still retaining its aspect of trials vanquished.

By the beginning of the 18th century there are references in medical tracts and literature to the 'disease of the labyrinth of Venus', a euphemism for venereal disease, and an apt characterization of the fear that men felt at the seductive power of women. The responsibility for succumbing to sexual temptation was laid firmly at the door of the woman, an attitude that has still not entirely died out. As women begin to explore their power, they become more conscious of their sexuality, and as they become more at ease with their sexuality, they become more conscious of their power. These twin aspects of being offer themselves for consideration, and each woman must find and explore her own labyrinth of complexity before she can harness and use both dynamically.

The dynamic use of sexuality and power is well demonstrated in the story of Ariadne. She is said to have helped Theseus (the Hero) to overcome the Minotaur (the Shadow) in the depths of his labyrinth by giving Theseus a ball of golden thread (her Divine instinct) with which he retraced his steps to the entrance. This echoes the idea of there being a "rope to Heaven" on which all things depend and are threaded. It also demonstrates the concept of there being a key, or 'right way', to traversing difficulties or reaching the hidden self.

The spiral

This highly complex symbol of woman's energy has been used since time immemorial and is found worldwide except, for some unknown reason, in Hawaii. More esoterically, the spiral stands for the veil of the Mother Goddess as she spins and weaves the web of life, controlling human destiny and weaving her cloud of illusion.

The various expressions of being, the journey that the soul makes in the physical world – and its return to its centre – are also shown within the spiral. As a great force it is the vortex and the cycle of creation and destruction; it therefore expresses within itself any two opposing forces – the irresistible force and the immovable object. It is accepted as the relentless 'patterning' of nature.

In mathematics the spiral is accepted as the principle behind the repetitive character, or pattern, of certain equations. The spiral personifies the androgen – the essential balance between feminine and masculine. It is also linked with the caduceus symbol – the entwined snakes symbol representative of healing – and which is now accepted as the symbol for DNA. It signifies duality of movement (both upwards and downwards). As a flat pictorial representation, the double helix or spiral becomes the yin-yang symbol, containing untold potential.

The spiral is seen within nature in the horns of animals such as sheep, the protective shell of animals such as snails and marine molluscs and in plants such as ferns and ivy. It is also seen in the cloud formation of tornadoes and other types of storm phenomena. In these manifestations it gives expression to the feminine as Mother Nature at her most powerful. Within the spiral – echoing the forces of nature – rather than struggling towards the centre as in the labyrinth, the individual has actually reached that centre in herself, has recognized her own inherent power and is ready to move onto a different and higher plane of perception.

Designs for Life

As we have seen, our journey as women occurs on two levels: the mundane and the spiritual. Only when we have accepted our right to undertake both these journeys, to recognize the validity of the gifts and talents that we bring into our everyday existence and couple it with our innate knowledge of 'all that is' do we truly step into our own power and use ourselves wisely and well. Mankind's spontaneous designs of the labyrinth echo this duality of spirit and secularity. We touch only briefly on this concept here and show how it can be developed more fully later in the book. There are basically two forms of design, one very simple and the other more complex.

The unicursal

In this a single path leads to the centre and back out again. There are no alternative routes and and nothing to confuse – except the decision to go back. The path extends towards the centre of the enclosed space then turns back towards the outer boundary before doubling back on itself. This pattern is repeated, with the path gradually working closer and closer to the centre and then out again. The individual travels over the maximum possible area without ever walking the same path twice, except by her own volition.

The multicursal or maze

For the last 1,000 years this has been intended to confuse and create disorientation. There are many blind paths and wrong turnings requiring repeated retracing of one's steps if the solution is to be found. Because the solving of the problem can be achieved by entirely logical means, once it is known the passage becomes easy to manage and the irrelevant paths can be ignored. This is a complex symbol and can often be best solved by getting above it and viewing it from a distance.

A labyrinth can be represented in many different ways. Often it is depicted as an underground space, and dark, to emphasize its hidden, mysterious nature. According to myth, the male descends into this underworld, the home of the Great Mother or Woman personified in her most destructive aspect. The labyrinth also suggests the meeting of the Shadow as seen in the archetypes or of negativity as in the Greek and Minoan legends which we look at in relation to understanding the feminine. (The entrance to the labyrinth is often pictured guarded by a woman, while the masculine Lord of the Labyrinth holds the centre.) These figures are the stuff of which myths and fairy stories are made, and you are beginning to lay down the basis of your own personal myth.

Myths and Personal Myths

The Oxford English Reference Dictionary definition of a myth is 'a traditional narrative usually involving supernatural or imaginary persons and often embodying popular ideas on natural or social phenomena'. A legend is defined as firstly 'a traditional story sometimes popularly regarded as historical but unauthenticated' and secondly as a 'popular but unfounded belief.'

A myth or legend arises from the traditions of a society; both are unauthenticated, primarily because initially they will have been handed down orally. Almost always myths and legends are to do with aspects of conflict between two polarities, whether good and evil, positive and negative or masculine and feminine. These conflicts have become romanticized, but are so basic to human understanding (archetypal) that the same themes and origins appear in the myths and legends of different countries, cultures and religions. Giants, for example, are to be found in the folklore of virtually every culture, from the ogres in Norse fables to the Cyclops in Greek legends. Not only physically large, these entities are often presented as having an overpowering, frightening aspect which, when tamed, becomes gentle or metamorphoses into something else.

Strong patterns of behaviour can be seen in the masculine and feminine archetypes of myths and legends. If we look at them carefully they show us how to relate to others in our search for Self, and how to understand and formulate our own personal myths.

Such stories offer a rich source of material with which to feed the inner being. Hopefully, this book will give an easier passage into that area of ourselves. When later in the book we look at the hidden masculine and feminine, and how we use them in relationships, you will begin to appreciate the ways in which you 'write your own story' and act it out in everyday life. Generally the masculine attributes are assertive and sometimes combative, whereas the feminine ones are passive and receptive.

The Hero's Journey, in which a young man leaves the safety of home and ventures out into the world to overcome seemingly insurmountable obstacles, is one of the principal themes of myth. The young man usually wins his badge of manhood or maturity by slaying an ogre or rescuing a princess. This is demonstrated in the epic story of Beowulf, which dates from the 6th century AD. Beowulf challenges a water monster and its mother but is himself killed by a dragon. (Later we examine what such actions mean psychologically in terms of the anima and animus – see page 94.)

There is also the Heroine's Journey, which takes an altogether different form, although the qualities required to win through are the traditionally masculine ones of bravery and strategic thinking. The bravery is usually more immediate and spontaneous than planned and the strategy is often accompanied by an intuitive awareness of the situation. Frequently the outcome in these tales benefits the community rather than the individual woman whose exploits have brought it about.

Myths and fairytales can help us explore the inner balance of masculinity and femininity and our own destructiveness, but it requires that we look at them not as we did when children but in a totally different way.

- Choose a fairytale or myth that appeals to you. You could try conventional ones such as Sleeping Beauty, Rapunzel, Hansel and Gretel or any of the Greek legends.
- After you have read the story, think about it from the viewpoint of the character that is most important to you. Try reading the tale from that person's perspective, using the personal pronouns 'I' and 'we'. For instance, you might say 'I let down my hair' or 'We approached the citadel'.
- As you do this, note carefully your reactions and emotions as well as anything unexpected. You might find, for instance, that you do not trust your prince or that the monster is not so frightening after all. These personal idiosyncrasies can be put to good use later. You may find it easier to keep a written record of your thoughts.
- At this stage you can continue the exercise in one of two ways. You may wish to explore other myths and stories in the same way. Then you can make an assessment of your own particular style of being the hero or main character in challenging situations. Alternatively, you may wish to go back to your first tale and look at the story again from the perspectives of other characters in the tale. How, for instance, would the witch feel in the story of Rapunzel? How does the prince feel as he travels through the jungle in the tale of Sleeping Beauty? Your reactions may surprise you.
- This exercise should be fun as well as illuminating; so stop when you feel you have gone as far as you need to on this particular occasion. You can always return to the exercise later.

Many myths and stories have been sanitized over the years to make them suitable for children. Through such stories children learn what is feasible and what is not, perhaps who can be trusted and who cannot. Used in the way we are suggesting, the stories become meaningful in a totally different way. For instance, a child may simply pick up on the fact that Red Riding Hood's grandmother was eaten by the wolf, whereas your work may reveal your feelings about being consumed by a negative aspect of the masculine.

By looking at the various characters you will begin to get a feel for the type of characters you like and those that you don't. The latter are the ones who present you with the greatest challenge. They could broadly be said to represent the more negative parts of your own personality or those aspects with which you have not yet come to terms.

Often we project these aspects onto others around us or attract people to us in ordinary everyday life who have these qualities. When we come to terms with these parts of our own personality, they no longer bother us and we are able to use their qualities to help us in everyday life.

Let us assume that one of the characters you have discovered is a 'wimpy' princess – a young girl who is too frightened to meet a challenge. In no way would you feel that you are like this and yet somewhere within yourself you feel that your dislike of her is out of proportion. It is therefore quite important that you get to know her and understand her. You can do this by using her in a story that might become the basis of your own personal myth.

Creating your myth

To develop your own personal myth it is best to start simply and to include in your story positive characters who will help rather than hinder. You might work in this way:

• For the moment start with only three characters, yourself as hero or heroine and two others, one of whom is, for example, the princess and one who is a helper. Your task is to assist the princess to escape from her present situation. (You can decide on the reason for this.) You can bring in other characters and helpers or hindrances as you wish. You might wish to bring in, for instance, characters you have used in the last exercise.

• Try not to monitor the process too much but allow it to happen spontaneously. As you become more proficient you will find that your imagination expands to take in other aspects of the person you are and your way of being. Nor does it matter if you seem to be stuck at a particular point in a story. Simply note where you have got to and come back to it another time.

• When you have tried this method with a number of your inner characters, you will probably become aware of certain themes emerging and over time start drawing them together. When you have got a better idea of those themes and how they fit into your life (your own personal focus) you will be able to clarify for yourself your own myth – the story by which you live.

From time to time thereafter you may wish to take a look at this story and make adjustments to enable you to live more fully. For instance, you may discover that the 'wimpy princess' – the part that hates making decisions – may make very good ones if she feels supported, or that a stronger part of the personality, another character in your story, is better at making decisions and she is better in supporting you in what you have to do.

One aspect of personal myth that does need to be considered is what might be called 'family myths'. As children, we may often perceive ourselves as having certain characteristics, or indeed these might have been attributed to us by members of our family. To be comfortable, we accept this view of ourselves and often try to live up to it or to manifest the particular aspects attributed to us.

For instance, one child may be perceived as a dreamer or as 'creative' and capable of learning to respond to certain triggers. Other members of the family will then consciously or unconsciously use these triggers, thus perpetuating the 'myth'. It is only when an individual begins her own journey of self-discovery that she realizes, with some shock, that 'I am not like that at all!' She is then able to rewrite her own story and let the behaviour that has helped her to buy into the myth disappear.

For many women it is during the times of transition between the stages of femininity of Maid, Mother and Crone that behaviour seen by others as erratic – and in need of rational explanation – can give rise to family myths. Other family members may suggest that such behaviour is 'just like mother's' or 'following in grandmother's footsteps'. We often internalize observed behaviour without realizing it, and inherit certain other traits of character. Other people then make comparisons which may not be accurate. In fact, the woman is more than likely simply experimenting and finding her own individual way through these transition periods. It is these that we consider next.

CHAPTER 4

The Way of Everywoman

'She wavers, she hesitates; in a word, she is a woman.'

Perhaps the easiest way to think of these transition periods is as being similar to airlocks. You enter the airlock, for instance as a child, knowing that you will emerge from the other end as a maid. During the time that you are in the airlock, you will receive influences from both states of being in varying degrees. Firstly you will be more child than maid, secondly you will find difficulty in differentiating between child and maid and thirdly you will emerge as fully-fledged maid as we have described her previously.

Rather than being in a state of suspension, such times are full of promise and full of energy. Some of these energies may conflict with one another and you will need to learn how to handle them. Not only will you be handling physical energies, you will also be handling spiritual energies and you can see that there can be a great deal of confusion which arises.

The transition from maid to mother, from mother to crone and the final transition of death equally all need handling in a practical manner and it is this we demonstrate in this section.

For each stage there is a need to understand and care for the body in specific ways. The more a woman can keep the energy at a positive vibrant level and not descend into negativity and wild behaviour the better it is for her and those around her. Disciplines laid down at times of change will always stand her in good stead.

Puberty

Girls become more aware of themselves and of being 'different' from boys during the teenage years. From a purely physical point of view, the growing girl needs to know that the biggest spurt in her physical growth usually takes place around the ages of twelve to thirteen, when she will also begin menstruating. This first period marks the beginning of her transition from child to woman and, depending on the attitude of the women around her, will be greeted with anticipation, fear or distaste.

It is also at this time that the girl's body image may become set for life. There is no 'normal' size or shape, but a fair estimation of what the youngster will come to accept about herself can often be gained from photographs of older members of the family at around the same age. It often happens, for instance, that father's family are taller/thinner/fatter than mother's and such things must be taken into account. Also, it is important that the girl is allowed to develop her own ideas about herself and not have projected onto her the parents' attitudes towards such matters as food or what constitutes appropriate behaviour.

This does not mean that she should be spoiled or that she should be allowed total freedom. It does mean that she can be encouraged to view herself and what she does in a positive light and can be encouraged to experiment. Almost inevitably, at some time, her image of herself will become somewhat distorted – this is part of growing up. It may be that some part of her body will give her problems – for instance, a nose that is the wrong shape, a spotty face or an over-large bottom. The apparently grotesque, the bizarre or the out-of-place can be quite disturbing to a young girl, since her body is probably doing some very strange things as it prepares for adulthood and is therefore a focus for attention. She will need time to grow into herself. This process is often helped or hindered by experiments that may make parents and other family members cringe with apprehension. Such experiments are simply ways of her trying out different identities in an effort to become the woman she senses herself to be.

It is often helpful at this stage to develop the notion of self-respect. Self-respect is accepting yourself as a good and worthwhile person and appreciating who you are the way you are. You are no different from anyone else in that you have both good and bad qualities, are just as likeable and have just as much right and ability to be a successful person. As the teenager grows up, accepts and cares about herself, she can develop self-belief. Hopefully this attribute will help her to become an able mother and mature into a confident older woman.

For the time being our young lady is beginning to learn that her response to events will not necessarily be the same as that of her parents. She is realizing that her actions will have consequences, of which she will not necessarily be aware. She is also learning to appreciate that she can control certain aspects of her own behaviour and that at this stage she will not necessarily understand the way in which other people's emotions and feelings have a positive or negative effect on her. Almost inevitably she is learning how much she needs praise and encouragement, and hopefully she will be prepared to give like support to her friends and family. She is coming to appreciate that people mature at different rates and make choices and choose alternatives by weighing up both the long-term and short-term outcomes. The chances are that she will also need – and learn – to be very honest with herself.

Some of the choices facing her initially will appear to be negative ones. Her friends and peers – or even she herself – will no doubt pressure her to experiment with all sorts of substances and activities – from the use of tobacco to so-called 'recreational' drugs. Wise parents will have ensured that the youngster will recognize her personal responsibility for her own decisions and be aware of the inherent dangers. While it may seem 'cool' to experiment, she needs to be given the opportunity to develop appropriate understanding of the use of drugs – both medicinal and otherwise. She must decide whether she wishes to put herself at risk; only by being given the necessary knowledge can she make this decision.

Puberty is a time when mood swings are fairly prevalent. Knowledge and education about the reasons for them can be of inestimable value. One battleground that almost inevitably arises is that of food. The young woman may use food as a weapon in her search for identity, whereas her mother may be using it as a way of controlling her daughter. One type of rebellion may be the decision not to eat with the family, or to adopt a totally different diet – such as vegetarian – in order to prove a point. Provided that a good basic diet is offered and the child – for child she still is – understands that certain foods are needed for effective growth, she will come through this period relatively unscathed. She will eventually understand the relationships between food, body image and self-esteem and be able to analyse and evaluate her own diet.

On a practical level our growing woman will learn that she needs a balanced diet, and one which at this stage of her life contains protein, calcium, phosphorus and vitamin D for good bones, and complex carbohydrates, rather than sugary junk foods, for energy. With any luck she will lay down the matrix for the beautiful woman she will become, and will not develop the bad eating habits often found during the teenage years. If she is aware of the problems associated with eating disorders, with obesity and with skin complaints such as psoriasis and acne, she will also recognize the need for a good fitness programme.

This last requirement can be difficult to fulfil. We have already spoken of the mood swings associated with puberty; when these are compounded by fluctuations in energy levels, life can become somewhat fraught for both the young lady and her family and friends. Wherever possible it is helpful to instigate a suitable exercise programme, but one geared to the person concerned. It is a huge turn-off for someone who heartily dislikes weight-lifting or circuit training to stick to such activities when they would rather be swimming or dancing. Often, simple natural encouragement will do more good than nagging and ridicule.

One of the areas in life most fraught with difficulty for the young woman and her parents is that of sexual activity. This draws together all of the 'problems' facing a teenager: moral values, physical appearance, biological aspects of reproduction, family planning, sexual behaviour and orientation, relationships and, finally, sexual harassment.

We have looked at the Maid earlier in the book in the sense of the young person's growing awareness of spiritual, religious and moral integrity. All of these things are important as concepts and ideas, but when faced by her own physical needs and awarenesses and those of an inexperienced – or even experienced – partner, the young woman can become very confused about a correct course of action.

All the advice in the world is not going to help her to make the decision as to whether she is going to allow someone to perform the act that will mean she is no longer a virgin. It is only her acceptance of her right to decide what happens to her own body, her confidence in herself and her self-respect that will put her in the position of deciding whether her femininity is the greatest gift that she can offer someone, or whether it is something that is of little value in today's society.

Again, the important point is that she has learnt to make personal choices. Only she is in a position to decide whether she is ready for the responsibility of a full-time relationship, the possibility of being a mother or of taking pleasure only in the moment.

As a quick checklist to assess the consequences of actions, we suggest that young women going through puberty (or anyone wishing to understand the process of puberty) ask themselves the following questions regarding any important decisions – sexual or otherwise – facing them.

- Do I think that what I am doing is wrong?
- Will what I am doing hurt or harm anyone?
- Is what I am doing illegal or immoral?
- Is what I am doing destructive and will the outcome be negative?
- Would I be ashamed or embarrassed to tell anyone about what I am doing?

These questions allow nobody else to stand in judgement over you. The only person who can do that is you.

With the advent of the contraceptive pill there is now in existence a whole generation of girls who have made decisions their mothers did not have to even consider. They may or may not have made the choice as to whether they will remain virgins, enjoy and experiment with sexual intercourse outside a stable relationship or, having experimented, will deliberately decide to remain celibate until the right partner comes along. Their decisions are made from a logical rather than an emotional standpoint.

It is the prerogative of every woman to decide for herself what she will do with her own body, just as it is her right to change her mind in the light of her own maturity and the circumstances around her. If, for instance, sexual intercourse leads to an unwanted pregnancy during puberty, the adolescent girl is going to have to decide for herself whether she is ready to become a mother or whether she must make a decision to terminate the pregnancy. She may also have to make a decision as to whether she will marry the father, or whether he is in a position to support her. Gone are the days when she had to have the baby and the decision was simply whether it would be put up for adoption or not.

Now there are multiple choices, since the young woman must decide whether she wants to have the baby, whether she wants to keep it, whether she can – or wants – to look after it, and indeed whether she can do so with help or without. All these decisions must be made with great maturity, and with a realistic, unsentimental eye to the future. The resolution to become a mother, having discovered oneself to be pregnant unexpectedly, is just as valid as a deliberate decision to opt for pregnancy within a stable relationship. This is as much deciding to become a mother as is a decision to become pregnant by a partner in the safe security of marriage or a stable relationship. The decision is simply made within a different framework.

At such an emotionally charged time it is sometimes possible to work out the action to take. Ask yourself the following questions:

- What do I want to do?
- What do I need to do?
- What do I believe I should do?

There are, of course, other decisions which the young adolescent must make for herself, and this generation of young people have one decision to face that was not even considered when their parents were young. This is the whole question of safe – or rather unprotected – sex and the AIDS/HIV problem. In less than a generation we have seen an initially unidentifiable killer disease rampage through a whole section of society. Despite this syndrome's known risks, in that it is transmitted through unprotected sex, it would seem that some young people are still prepared to run the risk of developing the disease.

While the attitude of 'it'll never happen to me' is fully understandable, it is inappropriate in these particular circumstances. Young people need to ask some intelligent questions about the drug habits of their sexual partners and not be prepared to have unprotected sex. Otherwise they are putting themselves at risk. Provided a young woman has been given the facts and is aware of what can happen, she can decide whether she will protect herself and her partner by making good choices. When a girl has developed a good sense of her own body, a strong self-esteem and is comfortable with her own belief system, she will not go far wrong.

Pregnancy
The good practices that a girl has laid down in her teenage years will hopefully stand her in good stead in later years when she enters another transitional stage in her life, that of pregnancy. This is truly the transition stage from 'maid' to mother, from a young woman without responsibilities to a more mature person who is taking on responsibility for another life. We have already mentioned teenage pregnancies. Now we are considering pregnancies undertaken willingly and after planning, as a further stage in the progress of a loving relationship between two people.

Pre-pregnancy
Recognizing that her body will be providing a 'home' for her baby for nine months, ideally there will have been some forethought before a woman opts for pregnancy. At this stage it often helps to look at pre-existing health conditions in both families. There are some conditions that might cause concern – high blood pressure, diabetes or thyroid problems, for example – even with the

intervention of modern medicines. Also, should a woman who is HIV positive wish to become pregnant, she must consider very carefully how this is going to impact on her caring for herself and her baby. She will have to deal with a Caesarian birth and foregoing breast-feeding to minimize the baby's chances of becoming infected.

It is also worthwhile finding out if there has been post-natal depression in her mother's family since, although it is not inevitable that the new mother will suffer in this way, steps can be taken by learning to use relaxation methods and yoga to minimize the effects.

Given that neither the consumption of alcohol and other recreational drugs nor smoking creates the best environment for the baby, the new mother may wish to make adjustments in her use of such substances.

Difficulty in conceiving

Sometimes there is difficulty in conceiving a baby. This can be a trying time for everyone and can put a woman in the position of questioning her own femininity. There are the endless tests that she and her partner must go through firstly to establish what the problem is, then the treatment to deal with it, and finally, if appropriate, the fertility method itself to be undergone. All this, even if it is contributing to a positive outcome, puts a tremendous strain on a couple, especially the woman. A wise couple will seek assistance to strengthen their relationship in order to weather the difficulties.

The woman's sense of self will need building up; some of the suggestions later in the book may help in this regard. She will, in particular, need the support of her family and network of friends to help her achieve a proper perspective on the difficulty. Encouragement and support in helping her to reach decisions will be invaluable. Often a patient, sympathetic ear is all that is necessary. Those of her friends who have experienced childbirth may be able to create an atmosphere that enables her to work through some of the issues, fears and doubts that she may have. If fertility is not an issue, our hopeful mother may need to explore whether there are any spiritual or psychological barriers to pregnancy. She may, for instance, have become aware during her own childhood that pregnancy and birth is a painful process, but had not realized this had become a difficulty for her. This is not to say that all the problems are necessarily to be laid at the woman's door, but where there is a difficulty she has the opportunity to undertake, and encourage her partner to make, some in-depth explorations that may help them both. In the workbook section there is a checklist that might provide a starting point for such thoughts, and also a practical visualization/meditation that might help to release tension.

First pregnancy
Assuming that all has gone well, and the woman has become pregnant for the first time, this can be both the most exciting and the most frightening time of her life. Even if she becomes pregnant again she will never be able to replicate this first occasion, with its numerous changes, thoughts, ideas and apprehensions. Her body will never be the same again, and – though the old ideas were that it is probably all downhill from now on – with today's much enhanced natal care she will learn to be aware of just how special she really is as she carries her baby, and will be able to take the proper pride in her new state of being.

Instinctively, she will recognize that she is receiving a great deal more attention than before. For instance, a shy person may have difficulty in becoming accustomed to medical examination, whereas someone who has been proud of her well-toned body may hate the idea of the changes occurring. There can be a sense of humility that she has been enabled to bring a baby into existence, or a sense of arrogance that she has taken a step forward into another facet of her life. It is impossible to predict exactly how she will react to both the thought and the reality of a new life growing inside her, but react and respond she certainly will.

Many women find it helpful to keep a diary or journal of what goes on emotionally and spiritually as pregnancy progresses. This need not be done on a daily basis, but just when it feels right. The record may be of interest after the birth of the baby, during later pregnancies and even to the child or adult the baby will become. Such a journal may also be of use in recording the dreams that a woman has at this time. We have spoken elsewhere of the dreams and aspirations that a woman may have as a mother.

Pregnancy dreams

It is important to realize that dreams during pregnancy do play an important part in assisting the pregnant woman to accept the changing relationship between her body and her mind. Studies have shown that in early pregnancy dreams contain many hidden references and symbols of the woman's condition. Dreams of playing with small fish are very archetypal and are clear symbols of the embryo within the womb. Often a pregnant woman will dream of baby animals, or of planting seeds. Water is almost inevitably a strong symbol in dreams, both representing the flow of emotion and the idea of the womb and its inner environment.

Pregnancy is such a key transformation for women that fear of the unknown has to be dealt with in some way or another, and this can be done with the help of dreams. The grotesque, monsters and an all-engulfing wave are all representative of fear. Dreaming of becoming massively fat or of symbolic images characterizing motherhood is also common. The Great Mother -- as in Mother Earth – is a recurrent symbol. It is as though the mind of the pregnant woman has hooked into a particular stream of information and is trying to make sense of hidden feelings and bodily knowledge.

During the following three months, or trimester as it is called, a woman will have dreams of the birth of her child. In the first pregnancy there will often be dreams about the child the baby will grow into; somewhere around the fifth month a woman will often dream of losing or dropping her baby. Spiritually, it is probable the mother is expressing an unconscious worry that she may not be able to handle this new life, or has some ambivalent feelings which need to be appreciated.

As a woman becomes more involved in the changes affecting her body and gets closer to the birth process, particularly of a first pregnancy, she will often have what might be called a progression dream, finding herself in dark places, such as caves or cupboards, and having to pass through a dark passage or negotiate obstacles. These dreams, it is thought, may be echoing her own birth process or be a perception of how her baby will achieve the passage to life.

In the last months, a woman's fears about her attractiveness and the changes in her appearance may be echoed in dreams. Anxiety dreams of the baby being deformed do sometimes also occur and there is reason to believe that there may be some link between an easy birth and such dreams during pregnancy. It is almost as though the woman has dealt on some inner level with her apprehensions. If she has been allowed to face her fears and to deal with them, she is able to concentrate her efforts more fully on the task in hand.

After the birth

Creativity has many facets. During pregnancy, a woman is forming something totally unique. She is quite literally growing both a new life within, and cultivating a new way of being for herself. In this waiting period she will take time to strengthen the bond between herself and her new baby by communicating with it, through words or music, strong thought patterns or even by writing a letter that can be read by both baby and mother in later years. She may find that she is daydreaming of times to come. Of course, in this process her partner should not be forgotten. It is worth remembering that – if the partner is willing – many issues that she and her partner may have either together or separately can be addressed with love and integrity. After all, just as she becomes a new mother, he also takes on new responsibilities and a new way of life as a new father. There may well be fears that her partner may have for her, their new baby and for himself that need discussing before they cause problems.

It is now accepted that the division between a woman's spiritual and psychic side and the 'real' world in which she lives becomes very blurred during pregnancy and around birth. Of necessity, our new mother must be aware of both the inner and the outer reality, and for a time must handle both. She may have to deal with some unpleasant by-products of birth, such as post-natal depression and other disturbing symptoms. On a physical level post-natal depression results from tremendous hormonal turmoil. The appearance of 'voices in the head' and other such symptoms is one which must be dealt with very sensitively, since there is a spiritual dimension to this, too. This aspect is not always faced up to or the correct guidance given even today. Birth enables a woman to be part of a tremendous burst of joy that is both wonderful and yet untouchable. The aftermath to this may be a sense of loss, frustration and only partial connection to the spiritual dimension which she will experience as depression or even what is technically known as psychosis. Professional guidance from a medical perspective, coupled with spiritual counselling, can be of inestimable help in such cases. The new mother is, of course, also in part mourning the loss of the 'maid' or young woman she formerly was. Understanding these connections can help a new mother to come to terms with her 'loss' and adjust to her new situation.

Menopause

Another time at which a woman may find herself mourning for times past is during the menopause. This is traditionally a very difficult time for women, although for some more than others. Partly this is because it was once thought that many of the problems were 'only in the mind'. Only latterly, as more and more has become known, have doctors been prepared to admit that most of the difficulties complained of by women are due to the drastic hormonal changes occurring at this time.

Symptoms can be divided into two types – early and late, though not every woman will suffer from all of them.

Early symptoms:
- Dry vagina; genital irritation
- Formication – skin crawling
- Headaches, general aches and pains
- Hot flushes, night sweats
- Painful sexual activity
- Urinary frequency and urgency

Late symptoms:
- Anxiety, palpitations, panic attacks
- Curvature of the spine, joint stiffness
- Depression, confusion, mood swings
- Digestive problems such as irritable bowel syndrome and/or constipation
- Fatigue, irritability and/or aggression
- High blood pressure, angina

- Migraines
- Osteoporosis

There are many ways in which a woman can help herself to deal with these symptoms. It may be worthwhile instigating a programme of care before symptoms present themselves. As always, learning to relax properly and paying attention to a sensible diet are important. A diet containing calcium-rich foods – such as enriched milk, cheese and yoghurt along with oily fish, in particular herrings, mackerel, sardines, pilchards and salmon – is beneficial. It may also be wise to increase nutritional supplements such as iron, zinc and essential fatty acids.

Cutting down on alcohol and stopping smoking are sensible moves, although many women may use alcohol and smoking as 'protest mechanisms' in their search for autonomy.

The menopause tends to be regarded by some members of the medical profession as a condition made manageable by the increased knowledge manifest in modern medicines. In the menopausal state women cannot take their health for granted and, indeed, it is imperative that they learn to listen to the demands of their own bodies. Moderate exercise such as walking, keep-fit, yoga and t'ai-chi can be fun and form a new interest, and researching and experimenting with alternative therapies can help to minimize the worst effects of the menopause. Unfortunately, even though a woman may have been very good at looking after herself and others during the mothering period, she cannot escape the effect of the major hormonal shifts which occur at this time.

The physical changes are manageable and, with practice, many of the emotional shifts can be understood in the light of the changing body image. For instance, with the realization that pregnancy is less likely to occur and will shortly be impossible, many women begin to feel somewhat redundant and superfluous. Their function as mother within the family will also be altering as the children grow up and leave home or follow their own pursuits. There is less room within the modern-day family for the matriarchal role to be practised, since families may be widely separated by distance or children may delay having babies of their own for economic reasons.

Rather than being able to welcome having more time for herself, the poor lady finds herself becoming sad and depressed without being able to understand her reactions. Once she understands that she is mourning the loss of a way of life, she can allow the process of grieving to take place and come through to a new peace and tranquillity.

Menopausal women are now starting to take control of their health worries and are looking for alternative methods of treatment and ways of living healthily. One way in which they can help themselves is by joining together to offer one another support. Many women dislike the idea of such self-help groups, but it need simply be a way of networking and encouragement to continue with a sensible regime of exercise and healthy living

A number of women are concerned by the lack of sexual desire at this time, and other physical symptoms making sex difficult. If she remembers that a lot of the energy which previously went into a successful sex life is now being used to prepare her for perhaps the most exciting phase of her life, it is understandable that for the time being she will not necessarily need the closeness of sex as much. For perhaps the first time in her life she has the freedom to follow her own pursuits without having to worry too much about the effect she has on other people. While it may seem that she is totally self-involved, she may in fact be exploring a new dynamic within herself that has never been apparent before.

On the other hand, our menopausal lady may find that her libido increases considerably for no particular reason, and she finds herself involved in activities, sexual or otherwise, that previously she would have found unlikely. It can be quite distressing to discover that to all intents and purposes she has little or no control over her emotions or her thoughts. At this time it is worthwhile trying to apply as much rationality as possible and to ask herself the same questions that were suggested for the young person at puberty. These were:

- Do I think that what I am doing is wrong?
- Will I be hurting or harming anyone by what I am doing?
- Is what I am doing illegal or immoral?
- Is what I am doing destructive and will the outcome be negative?
- Would I be ashamed or embarrassed to tell anyone about what I am doing?

In the light of the experience that the older woman has, other perhaps more important questions are:

- What do I want to do?
- What do I need to do?
- What do I believe I should do?

When she can honestly answer all three questions, her sexual responses have all the power of her self-knowledge and wisdom. She has choices in her management of herself, and can choose, if she wishes and understands the consequences of her actions, to give in to her sexual desires. She can, if she so decides, dedicate those desires to a higher purpose and learn to connect to her own spiritual source, sublimating the energies to the point where – like women of medieval times – she works to make the world a better place in which to live. Then she truly becomes the Crone or Wise Woman.

Death and Dying

A further stage of transition which does have to be dealt with, albeit in several different forms, is that which eventually comes to all of us – that of death and dying. Traditionally it was the older women of the tribe – the crones – who were intimately concerned in helping others effect the passage from this world to the next. They had experienced grief at the passing of family members, had grieved for children lost before they were born or through accident and illness, and knew the rituals and customs of their community which set the soul free on the next stage of its journey.

As crones they knew that their active lives were coming to an end and could face with a degree of equanimity the idea of moving on to something better. They were able to sit with the dying person and comfort their fears. In many societies, they would help the soul on its journey, reminding it that it need not be caught up in the illusions of the physical realm.

Today we are returning to the principle that everyone has the right to die with dignity. Over the last twenty years or so changes in pain management and grieving, whether for the individual or their loved ones, have resulted in profound changes in how we manage the process of dying.

For the dying person, mixed up in this process is a multiplicity of emotions:

- Feelings and fears about the next world
- Difficulties with the physical body
- Embarrassment over loss of control over major aspects of one's life

- Dependence on others
- The facing of the unknown
- Isolation and loss
- Separation and rejection

Certain stages have been identified that the dying go through before coming to terms with the inevitability of death. They are not experienced in any particular order, nor necessarily may they all be experienced to the same degree. It is somewhat unfortunate that since the stages have been identified there is a degree of pressure to experience a 'good' death by going through each one. The 'wise woman' given the task of assisting death will honour the individual and his or her own particular way of facing death. The seven stages are:

1. *Denial and Isolation:* Denial is experienced by almost everyone in some form or another when faced by death. At its most profound in terminally ill patients, it is a reaction to the shocking news that death may be imminent. Isolation is experienced when people, perhaps even family members, cannot cope with the idea of death and end up avoiding not only the issue but also the person concerned. When there are new developments in the illness or the dying person is aware of a worsening of his or her condition, it can be of tremendous help to be asked a very simple question like 'What do you need me to do or be?' By doing this you are giving them the opportunity to have a degree of control over what happens around them.

2. *Anger:* There are different ways of expressing the anger that arises at this time, and these depend on the personality and beliefs of the person concerned. There may, for instance, be resentment of others: this often manifests as a sense that others don't care or understand i.e. 'It's all right for them!', 'It's not fair' and other negative thoughts. This is a perfectly natural state, but might be made bearable by using some of the forgiveness techniques shown later in the book.

There may also be anger towards doctors, nurses, helpers and family members. Anger may also be projected on to the environment or other aspects of society.

Almost inevitably there will be anger at God or at a personal concept of a greater power. Here the question is often 'Why me?' or 'Why not someone else?' Help here is often best given by simply allowing the dying person the opportunity to express themselves without restraint.

3. *Bargaining:* This is a brief stage, and often consists of trying to find some trade-off against the inevitability of death. The person may be looking for excuses to postpone death or reasons to be good so that they gain the co-operation of the Almighty. If there has been no system of belief in God, this may result in the need to find some kind of meaning in one's life.

4. *Depression:* There may be a profound mourning for opportunities, skills, abilities that have been lost and for things that have supported one in the past but do so no longer.

These last two stages can be made easier if an able listener is capable of helping to guide the patient into a better – and perhaps more realistic – state of mind without distressing them. Therapists and carers can help in this process by giving the patient the chance to talk about their feelings, doubts and difficulties in an open and honest manner. They can also help – both practically and spiritually – the person approaching death to make peace with themselves and others, as far as they are able. Often members of the family will not have enough objectivity to be of assistance in this.

5. *Acceptance:* This last stage for many is not a joyful one, but is more likely to be somewhat empty of any particular feeling. Sometimes even those who have not consciously become alert to the approach of death show some awareness of impending events, often through dreams – perhaps of a machine slowing down or in the process of breaking down. It does take a while to reach acceptance and a person who chooses to fight until the end will not necessarily always reach it. It consists of resigning oneself to the inevitability of death.

6. *Reaching the inevitable:* The surrounding environment can have a great effect on a person's acceptance of death. We now know that a patient in a positive and supportive environment is likely to cope better with difficulties than someone who is left in an uncaring and unsupported one. The wise women of old, of course, recognized this and knew that while a person lived they must be given the chance to try out their own strategies and, if need be, reject them. They also needed to understand what today would be called their own life themes (the way in which they lived their lives) and develop their own ways of coping. It is the individual who must be given the dignity to complete their own tasks. This still pertains today – perhaps even more so as life becomes more complicated.

One important task is to deal with the fears linked with what is going to happen after death. By working with dreams (see page 205), a great deal can be done to achieve a better perspective and lessen the fear. The practical technique of Keeping a Journal (see page 204) will help you to do this.

Dreams associated with death are often beautiful, depicting wonderful landscapes, streams and fountains or places of learning. It is as though the spirit or soul of the individual is giving glimpses of what will happen to the Essential You – your Life Force. Hope is a necessary part of everyone's makeup, and belief or awareness can help people through difficult times. For instance, putting one's affairs in order in this life can leave room in what time is left for more spiritual concerns.

7. *Grief and bereavement:* It is a fair bet that anyone faced with the death of a loved one will experience to a greater or lesser degree most of the following:

- Shock
- Emotional release
- Depression, loneliness and a sense of isolation
- Physical symptoms of distress
- Feelings of panic
- Guilt
- Anger or rage
- Inability to return to usual activities
- The gradual regaining of hope
- Acceptance as life adjusts to reality

These feelings will not occur in any set order and some may be stronger than others, but no one should be too hard on themselves as they go through this very necessary period and should recognize that they have the right to grieve in their own way. The mother who has had a miscarriage, for instance, will experience a different kind of grief to the wife who has lost a lifelong companion and husband. Each person copes in their own way, and whereas in earlier times the tribal structure allowed for a natural kind of support, today it is perhaps even more necessary to make an effort to ensure that those around us are not suffering too much.

As women, with the ability to empathize with grief and perhaps to intuit a friend's needs, we have in place a unique system of support on which to draw. It often helps to identify in ourselves the coping skills we have for moments of crisis before an actual crisis impinges on our lives, and also to understand how we react to grief. Do we throw ourselves into whatever daily routine we have? Try to hide from it? Or react with anger and resentment to what is happening? There are many responses, none of them more right or wrong than any other. Understanding them and recognizing that certain of those responses may put our own health at risk enables us to monitor ourselves and those around us and deal with the consequences. It is important to realize that grief is itself part of the transition stages of death – a movement from having the presence of the person in our lives to having only memories to sustain us. Not everyone has the comfort of knowing there is life after death and that the loved one's energy and sense of being will remain with us.

Dealing with one's own death

The final way in which death needs to be dealt with is in dealing with our own demise. No one at any age – young or old – likes to consider that life as we experience it will not continue indefinitely. Yet it is also true that we must all make that final transition from the physical to the spiritual realm. We have spoken of the pressure to have a 'good' death, but it is probably be more correct to try to have an 'easy' death. There is a lot that each of us can do individually to help in this process, to help both ourselves and those around us.

Perhaps the first thing that needs to be considered is making it easier for others to accept our death by preparing them for when we are not around. This means encouraging them to develop lives of their own which do not include us in any physical way whatsoever. This process should begin long before we are incapacitated or incapable of making decisions. Hopefully in that way our loved ones are not going to feel so guilty at having to leave us alone or with other carers.

The second thing we should ensure is that we put our affairs in the best order we possibly can. This may mean deciding which of our treasured objects are to be given away to friends or family before we die, and which are to be disposed of afterwards. We also need to think very carefully about who may or may not need support materially, emotionally or spiritually, both before and after our death. While we are still capable of thinking clearly, it might be a good idea to instigate this support by making suggestions to others without necessarily appearing morbid. Nor, of course, should we deliberately try to interfere in the lives of those we love, by trying to make them conform to our wishes.

If we are so minded we also need to ensure that we have some control over our process of dying. This might mean writing a Living Will, giving instructions for our terminal care – if, for instance, we do not wish to be revived after a major collapse, whether certain medications are to be continued or withdrawn, how we wish to dispose of our internal organs or other matters important to us. At the very least, our family or carers should be made aware of our wishes.

We may also wish to decide on the form of our own funeral. Nowadays many people do not subscribe to any particular type of religion. Yet some kind of ceremony, a way of saying goodbye or a celebration of the person's life is helpful to the grieving process of those left behind. Favourite readings and pieces of music remind others of the person we were but also mark our passing into another state of being.

For those who have not thought about their own transition, or who have never considered the idea of such a personal bequest to their friends and loved ones, some suggestions for suitable readings and simple ceremonies are given later (see page 299).

CHAPTER 5

Adam and Eve and Everyman

'Equal rights for the sexes will be achieved
when mediocre women occupy high positions.'

– François Giroud

We are all, if the truth be told, androgynous. We hold within us a series of opposite polarities and have a hidden part of ourselves that is of the opposite gender. Each little boy has a part that is intrinsically female and each little girl has a part that is male. We inherit our genetic makeup from our parents. Our psychological makeup is such that the unconscious side of ourselves – the hidden masculine in the case of a woman, or the hidden feminine in a man – gives certain attributes which, when used positively, can be of great assistance in living life with full awareness. These hidden parts are known as the Anima and Animus.

Before we explore more fully the balance of the masculine and feminine, we need to have some understanding of the theory of archetypes and of the archetypes themselves, which we are bound to encounter on our individual journey through life. Such an understanding can save us from a great deal of confusion.

The theory of archetypes is a concept of life that enables us to differentiate between diverse aspects of behaviour in ourselves and others. While Jung was the first to give any coherence to the idea of archetypes, many others have expanded and enhanced his original work. He said of archetypes:

I have not been able to avoid recognizing certain regularities, that is types. There are types of situations and types of figures that repeat themselves frequently and have a corresponding meaning.

Others have compared the archetypes to a blueprint or a code which is recognizable in each of us to a greater or lesser degree, not only individually but also across cultures. They are not part of the personal unconscious, but belong to a wider sphere that Jung called the 'Collective Unconscious'. Philosophers and religious thinkers had already theorized about there being a common source from which we all draw, before the notion was brought into the arena of psychology.

Archetypes seem to offer a structure or group of behaviours that allow us to understand our own makeup and the challenges we set ourselves. The way we handle these archetypes seems to arise from a deep intrinsic recognition of basic natural patterns. There are many identifiable archetypes. We shall later explore two of them in the Dragon and the Witch, two deeply held characterizations that hold intrigue or fear for everyone. An archetype that has a similar effect on us is the Shadow.

The Shadow

By and large we tend to be fearful of anything we do not understand; negative and hidden aspects of our personality can be very scary. These aspects have been designated the Shadow which, in dreams, often appears as a member of the same sex as us. This figure is often dark – that is, dark-haired or dark-featured or even dressed in dark clothes. It is the part of ourselves that we only come to terms with after great difficulty and might be thought of as the bit we have hidden away behind all our other characteristics.

We all have an ordinary everyday personality that we slip into very easily when we are in public or on show. All the difficult and nasty bits are hidden away from others and, more often than not, from ourselves as well. A little bit like Peter Pan, we will often need help to find our Shadow and deal with parts we cannot face or make use of. When we do come to terms with this Shadow, with all its negativity, and begin to understand how it has been hindering us, much more universal energy becomes available, allowing us to become the people we really want to be.

An easy way of checking on your own Shadow and the actions it dictates is to make a list of all the things in other people that distress and disturb you and then, being painfully honest, look at those qualities in yourself. You will tend to deny that you are at all like that, but if you can check with a good friend you may well discover that others have a clearer view of you than you do of yourself.

The good news is that, because these aspects are unconscious, you have not needed to deal with them up until now. When you do become aware of them you can begin to bring them under your direction rather than suppress them. Sooner or later you will be able to transcend them and use them. For instance, if you discover that you are argumentative, you may be able to train yourself to be so only when you perceive injustice or some other wrong. You might find that rather than being afraid of being thought foolish, you are able to speak out on behalf of others. There are many ways in which your behaviour will change – slowly at first but then with increasing confidence as you are able to see positive results from what has previously seemed like negative behaviour.

We tend to project our Shadow onto others, but it can also manifest in behaviour that is far removed from our norm. Often at these times it erupts with such passion and force that it appears that something else has taken over. Other people might well pass comment on it, such as 'I didn't know she had it in her!' In many ways this is quite true, since probably neither did you! The trick here is not to try to bury whatever the outburst was, but to look carefully at it and try to learn a little more about yourself. What triggered the eruption? What feelings were there? You might also ask how old it made you feel; often we can deduce from this at what age you first began pushing inappropriate feelings or thoughts out of the way. With these insights you can begin to give fresh expression to the hidden sides of you.

The way you express those hidden sides and turn them into positive attributes will depend on personal factors, such as the way you have been brought up, how you intuitively perceive yourself and also your ability to analyse – or have analysed – what is happening to you. It will also depend on other cultural factors, such as how your own community deals with the Shadow, what stories and myths help in this process, what symbols you have to represent it and so on. Examples of this might be, for instance, how various cultures deal with the demoniacal side of their beliefs – the demon being one manifestation of the Shadow. Some believe that it must be faced with some bravery, some that it must be absorbed or consumed, some that it must be conquered in battle and others that it must be banished to the underworld. These disparate examples show us that, in one form or another, the Shadow is a universal symbol.

The Great Mother
Another archetype that helps to move both men and women to a better understanding of themselves is that of Great Mother. Previously in the book we have recognized her in the form of the Goddess, and as Mother Earth. She has also, of course, a destructive element. It is this archetype which, when recognized and handled most successfully, highlights the difference between a Man's Self and a Woman's Self – that is, their truly integrated personalities. Perhaps the easiest way to understand the

perceptions of the Great Mother's function is to suggest that, for men, the archetype represents an external influence which he has internalized, while for women she is an internal connection.

One particular myth demonstrates how this archetype is capable of operating within the male. This is the Welsh tale of Arianrhod, Virgin and Mother. One of the peculiarities of Math, lord of Gwynedd, was that, unless at war, he had to have his feet resting in the lap of a virgin. Arianrhod undertook the chastity test, but stepping over Math's magical wand – actually a symbol of masculine potency – she gave birth to two infant boys, one called Dylan, who slipped away into the sea, and another whom Arianrhod's brother Gwydion took under his protection and named Lleu.

In an action prevalent in the more destructive aspects of the Mother archetype, and demonstrating the total power that is held by this archetypal figure over the masculine, Arianrhod imposed three curses on the boy. He would never be named unless his mother decided to name him; he would never bear arms, unless his mother decided to equip him nor would he ever possess a human wife.

She was clearly a powerful figure to be able to place such impositions on her son, and this echoes the power that every man senses in a woman, particularly his mother. The tale also provides a good example of the paradox that is so prominent in myth. Arianrhod was, like the Virgin Mary, apparently both a maiden and a mother, conceiving and bearing a son of divine status while still a virgin.

It is this paradox which must be faced by every man and is never really resolved until he understands, comes to terms with and begins to use the feminine qualities within himself. The balance of power between virgin and mother is only one aspect of a man's understanding of the feminine, but it colours not only his own perception of feminine, but also – as we shall see – the woman's perception of herself.

The Ego

The ego, being the conscious part of us, is another element we meet in the journey of self discovery. It is the ego that must eventually assimilate and understand the various aspects of ourselves. The integration of these facets gives us a more fully rounded personality or Self. Jung showed that knowledge of the ego-personality is often confused with self-understanding. He said:

'People measure their self-knowledge by what the average person in their social environment knows of himself, but not by the real psychic facts which are for the most part hidden from them.'

The ego experiences itself as the centre of the psyche, but it is an expression of our personality that is inferior to the self and in fact is a very poor reflection of it. It is that characteristic which is by and large self-important and bombastic. As we begin to discover our inner selves, and particularly the animus or anima, it becomes threatened and must be open to change.

The Anima and the Animus

To understand all of these archetypes we must return to the idea that we are androgynous. However 'masculine' a man may seem, however feminine a woman, within each of them is an unconscious part of the opposite gender. In men this feminine side is called the anima and in women the masculine side the animus. By and large this part is outside our consciousness and, like the Shadow, remains so until deliberate attempts are made to bring it into consciousness or until trauma or advancing age awakens the power within.

The anima

Initially recognized through the primary relationship that a man has as a child with his own mother, the anima is then perceived in other women and is seen as an omnipresent influence throughout his life. The problem is that the anima is, for a man, both a personal construct based on his perception of his own mother and an archetypical image of woman buried deep within his psyche. It is thus an unconscious factor requiring some form of expression if it is to be understood properly.

When given full and proper acknowledgement within a man's psyche, the anima brings to him all the attributes of femininity in full measure. He is then not fearful of his feelings and emotions, or of tenderness and gentleness. He has the ability to relate properly to others, and is capable of a whole range of finer feelings including love and compassion, devotion and friendship. He is able to use the tools of imagination, romance, intuition and creativity and has a strong appreciation of beauty.

If, however, a man cannot come to terms with the feminine within, all those finer aspects become twisted and, as the anima is rejected, her traits are warped. There is instead moodiness, banality and hysteria. His possessiveness, turbulent relationships – or complete withdrawal – means that a man puts his masculinity in jeopardy. The anima when thwarted not only forces the man to express the feminine, she also disturbs the man's masculinity and he may become a parody – macho, power hungry and far too competitive.

In the story of Arianrhod and her son Lleu, she is seen to have power *over* him, rather than giving him the power to be all that he could. This story illustrates another paradox that must be resolved by all men. Each must learn that no woman, particularly his mother, need emasculate or minimize him in an attempt to prevent him from reaching his full potential, and also that every woman has the power to encourage him to develop the feminine qualities of wisdom and compassion. That way he earns the right to 'name' himself – to give himself an identity; so in this sense it could be said that Arianrhod was doing her son a favour.

Each man perceives his anima in four different and distinctive ways. Initially, in the first stage, which Jung named Eve, the anima is impossible to differentiate from the mother on a personal level. He is unable to function without a close attachment to a woman. He is likely to perceive all women in terms of him being mothered or looked after.

In the second stage, which was embodied by the figure of Helen of Troy in days of old, the anima comes across as an idealized sexual image, one on whom he can project all his daydreams and fantasies. At this stage the outward projection on to unattainable figures such as film stars can seem more real than the woman he is in actuality having a relationship with.

The third stage, which Jung designated as a personification of Mary, reveals herself in strongly religious feelings and a capacity for fulfilling and meaningful relationships. The projection can become that of the pure, universally maternal being without sin, an impossible task for most women to live up to.

In the fourth stage, we again meet Sophia when a man's anima serves as a guide to the inner life, acting as a go-between connecting consciousness and the contents of the unconscious. Men and women do, however, perceive Sophia differently. When a woman understands her own inner Sophia, she can co-operate with her man in his search for meaning and can be the Creative Muse in his life. When a man truly understands his inner Sophia he has no need to project the disappointments in his life onto his partner, but can take responsibility for himself. He then has no fear of his more sensitive side and can express his search for spirituality in whatever way is appropriate for him. Perhaps his greatest gift to the woman in his life is then his ability to recognize when he is projecting his anima onto her, when she is projecting her animus onto him and when there is some kind of joint 'game-playing' going on.

It is often during the maturity of mid-life that the animus or anima is recognized and it is appreciated that we no longer need project onto others but can reclaim those parts of ourselves which we have suppressed (or even forgotten existed) and can enhance our lives by becoming much more rounded personalities.

The animus

Jung's disciples also described four separate stages of the development of the animus in a woman.

This inner masculine first appears in both dreams and fantasy as the physically powerful male, perhaps as an athlete or bodybuilder or, more negatively, a thug or villain. At this stage the projection is often manifested as the desire, or need, to relate to an embodiment of perfect physicality such as is seen in the Adonis type so beloved of show business.

In the second stage, the animus is behind a woman's desire for independence and a career of her own. He demonstrates to her the initiative and capacity for planned action seen in successful businessmen. He will often manifest in dreams as requiring the woman to develop qualities normally associated with men, such as power, objectivity and the capacity for fast decision making. In waking life, these abilities can enable a woman to recognize and handle the obstacles to career success which have restricted her previously.

In the third stage, personified in dreams as a knowledgeable male such as a professor, priest or clergyman, a woman's inner masculine allows her access to logical thought, the assimilation and codifying of ideas and concepts. The projection of this stage often occurs as a truly platonic relationship with an older, wiser figure. When such a projection becomes distorted, it may be perceived as the need for a relationship with a father figure.

In the last stage a woman's animus permits access to spiritual concepts without the clouding of an emotional content. This aspect thus mediates between a woman's consciousness and her unconscious self. The dream figure often appears as a messenger or as Hermes, who was, of course, the messenger of the Gods. The projection at this level of understanding can often be onto known – albeit unattainable – figures of wisdom from the past, which makes relationships with the masculine in the present somewhat unsatisfactory.

When used positively, all of these aspects of masculinity can give a woman a desire for achievement and the ability to focus on matters in hand and the right priorities. She, through the use of her animus, can develop decisiveness and analytical thought, courage, strength and vitality. If, however, the animus is thwarted, all these qualities turn negative and result in such character traits as aggression, argumentativeness, ruthlessness and action for the sake of action rather than strategy.

One of the biggest difficulties many women have is that of learning to be themselves. It is so very easy for women to recognize from an early age that pleasing other people brings its own rewards. Men, usually their fathers, often put them in the position of being 'Good Little Girls' and those same Good Little Girls grow into women who respond to men's needs and requirements rather than their own. They become aware that submissiveness is a very valuable tool, without necessarily realizing that they also need to develop the qualities of straightforwardness, courage and feistiness that understanding their inner masculine (the animus) can bring. If a woman falls into the trap of accepting the projection of her man's anima (his inner feminine) onto herself, she can stunt her own development to the point where she stands in danger of losing her own identity. She becomes something that reflects the fantasies of the men around her rather than her own real person.

If she has been brought up to believe that she is 'Daddy's Little Princess', for instance, she may learn that being manipulative works in her dealings with men, but is unable to develop any proper sort of relationship with them because she continually regards them as her tools. If, on the other hand, she has been led to believe that nothing she does is ever good enough for men, she can end up never being prepared to take risks. She does not realize that it is her animus in its most negative form that is preventing her from moving forward.

It is important that she learns how to develop the more positive aspects of her masculine side, otherwise she is likely to experience dreams that contain a good deal of violence. This violence often gives her the sense that she has been abused or turned into a victim in some way. It is, however, the masculine side of her that is clamouring for attention. She can develop the rational, logical side of herself through creative pursuits which need such attributes. She might wish to work with metal – which requires strength – or to undertake a research project requiring method and logic. When violence concerning a female figure does appear in her dreams, a woman may be able to identify how she is suppressing her animus and how it is reacting to this suppression.

Some aspects of dreams that occur during pregnancy can give women cause for concern. Dreams of loss or conflict can occur, for instance. We have already remarked elsewhere on the relevance of such transition dreams, but, in addition, as a woman settles into motherhood and family life she may find that, as well as having to relinquish certain of the temporarily unnecessary parts of her femininity, she must also cope with her animus as it adjusts to a different status. Many women complain that following the birth of a baby they feel particularly stupid and unable to think clearly. While some of these changes are hormonal, they are also caused by the fact that the ability to focus on essentials – an attribute of the animus – is at this stage in abeyance due to the demands of the new art of mothering. Often a woman will blame her partner for this, but really this is a projection.

Perhaps one of the best stories to illustrate the whole spectrum of woman's relationship with her own animus is that of Rumpelstiltskin. In this story the princess is set the task of spinning straw into gold – worthless material into useful resources – by her prospective husband. (This is, of course, well-nigh impossible and represents his projection on her.) Only by enlisting the help of her stunted animus (the dwarf - which has at that point no name) can she succeed at this task. Later when she has gained new status as Queen and is therefore adult, this comes back to haunt her. This stunted aspect of herself will claim her child if she does not confront him in the correct manner – that is, by naming and recognising him for what he is. By calling upon the helpful masculine aspect in herself (the woodcutter), she is able to treat the more negative side properly and overcome its stunted nature. She is now able to treat it with some amusement, since she no longer fears it.

This brings us to the next aspect of the animus that needs to be understood. If, as a girl, a woman has perceived her father in a negative way, she is likely to see all men in this light. She may not like men or find them overbearing, frightening, controlling, lacking in understanding or having other negative traits. She is most likely to project this perception on the men around her and may well find this is the type she is unconsciously attracted to. She may also find that she is overly critical of herself and others and resists being loved or cared for. She will have a habit of sabotaging relationships in a particularly destructive way. This can also include relationships with her own family, since she dare not allow herself to feel genuine emotion. She can thus deprive even her own children of much rich experience.

She may also shut herself off from meaningful relationships in an attempt to remain focused on her own objectives, being fearful that such relationships will distract her from being herself. This type of behaviour will, however, only work for her if she substitutes another passion (such as a career or religion) for a male/female relationship. That way she can develop all the qualities of the animus by projecting them on the task in hand. This is not always the best way to deal with this side of herself, unless it is done with full awareness of what she is attempting to do, since other men, for instance work colleagues, can also get caught up in this projection. She may, for instance, choose a kind of trophy lover who adds cachet to her portfolio of skills.

Another form that the animus might take is that of a fantasy lover, who is fated to sweep her off her feet and whisk her off to some far-flung shore. This is most likely to occur when a woman is unhappy with other aspects of her life, such as her position within the family or her working life. It can be particularly dangerous when she projects this onto some poor hapless male who does not have the ability or the inclination to fulfil her dreams. Again, if a woman recognizes that this is a projection, she is able to work it through and later internalize the sense of adventure and derring-do she perceives to be important.

When we start uncovering the 'psychic facts' Jung referred to when talking of the Ego, we begin to realize that those hidden characteristics have an extremely important part to play in the way we live our lives. Jung and his followers designated the feminine attributes as Eros, associated with human relationships, earthiness, receptivity, creativity and passivity; and the masculine as Logos, acknowledged as being to do with power, abstraction and action.

In bringing these aspects through to full expression, whether we are male or female, we can only enhance our lives. If, prior to middle age, we have made no attempt to uncover these hidden parts, they will most likely force themselves upon our consciousness at that time anyway. It is almost as though there is a last-ditch attempt to balance the personality. For instance, the man who has been the hard-headed businessman up until then may discover his more compassionate side and resolve not to carry on in a competitive arena. The woman who has previously been a rather scatty, unfocused type may discover a business brain of which even she was unaware.

If we do not give these traits full expression we will inevitably project them upon the people around us. We undergo the same problems that crop up whenever we bottle up or misuse our potential. A man who finds it impossible to use tenderness when that is necessary or a woman who is incapable of applying logical thought to a problem both miss out on the opportunity to support their partners and therefore deny themselves an important aspect of closeness within a relationship.

When we have made an effort to understand the hidden sides of ourselves, and this goes both for men and women, we project firstly the image we took from our earlier experiences with people of that gender. A woman with a weak father figure will tend to see all men in that light, whereas a man whose mother or first girlfriend was somewhat ineffectual will perceive women to be similar.

A second projection is that of an image that fits our level of understanding of our own animus or anima at that particular stage of realisation. If a woman has reached the point where she senses the animus as messenger, she may project this aspect onto her men friends and perceive them as, for instance, being capable of interceding on her behalf in arguments and other such situations.

A man, on the other hand, might credit his partner with a wisdom that she has not yet attained, if he senses the potential for that wisdom in himself.

At the next stage we stand in danger of projecting, without awareness, the animus or anima onto a suitable person of the opposite gender. This occurs when that person already has all or most of the qualities of our own animus/a and is, as it were, a ready receptacle for our projection. This creates a tremendous amount of highly charged energy that can be very heady and intoxicating. It is dangerous in that if we do not realize that such projection is occurring, we run the risk of investing the other person with powers they do not have rather than developing that energy within ourselves. It is also hazardous if the projection is happening in only one of the partners, since there can be difficulties in the day-to-day relationship, and the management of our expectations of the other person.

The almost inevitable outcome of such a highly charged situation is that we fall in love with or – at the very least – are sexually attracted to the other person. In reality, we are firstly attracted to the image and energy of the situation, then are actually making a connection with our own animus or anima – falling in love with the opposite gender in ourselves. Once we appreciate this fact it actually makes life very much easier all round. When our opposite number does not come up to our expectations, we are able to be level-headed about it. When we move from being 'in love' – and in lust – we can develop a real relationship that is meaningful and we can dare to be ourselves within that particular scenario, whether with that person or someone else.

This ability to be ourselves only really occurs when we stop projecting onto the other person altogether. Our projection will inevitably fail anyway because no human being is capable of living a life that fulfils someone else's dreams and fantasies. Each of us is unique and, while we can co-operate with others, we cannot manipulate them. We must first take responsibility for the relationship we need to have with ourselves. We cannot afford to lose ourselves in a co-dependent relationship where we perform to someone else's music, nor can we simply become one half of a couple. It is so much more powerful when two whole people unite in harmony.

On the subject of one's relationship with oneself, perhaps the most vital thing to realize is that initially we are not conscious of the part of opposite gender within ourselves. However, as we become more aware of it rather than fighting against it, we are able to use it as a source of energy within and also to combine it with the conscious self, the persona, and become a person of considerable depth of character. The diagram below illustrates this particular dynamic.

Persona ——————— **Self** ——————— **Animus/Anima**

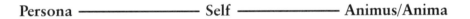

It is considerably easier to put oneself in touch with these depths once one has formed a strong relationship with the inner opposite. As a matter of interest, an easy way to check on the psychic health of the inner you is to ask yourself what you would do in the same circumstances if you were the opposite sex. With practice you will learn to highlight your weaknesses and fears. You will continually be surprised by yourself, because no-one can ever know themselves totally. You will find yourself capable of setting challenges which it will please you to overcome.

Wherever a person is in terms of psychological development, he or she will always be prone to seeing aspects of his anima or animus in another, and will either search for or admire those aspects in someone else. No matter how hard a person has worked at integrating these aspects, no matter how well they are understood, they will continue to exist at a level that remains largely unreachable. Jung himself said:

'Though the effects of anima and animus can be made conscious, they themselves are factors transcending consciousness and beyond the reach of perception and volition. Hence they remain autonomous despite the integration of their contents, and for this reason they should be borne constantly in mind.'

When we are younger we can afford to ignore the animus and anima. However, if we are to integrate either of these into our personalities so that we become aware of our inner power, we do need to recognize the dynamic that occurs when we are in relationship with someone, whether male or female. This is best illustrated by the following diagrams. The dynamic is slightly different regarding assertiveness and passivity in same-sex relationships, but still requires a balancing of the elements. In male-female relationships the dynamics of the relationship are most succesful when the man understands his own anima and the woman understands her own animus, as shown:

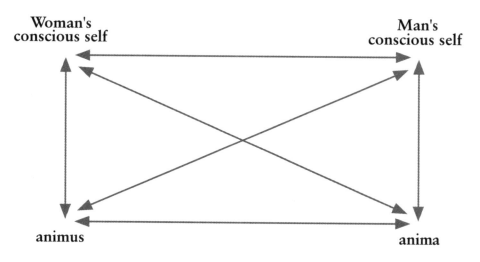

Our individuals will be aware that while their conscious selves are relating to one another, their animus and anima can carry on a relationship in the background.

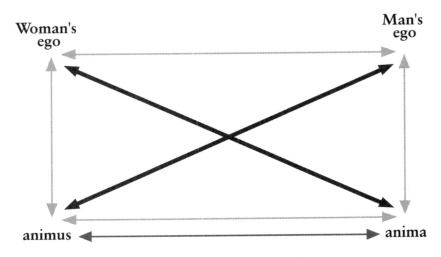

The relationship between a man's conscious self and a woman's animus and a woman's conscious self and a man's anima add certain subtexts to the interplay between them. Each person needs to learn how to 'manage' these various subtexts and background scenarios.

Only someone who has developed supreme confidence in themselves and has integrated all the subtexts will manage these things totally successfully. Perhaps therefore the art of relationship is in managing the various aspects of our personality and the subtexts they produce as successfully as they will permit us to do.

Natural dreams

Dreams are often the easiest route to sorting out problems we may have with the inner masculine or feminine. Unless we understand the meanings of dreams with apparently sexual or erotic content, we are liable to find them both distressing and frightening. We have to accept that although many dreams can have in them elements of what seem to be deviations from normal practices, this does not mean that the dreamer is perverted. This material is simply the mind's way of presenting a process that is going on (or perhaps needs to go on) at an internal, mostly unconscious, level to ensure the dreamer's health. Fantasies – that is, daydreams – that have an element of perversion in them should be thought of as a more conscious process. This may have some danger in it for the dreamer, since it is a more directed and controlled activity. In other words, the deviation from what might be considered normal has been deliberately brought through to consciousness.

Very occasionally, we may have dreams containing practices that are totally alien to us. Such dreams are simply the mind's way of translating and presenting in graphic terms aggressive or inappropriate impulses that could be harmful. The dreaming mind removes the taboos and restrictions imposed on the conscious self so that the individual can recognize the power of their instinctive urges. It is interesting that what now may be considered an unnatural practice, such as wearing an animal's head, was believed by pagan societies to give one greater power, or to give one the power of that animal.

Fetishism – or fastening on a particular object as part of a sexual 'ritual' – can occur quite frequently in dreams as we sort ourselves out. In such dreams the mind is actually giving us the opportunity to concentrate on the object, and thus it is the symbolism of the object that needs to be grasped. (The practice of fetishism in real life is centred on the sexual act itself.) The information is that we cannot do without this 'thing' in our lives, and must do everything we can to provide ourselves with it. For instance, dreaming of a fetish over women's clothing would suggest a need to develop the more feminine, sexually sensitive part. Dreaming of a cuddly toy might suggest the need for more tenderness. The use of a fetish suggests a kind of displacement mechanism, a way of directing the mind away from an actual activity. Such a dream may be indicating that we should pay attention to sorting ourselves out and understanding our basic drives before we attempt to integrate our masculine and feminine sides – for example, the fundamental differences between the way we as individuals handle enthusiasm and passivity or logic and intuition.

For young people, dreaming of sexual activity with – usually – the opposite sex parent or member of the extended family is a perfectly natural part of maturing. The teenage girl particularly may go through a process of being erotically attracted to her father, only to realize that that attraction is inappropriate and should be directed outward beyond the family. When the dreams are of sex with – or a sexual attraction to – other members of the family, the dream self is creating a particular scenario in order to highlight the information it is attempting to give. This is most likely so that the conscious mind can come to terms with society's taboos and restrictions. The young person has to learn to accept or reject those embargos and understand the reasons why they may have been imposed. On a slightly more esoteric level, the dreamer may recognize the fact that he or she needs to assimilate many of the qualities belonging to the other person in the dream.

Incestuous dreams can also highlight different types of abuse, not necessarily sexual. Sometimes inadvertently other members of our family can hurt us by not loving us in the way we need to be loved. They can penetrate our personal space in a way that may be hurtful to us. When we are ready to deal with that type of hurt, dreams of incest may surface. It cannot be stressed too strongly that such dreams do not necessarily mean that the individual was in fact abused. It is the perception of the individual that is relevant. (When working with dream interpretation, care should be taken not to develop 'false memory syndrome', where a 'memory' is accepted as a fact, when it is simply a perception of an event.)

It is also possible that incest in dreams can alert us to situations that occur in waking life. For instance, if our partner has similar qualities to one or both of our parents, dreams of incest may occur to alert us to certain patterns of behaviour either in ourselves or our partner. We may perhaps have a tendency to be a victim within certain situations, and need to handle these more positively.

Sadism is the need to hurt someone else. Masochism is the ability to accept hurt from another person. When the aggressive tendencies in an individual are curbed for whatever reason, dreams of sadism or masochism can arise later. It could be, for instance, that anger or cruelty was not seen as appropriate when the dreamer was a child, causing them to suppress some very natural feelings. In later life this can manifest in dreams as the opposite side of an individual. Thus a meek and mild person may have sadistic dreams because the self-imposed inhibitions do not apply in the sleep state. Sadism in dreams can take many forms, ranging from childlike physical cruelty such as poking at a person to a representation of domination using tools such as handcuffs, whips and so on. It could be said that sadism in dreams actually indicates a need to be in control.

Masochism highlights even more strongly the dreamer's ability to become a victim. Once again this need not necessarily be only in a sexual sense. Many people are aroused by rough treatment, and such a dream may suggest the need for some kind of balance. Sado-masochism, where both sadism and masochism are inter-linked, is a perversion of the ordinary give-and-take that occurs in relationships. To have such a dream can alert us to extreme behaviour in either ourselves or others.

Dreams do occur in which there is a strong concentration on some kind of union with a child. Sometimes this can be simply a yearning for a particular child, or can be a desire for closeness that in waking life is inappropriate. This is in reality the need to come to terms with, and to understand, the child within ourselves. Often in the process of growing up we lose touch with a part of ourselves through difficulty and trauma. Through dreams it is possible to reconnect with that part of ourselves.

To dream of being raped suggests that one's personal space has been penetrated in an inappropriate way. While in law it is difficult to prove rape, any sexual activity that goes beyond the bounds of normality may be translated in dreams into sexual violation. Technically, it is not possible for a woman to rape a man. However, in dreams a man can feel just as violated as a woman, and can experience a woman's inappropriate behaviour as rape or violation. Conversely, a woman can become aware of her need to treat a man roughly through dreams of raping him.

In dreams it seems that the inner self is more in touch with ancient ceremony and ritual than we are consciously aware. (A ritual is defined as a prescribed order for a ceremony or service.) Many of the original pagan rituals were fertility rites and often had a sexual symbolism which appears in modern-day dreams. For instance, the lighting of a candle in dreams might hold both religious and sexual significance. The flame represents the life force, while the candle is phallic. Often such rituals appear in dreams as a way of alerting the dreamer to deeply buried information and knowledge. Most rituals are only harmful if they include sadism or masochism.

In sexual dreams, sacrificial acts – such as blood-letting, placing a partner upon an altar, symbolic bondage and so on – usually signify the need to make some kind of dedication. This can be either dedication to the person, or turning the sexual act itself into an act of worship. This suggests that the dreamer is aware of a need for a heightened state of consciousness. Such an act represents the coming together of the sacred and the profane.

A particular type of dream can highlight certain aspects of a character or personality. This is role-playing. The most commonly recognized roles are those associated with female domination, and in dreams these images usually arise in order to make the person aware of their true inner feelings. In fantasy the images are used to consciously create a sense of power, whereas in dreams they can highlight a sense of power that is not apparent in everyday life.

Finally, in the type of dream that deals purely with the unification of the masculine elements, or of the purely feminine, within us, we are often watching either ourselves or others. When this type of dream has sexual connotations, it usually suggests that we are removed from our own sexuality and may be dealing with an inner need to integrate the qualities rather than an external sexual desire. Sometimes voyeurism can be represented in dreams by watching ourselves in a mirror. In this case there may be some connection with eroticism or pornography. It is possible that the dreamer has difficulty in waking life in giving him or herself over completely to enjoyment of both their partner and the physical act.

Different Approaches, Different Results

It is not only sexually that both women and men have difficulty in giving themselves to their partners. From a psychological point of view, many people find it extremely difficult to let go of fears and doubts and give themselves up to the pleasure of a good relationship. We have already intimated that as people we are constantly attempting to reconnect to a part of ourselves that we have lost – or, perhaps more correctly, have mislaid. Through other people we can attempt to reconnect the masculine and feminine parts of ourselves to form one coherent whole and live as vibrant human beings, and yet the very idea of that is somehow frightening. This paradox is difficult to solve, because what we most want – a kind of autonomy – is also what we most fear.

It really does not matter whether we are masculine or feminine: we will still seek that autonomy and internal union and will reflect that in the way we handle our relationships with others. However, in this seeking outwards, men are more likely to use logical reasoning backed up by intuitive feeling, whereas a woman will use intuitive feeling backed up by logical reasoning. For example, a man might say, 'I like this woman because she has a sense of humour and therefore she makes me feel good', whereas a woman will say 'This man makes me feel good because he has a sense of humour'. Such examples are, of course, simplistic but a little thought will show the differences in the approach that men and women take to relationships.

The way that men and women have hitherto handled their sexuality is, of course, also very different. To introduce a little humour, it might be said that by nature men are hunters and women gatherers; men are seekers and women receptive – a truly stereotypical viewpoint. We can no longer rely on stereotyping, and certainly our behaviour differs at various times in our lives. As women begin to understand themselves better, they recognize their own assertive qualities and demonstrate them within the sexual arena. As men are faced by that assertiveness, they are forced to become more aware of their more sensitive sides.

This inevitably gives rise to more fears and doubts on both sides and results in some of the projections onto a partner about which we have spoken earlier. A man can often initially allow himself to be lulled into a state of false powerlessness by an assertive woman, or even by someone who has not understood the need for a true balance within the personality. This means that he loses contact with his own true qualities of wisdom. Only when he recognizes that he is allowing himself to be emasculated will he come out of his stupor and appreciate that by developing wisdom and sensitivity he can come to terms with and empathize with those more difficult aspects in his partner.

A man, too, can be betrayed by his own perception of what he should be. The perception of the rough, tough manly man – the sort of man who, if we are honest, is perceived as a woman's saviour – is such a potent image that many men will have believed that this is how they should behave. To find that they are not cast in that mould, but have feelings and emotions that can be overwhelming, is very scary for them. Often, a man only recognizes this rough, tough manly man image as a chimera at the time of divorce or at the breakdown of a relationship. The code of masculinity expects that men will be able to handle problems on their own, yet most men do not have the personal skills to achieve this and find it difficult to be open and talk about themselves and what is going on. A man's emotions will be very intense and will run the gamut of grief, shame, helplessness, disbelief, anger, betrayal and loneliness. He will no longer feel in control of himself or the situation, and this feeling may be heightened if the woman has left him rather than vice versa.

Several myths about men and broken relationships have arisen over the years, and these have become even less valid as economic and cultural mores change. Here are a few of them:

He is stronger financially while his partner suffers. Modern divorce laws and better arbitration make this much less likely, particularly as more women return to work. Both may be less well off as a result of a breakup.

He is now free of all responsibility. Many men are prepared to take responsibility for their children and other aspects of joint ownership, but a woman who feels or finds herself to have been wronged will often argue over child access and possessions, clouding the real issue, which is the welfare of everyone concerned.

He relishes his freedom to date as many women as he wants. His problem initially may have been one of commitment (or lack of it) and he needs time to adjust to a different way of life, to find out who he really is.

He may have had a mistress before the divorce or breakup. Statistics suggest that about eighty percent of new relationships begun before the breakdown of an existing relationship do not last, but are part of the growing realization that all is not well with the existing relationship.

He will probably grow distant from his children. Often this is because he cannot handle the emotional trauma and is forced eventually into accepting that a clean break may be the only answer, however painful.

He is likely to be more violent than his partner. Studies over the last 15 years have shown that 'women reported the expression of as much or *more* violence in their relationships as men.' Also it is suggested that male violence decreases with better education, whereas the reverse is true of female violence – better educated women tend to be more violent.

In actuality, it is far more common for a man to simply feel confused, scared and lonely. Therapy does not always help, unfortunately, particularly in the short-term, because men find it difficult to take a long, hard look at themselves. If they are prepared to take the risk of adopting this course, they will – in common with women – often have to go back to childhood in order to find reasons for a particular way of behaving. This can sometimes give a completely different perspective on who they thought they were. They too must confront their own particular dragons.

Two Potent Archetypes

Every woman will recognize the archetype of Destructive Mother and Focused Power without necessarily being able to give them a name. These are also the two aspects of femininity which most frighten men and therefore have often been given the name of the Dragon and the Witch. These two aspects of the feminine seem to present themselves as negative and destructive. However, once they are tamed and understood they can become highly creative, both for the woman and those around her. Without an integration of these qualities within herself, a woman cannot aspire to fully appreciate either herself or the men in her life, or to give herself permission to use what is hers by right – the power to act with wisdom and integrity.

The Dragon

In folklore the dragon is depicted as a reptile-like monster not unlike a crocodile. It was usually described as having huge claws, wings and breath which belched forth flames. In a number of tales associated with ancient cultures the dragon stood for all aspects of evil and destruction. Perhaps the most important of these tales for our purposes of understanding the feminine is a Mesopotamian epic, written in about 2000BC, explaining the creation of the world. In this tale, the goddess Tiamat is a dragon-like characterization of the powers of the oceans and the forces of chaos. She has to be destroyed to bring order to the universe.

The Greeks and Romans believed that dragons could understand the secrets of the Earth and convey them to mortals. In Christian imagery the dragon represents paganism and is often shown being crushed under the feet of saints and martyrs.

Stories originating in northern Europe depict dragons as both objects of terror and as beneficent. Most cultures have in their stories dragons of one sort or another. They also figure prominently in the mythology of the Orient, especially China and Japan. In China the dragon is traditionally regarded as a symbol of good fortune and was chosen as the national emblem of the Chinese Empire. It is deified in the Daoist (Taoist) religion.

As recently as 1608 the existence of dragons was accepted as scientific fact, with their supposed natural history and anatomy being carefully recorded, although it is now suggested that the skeletons thought to be of dragons were probably of dinosaurs.

It is when we come to look at Jung's archetype of the dragon as an adversary to be overcome that we begin to appreciate why the many myths and stories which we inherit have, as a central motif, the appearance of such a beast. The Babylonians' fight with Tiamat, Minerva's throwing of the dragon's serpentine body into the sky before it had time to unwind, and the labour requiring Hercules to kill the dragon in order that he could win the golden apples – all have the same theme of the overcoming of an arch enemy to give the hero or heroine untold riches. Jung himself said:

'In myths the hero is the one who conquers the dragon, not the one who is devoured by it. And yet both have to deal with the same dragon. Also, he is no hero who never met the dragon, or who, if he once saw it, declared afterwards that he saw nothing. Equally, only one who has risked the fight with the dragon and is not overcome by it wins the hoard, the 'treasure hard to attain'. He alone has a genuine claim to self-confidence, for he has faced the dark ground of his self and thereby has gained himself. . . . He has acquired the right to believe that he will be able to overcome all future threats by the same means.'

Jung viewed the dragon as a Great Mother archetype which must be defeated before any man can become a 'king' in his own right. The over-controlling, protective mother appears in the dreams of men, in particular, in various guises, such as the spider, dragon, and vampire. The need for independence from this aspect is seen as paramount in a man's spiritual growth. It is also true that any woman must understand and control this side of herself. She must do this for her own psychological and spiritual health, lest she accept too readily the projection of this archetype by the men around her. In order for the energy and power inherent in this archetype to be released for her own use, she must also recognize that this aspect of herself is largely unconscious. As in the story of Tiamat, it is beneath the 'sea', a common symbol for hidden emotion.

Bringing this aspect into her consciousness can be very frightening for any woman and those around her. The more outgoing personality may risk the danger of breakdown and of alienation from the world. The more introverted type will probably experience her dragon as terrifyingly powerful.

One way of coming to terms with these manifestations is to transfer them into powerful playmates by using a form of active imagination. This means that you visualize yourself confronting your own particular image of the dragon, taking careful note of how it first presents itself, since there is much to be learned from this. Then visualize yourself gradually befriending it, overcoming your apprehension along the way. This may take some time and several attempts but do not be discouraged. Eventually you will learn how to have your dragon co-operate with you and even to be playful.

Jung was later to accept the image of the dragon as the main obstacle to progress in any psychological or spiritual journey. Classifying each type of personality as having a particular 'dragon' to overcome gave different constellations of types of difficulty that seemed to be common to many. The basic premise is this: the Hero is the person who recognizes the necessity of embarking on his or her inner journey and of undertaking a particular quest. At this point our Hero may not be aware of any particular task – he or she simply realizes that a journey is to be made and this urge cannot be denied. Later the task to be performed is also appreciated and understood. Failure to succeed at this task means that the Hero may metamorphose into all that he fears – the negative side of him or herself. Success means that the dragon – or main difficulty and block to progress – has been overcome. Complete success occurs when the hero earns the rewards that are due and desired; these usually being a sense of integration, a suitable partner, riches (personal or material) and a sense of achievement.

This Hero's quest remains the blueprint for numerous myths and stories today. Reading and understanding these myths can give us a better insight into our inner self. The stories that draw us most strongly are the ones that most closely approximate to our own inner quest. The acting out of our own story and the appreciation of how we handle our dragons in everyday life can motivate us to understand our lives as we must lead them. Similarly, it behoves us all to become familiar with, and to understand, the second important aspect of femininity – the Witch.

The Witch

Wise women and witches (the terms are synonymous) were cherished members of their communities until the 16th century and what has been called the 'burning times'. Their wisdom was fundamental to the well-being of the people they helped, through healing, herbalism, midwifery, clairvoyance and counselling. The witch or wise woman was concerned with both ordinary day-to-day living and the spiritual health of individuals and the community. She was mistress of the art of being powerful, drawing on sources of knowledge from within the family.

A witch viewed as a sacred trust her responsibility to pass on whatever wisdom she had accrued so that it would not be lost forever. For this purpose she would keep a grimoire, a manual containing all her knowledge. In common with other Shamanistic societies, a witch would recognize that, while the basic skills of her craft could be taught, the art which made them unique could not, for this entailed personal dedication and inclination. The rituals, charms and talismans which were used had been proved over generations of usage and had acquired an energy of their own; each witch simply put her own energy into what she was required to do. In addition to her own energy, a much subtler energy was made available to her by her use of the rituals. Thus she conformed to the requirements of what later became the archetype of the independent woman with a deep knowledge but lack of fear of the more intransigent inner environments and negativities of both herself and others.

The persecution of witches, which reached its peak during the early 17th century, was in many ways symptomatic of a pervasive fear of the power of women and their mysteries. It is worth remembering that just previously in Britain there had been a Virgin Queen (Elizabeth I) who had been in dispute with her relative Mary, Queen of Scots, and many saw this as a conflict between the two polarities in women, with the 'good' Elizabeth fighting the 'bad' Mary. There was still a great deal of conflict between the religious belief systems of Catholicism and the newly introduced Protestantism. Those who tried to maintain their own integrity and belief in the rituals of the Old Religion, paganism, were caught in the middle and persecuted from all sides.

More universally, Mother Church (Roman Catholicism) attracted to herself many men as priests who were bigoted and fearful, particularly among the Jesuits. As the essential connection with Mother Earth was lost to or suppressed in them, women who would not conform could be accused of having made 'pacts with the Devil'. If something went awry, be it major or minor, then it must be because an evil influence had been brought to bear and that could be blamed on certain women. Thus, the stereotype of the old, bitter and twisted witch who used her power for evil was formed.

Feminine power is not simply a hypothesis but is normally vibrant and dynamic. That magnetism and intuition is first recognized instinctively by most men in their mothers and then in their partners as an influence on their sexual senses. When it is thwarted or ignored it retires underground and does indeed become bitter and twisted. Representations of the Black Virgin or Goddess seen throughout all religions acknowledge the potential for the power of the negative. We have already explored elsewhere the principle of destructive goddesses such as Hecate and Lilith, and as archetypes these are very potent images for women.

Only by coming to terms with the aspects of destructiveness and with the bitter and twisted power within herself can a woman reach her full potential. This was recognized by Jung and his pupils in their development of the witch archetype. It is important, however, not to perceive this archetype in the same terms as the stereotype of the bitter and twisted woman, but rather as a feminine energy which is capable of using the power that it has, both emotionally and destructively.

The witch as an archetype is the lesser, more negative side of the priestess. The epitome of intuitive woman, the priestess has developed a close relationship with her own concept of the divine, and has dedicated herself to its service. The witch has an awareness of that intimate connection and the power that it confers, but she uses it for her own ends. The balance that a woman can achieve between the priestess and the witch – that is between altruism and selfishness – will ultimately help her turn into a wise old woman. When a woman becomes aware of the witch within, she begins to touch into her ultimate sense of being.

There is within each of us a universal energy, a very basic source of growth and healing that is experienced as the energy of the psyche. This can destroy or salve, rebuff or attract. However it manifests, it will necessitate the individual coming to terms with a force above and beyond the self. This energy is in no way a divine power but is what today might be called 'charisma'. It is indeed a manifestation of personal magic and in confronting the witch – the need to use this power from an emotional standpoint – a woman learns, among other things, to practise self-control in her dealings with the supernatural.

Later, as a woman loses her fear of her intrinsic power, she understands that she does not have to accept the projection of the masculine view that she is somehow evil, wrong or unruly. She is then able to establish and internalize her own personification of a spiritual guardian. Sometimes this is a figure of the goddess, sometimes a spiritual representation of a guide and sometimes the form of an angel. However it manifests, it can be accepted as a profound step towards the 'birth of personality'.

Often the manifestation can be of a witch-like figure that many would consider evil, but may simply signify ancient wisdom. We tend to develop a picture of the stereotypical witch as an old crone with her conical hat and her cauldron. Interestingly, the conical hat is now thought to be a representation of the headdress worn by ancient priestesses which was designed to assist their concentration and to give a better connection with the powers of the goddess. The cauldron is an ancient symbol of femininity, representing the womb and the potential of all things. It was also very necessary to the Wise Woman who was, as has been already mentioned, most likely to have been a herbalist.

The link between a magical cauldron and the goddess is well illustrated by a myth preserved in the Book of Taliesin, a 13th century manuscript which is transcribed from the work of the great Welsh satirical poet of the 6th century. Ceridwen, which means witch or sorceress, was the keeper of the Cauldron of Inspiration and Knowledge. Her son Afagddu was apparently not all that a mother could wish for. To compensate for his shortcomings, his mother brewed a cauldron of magical liquid intended to make him completely wise. Gwion, another son, charged with the task of looking after the brew, accidentally spilt some and licked his finger, thus receiving the wisdom intended for the other boy. Extremely angered by this turn of events, Ceridwen changed Gwion into a grain of corn, metamorphosed herself into the form of a hen and ate him. (This act is, of course, also symbolic of the devouring mother we have already seen in this chapter.) Nine months later the boy was reborn and Ceridwen set him afloat in a boat. He was given the gift of prophecy.

Ceridwen is often described as the 'Old One' or Hag of Creation. She is perceived as both creator and initiator, functions seen in all hags (holy women) and witches. She causes things to be reborn (changed, by having been given her protection) and at the same time is in charge of the actual process of generation. She has the power of knowing what is needed, whatever the circumstances.

This power is perhaps the most important with which today's woman must come to terms. In no way can she afford to use her anger as a destructive weapon, but she has the capacity – and indeed probably should be allowed – to express her passion for change in whatever way is appropriate. She thus moves away from the frightening archetype that appears so often in men's dreams as a reflection of their inner feminine and approximates most closely to the transformative power that is the birthright of the witch in every woman.

Today's true witches are those women who choose to make things happen in their own lives which will have an effect on – either now or later – the face of the world in which they live. Ceridwen recognized first her son's shortcomings and then her own mistake in entrusting a task, which after all was hers, to an inexperienced boy. In taking steps to remedy the situation, she took responsibility for her actions. When woman is able to take such responsibility, particularly for her own thoughts, she is in touch with her own inner power and acknowledging her status as witch.

To practise the art of being a witch – not to practise witchcraft, which is something completely different and requires a set of ethics, beliefs, rituals and philosophy – it is useful to try a type of guided imagery in much the same way as with the dragon. You might, for example, visualize asking your inner witch to show you how to make changes to some small things in your life. Suggest that she shows you first what needs to be done and then how to do it. You may find that you receive some very strong impressions, feelings or ideas. This is training your intuition. Only you can decide if you will then make those changes, but should you decide to do so, you can then ask your witch to help you to make them happen.

This sense of co-operating with an inner power can become quite exhilarating, and you must be careful not to let your ego run away with you. The best way of ensuring it does not is continually to ask yourself whether the change you desire is really necessary. As you become more proficient at bringing about change, you may find your internal image of the witch changing to become more akin to a Grecian woman or goddess. You are now working with the more positive elements of the witch and beginning to lose the will to destructive power that can get in the way of your truly creative energy.

A Powerful Combination

Having met and understood both the dragon and the witch within, it is helpful to see whether these two aspects of the personality can be combined in a positive, creative, dynamic way. As we have seen, the dragon epitomizes the initially negative obstacles to progress that we meet within ourselves. The witch, by contrast, is that destructive power within ourselves which becomes personal magic when harnessed. The relationship between the two can undoubtedly be exploited, but how? Many myths and fairy stories show us.

The hero on his journey often has no idea how he is going to overcome his adversary, until he meets the witch. It is usually a requirement of the story that no matter how hideous she may be, he is required to help her in some way, whereupon she either gives him various gifts which will help him or she metamorphoses into a beautiful woman whose knowledge can help him.

Put simply, this suggests that anyone undertaking their own inner journey must first acknowledge and have consideration for true feminine power – however much it is feared. Once this is accomplished, there are new perspectives to be gained and there is new knowledge to be assimilated. Only then can outmoded ideas, beliefs and concepts be tackled and overcome. The 'dragon' must be destroyed. It would seem, however, that as woman gains more and more understanding of herself, this dragon might be tamed rather than destroyed and the power and energy that is there in abundance might be used for what we have called the Greater Good. If the witch is allowed to use her energy properly, the need to use it destructively disappears and harmony can be achieved.

Your Own Journey

Using guided imagery, as has been suggested for both the dragon and the witch, try undertaking your own hero's or heroine's journey. Before you do, though, think carefully about what you wish to accomplish. This is your journey, so don't try anything too difficult initially. It may be enough just to make up your mind that you simply wish to complete this particular exercise to bring about a meeting between the dragon and the witch.

- Try to guarantee that you will not be interrupted; silence the doorbell and the telephone and make sure that you will not be disturbed by family and day-to-day concerns.
- Now, in your imagination, go searching for the witch. Remember that ultimately she is there to help you. However she presents herself, you will need to work with her to gain her co-operation. As though talking to a friend, try to ascertain why she appears to be so negative and what she (or you) needs to change in order for her to help you. It is important that you do not show fear but treat her with the respect she deserves.
- The perception differs between the masculine and the feminine. On the heroine's journey which we explored earlier, the witch represents all in the heroine that is potentially negative and restricts her ability to be powerful. On the hero's journey, she represents all that he fears in woman.
- When you have gained the witch's co-operation, you can move on to search for the dragon. Because of the work you have done previously, you will know that the dragon can be playful and act unexpectedly, but for now be aware that you are capable of dealing with anything that happens. Watch carefully to see how the dragon presents itself and, in your own mind, work out a strategy for bringing it under control. You may find that you wish to kill the dragon, but remember this would to a certain extent negate the purpose of the

exercise, which is to harness the dragon's power and not destroy it.

• At this point, it is good to become aware of how you deal with the problems and obstacles ahead of you in your imagination. This will help you to understand your own reactions. Do not try to force this part of the exercise, but allow the images and thoughts to arise spontaneously. As soon as seems feasible, try to bring the images of the dragon and the witch together and bring about their co-operation with one another. You might, for instance, envisage them performing a joint task as they learn how they work best together. Remember, this is supposed to be fun, so if nothing happens do not worry too much. This last part of the exercise (the joint task) could be done at a different time from the first if that seems easier.

In doing this exercise you are beginning to access some of the most powerful images there are. At the same time, as you grow in understanding, you will become more aware of the need for relationship as a step towards creating a union between the masculine and feminine sides of yourself.

CHAPTER 6

The Search For Union

'People spend a lifetime searching for happiness;
looking for peace. They chase idle dreams,
addictions, religions, even other people, hoping to
fill the emptiness that plagues them. The irony is the
only place they ever needed to search was within.'

– Ramona L. Anderson

As we have seen, the main focus of any work that a woman undertakes in order to discover her true self is the subtle balance between masculinity and femininity. She may achieve this balance privately within herself or in a more open, straightforward manner through her relationships. In this process she learns to integrate the two sides of her personality and to understand the duality of her own nature. What may start as an exploration of her sexuality often goes into perhaps hitherto unsuspected depths, requiring her also to reach an understanding of the true meaning of spirituality. Part of that search for spirituality can also be achieved through an understanding of partnership.

All of us have a need for wholeness through partnership, it being a perfectly natural side of our make-up – we are continually trying to become a unified whole while remaining consciously aware of our own inner duality, which is epitomized by the masculine and feminine aspects.

The impulses that have us seeking for union of one sort or another are very primeval urges that have to be understood if a woman is to step forward into her true power. On an internal level this seeking epitomizes the awareness that, in so many ways, we have become separated from our own beginnings and somehow must return to that source if we are to rest secure within it and also enhance it by what we have to offer.

For example, the child who seeks comfort from an adult is simultaneously trying to comfort that adult through an instinctive awareness of what is needed in order to give expression to that urge for comfort (expressing a mutual need). The teenager who flirts with the older man and with others of her own age is leading man back to a sense of his own identity through the age-old art of seduction. The mother who recognizes that her son must make full and satisfying relationships with others, the nun who seeks union only with God and the grandmother who waits for death so that she can rejoin her husband are all natural expressions of a woman's search for autonomy.

The search for independence is never going to be wholly successful until the individual accepts that independence also means interdependence – in other words, recognizing that none of us exists in a vacuum, that we need others in order to function properly as human beings and that we will need some people more than others. Our lives intertwine with others in many different ways, and not until we are deprived of meaningful contact do most of us appreciate how important this is to us on a personal level. For practical purposes, too, we need the skills and talents of others. We are indeed a global society and our survival depends upon the way we relate to the beings who share it with us.

Parental Relationships

We first learn to relate to others on an external level through our relationships with our parents. It was the norm a few years ago to blame (or praise) the attitudes and actions of parents for how the child grew up. If parents were demonstrative then the child would learn to be so. If the parents were abusive then the child would become so. To a certain extent this still holds, because the nature/nurture argument – whether one learns by example or whether one follows one's natural inclinations – has never truly been solved. However, in today's society there is much more of a climate for freedom and choice than previously. The right to choose her own destiny, which she had to fight for up until about fifty years ago, is now accepted by most young women as normal and no longer requires parental approval. Also, nowadays a young woman is in a position to make choices that a child cannot. She may repeat the same type of mistakes as her mother made – say, in her choice of mate or career – but, if she is sensible, she is much more likely than previous generations to wait and make an informed choice – and to acknowledge her mistakes. She will not allow others to influence her, but will be aware of her background, and particularly of her relationship with her mother.

The mother figure
The first relationship that any child makes is usually with its mother or with a substitute nurturing figure. Most children will internalize fairly early on what constitutes acceptable caring behaviour within their own environment. For instance, the little girl who is constantly chastised for supposed wrongdoing may well have recognized quite early on that this is the only way to gain attention, whereas another little girl may adopt behaviour based on a recognition that she can avoid chastisement by being nice or by blaming someone else.

Whether we like it or not, our mothers are our first icon of femininity, an illustration of a way of being. You may like to consider other female members of your own family and try to classify the differences and similarities in how they approach (or approached) life. How similar are these ways to those of your grandmothers? Who treats every excursion as an adventure? Who treats it as a trial of endurance? Who panders to men's needs and who expects them to be independent? Who tries to manipulate circumstances to their own advantage and who is content to let things slide? These are only a few examples and as you look more closely at your family, other comparisons will occur to you.

Now try to be very honest with yourself and look carefully at your own personality. How similar are you to your mother and how different? Why do you do certain things the way you do? Is it because you learnt the skill from your mother or did you experiment for yourself? Do remember that this process of examination is not one of self-flagellation or of apportioning blame; it is simply a way of assessing the subtleness of relationships in families, particularly between mothers and daughters.

The father figure
The second relationship that a little girl develops is with her father or a father figure. This is the cornerstone of all future relationships with the masculine in her life and sets the tone for the way that she thinks and feels about men. Gone are the days, thankfully, when inevitably father was a figure to be feared or was seen only briefly at the beginning or at the end of the day. Nowadays many men are more than happy to play their part in caring for their children and to be seen as loving, caring individuals rather than austere martinets. If a little girl experiences this first relationship with the masculine as hurtful or lacking in some way, that tends to set a level of poor self-esteem which is not easily eradicated later on. If she is given the confidence to believe in herself, perceiving herself as worthy of love, she will handle later male/female relationships more successfully. Often if a man has had a good relationship with the women in his own family, he is better equipped to deal with his own daughters. Conversely, of

course, if he has a family in which there are many strong women, he may feel himself to be inadequate and hampered in some way.

Just as a woman must consider her relationship with her mother if she is to understand herself, so also must she look very carefully at her relationship with her father. Was he someone with whom she felt secure? Did she experience him as being aggressive towards her mother or herself, or was he quiet and submissive? Was he used as a threat by her mother or was he himself threatening in some way? Was he a dreamer or a doer? Was he reliable or not? Again, all of these things are simply starting points for consideration, and you will develop your own set of questions to ask yourself.

Having done this, it is then important that you take time to look at the men with whom you have had – or are having – a relationship. How like your father are they and how unlike? Is there a particular overt characteristic belonging to your father that you can perceive in all of these men? Is there maybe a hidden trait that you seem to be homing in on? For now you are not going to do anything about these things; you are simply exploring a few ideas. Look also at the way that you tackle problems and difficulties or your own drives to succeed. Such things may owe a lot to your father and less to your mother. Incidentally, if, when in difficulty, you ask yourself the question, "How would I handle this if I were a man?", you may well find that your answer closely approximates to the way that your father would tackle the problem.

The next relationship to consider – and one that often gets lost when we are considering the way in which we learn how to relate to other people – is that between our parents. We are born into an already existing association that is changed forever by the very fact that we are the result of that association. The union between two people has, if you like, given birth to a tangible entity in its own right. This will almost inevitably cause some stresses and strains to which parents must make adjustments.

As children we are unlikely to give much thought to this, but as we grow up we need to look at the relationship between our parents for clues as to how we are going to act and react within the everyday world. Is this relationship a loving one based on respect and dignity or is it one in which there are subtle put-downs from one side or the other? Does each parent have or take the freedom to be themselves? Even on a very mundane level does the family unit come first or are one person's needs always put before those of the others? Such norms have a subtle but profound effect on the way we think of ourselves and later how we think of, and form, relationships. If parents are able to present a united front, is this done at the expense of other things? In other words, does the child grow up with a realistic view of relationship or is she led to believe that life is some fairy story that she will do her best to repeat within her own relationships?

Elsewhere in the book we consider how family myths develop, but for now you might like to look at how you have learnt to handle your parents' relationship. Did you feel included in it as a child or did you feel left out at times? Do you consider that your mother was a good wife or your father a good husband? Did they struggle to understand one another and to communicate and was there generally difficulty with these processes? Remember, again, that there is no blame attached to this process of review. It is not for you to apportion blame; you are simply looking for clues as to what has made you the way you are. There are subtle patterns of behaviour and expectations that you will have assimilated without even realizing it, which will have an effect on your own relationships both now and in the future. Take time to make a few notes as to where you think you might have been influenced both positively and negatively and resolve to explore these matters further.

Childhood perception is very different from that of an adult in that it is very clear-cut and innocent initially, but adult perception enables us to have insights in the light of further experience. Some of these insights may be painful, others joyful. All will allow you to drop or retain certain understandings that you have held on to until now and will allow you to experience yourself in a new way. Below is an exercise that might help you to do this.

Handing back the baggage

Having looked at your parents in the ways we have suggested to enable you to understand yourself in a new way, it is time to let go of the old patterns of behaviour and misapprehensions that you may have carried since childhood. One way to do this is to visualize yourself handing back those attributes to your parents so that your own personality can come through.

- First visualize yourself as a child surrounded by boxes. In each box is one of those old things that you now feel you no longer need. This might be, for instance, argumentative behaviour (an old pattern within the family), or the hurt of being misunderstood – something you have felt since childhood. The choice is yours.
- Now see yourself as an adult, wrapping the box up, signifying that you no longer require it and visualize yourself handing the box back to whichever parent you feel you have inherited it from. It does not matter that your parent is not present or perhaps is dead; it is your action of handing it back and therefore rejecting it as yours (unless you want it to be) that is important.
- Repeat this process at least three times until you really begin to feel that you are letting go of the behaviour, or characteristic.

In due course you – or others round you – should begin to notice changes in you, and you may well find that previous attitudes are no longer appropriate or acceptable.

Understanding these primary relationships allows us to take an objective look at the way a child grows away from very early influences.

CHAPTER 7

The Developing Personality

'If nature had arranged that husbands and wives should have children alternately, there would never be more than three in a family.'

– Laurence Housman

The preceding chapter has been designed to make you think about your primary childhood relationships – the basic building blocks that you have used to form your initial perception of the family into which you were born. To understand ourselves as women, we need to trace the way that we have grown up and how we have become the women we are.

Emotional Strength: The Child at Six

By the time a little girl has reached the age of six she is venturing out beyond the confines of the family. She is beginning to meet more adults, often as authority figures such as teachers, doctors and others who seem to her to be 'in charge' of her life. She is also meeting other children on a regular basis and hopefully beginning to make friendships and interact with them. She must expand her awareness of herself and recognize that other people can have an effect on the way she feels, whether that be good or bad.

At a slightly younger age she will have discovered if it is more important for her to rely on her own inner feelings or if she is more comfortable giving a perceived correct response to other people. This is the first awareness of introversion or extroversion in her and quite often sets the tone for her later life. Contrary to expectation, it is possible to learn to be more extroverted or introverted in later life. Wise parents, being aware of the possibility of emotional blockages, may like to take the time to ensure that their children learn to understand themselves and their emotional reactions quite early on.

By the age of six the little girl will be beginning to develop a sense of responsibility towards those she cares about. If this sense of responsibility is not carefully managed, and the child is overloaded, she may grow to become too responsible. The tasks she is given must be commensurate with her age, lest she ends up feeling that the world's problems are on her shoulders, or that 'everything' is her fault.

When we undertake to redevelop the six-year-old's natural curiosity and sense of adventure as part of our search for self, it is worthwhile reminding ourselves – with the help of photographs and family stories – of what sort of child we were. The questions you might ask yourself to get a sense of that time are:

- What do I remember, if anything, about the first year of infant school?
- Can I visualize my teacher and the classroom?
- What memories do I have of important events – eg, nativity play, sports day or special family occasions?
- Did I belong to any groups, such as the Brownies or teams in playground games?
- Was I popular with others or was I a lonely child?

Now, thinking about those times, try to remember what your feelings were. Were you excited, happy, sad, frightened, etc.? Reproduce those feelings as closely as you can, then try to remember other times when you felt the same way. For your own information, make a list of those times and try to find a common theme. This should help you form a better idea of what pleases you or what causes you problems.

While accepting that the feelings of the six-year-old you once were are valid and belong to that time, you will now be able to use the curiosity and innocence from that time in a mature manner. You may react emotionally like a six-year-old but you can respond rationally as an adult to the emotional moments in life. While you may find this exercise quite difficult initially, and sometimes painful, it is worthwhile and gives an insight into influences at a very impressionable time, when you were internalizing not just your perception of yourself but also a view of the world.

Often as an adult you will be able to remember a great deal about this period. If perhaps your memory is not as good as it might be, or you do not seem to recall everything fully, it may help to put yourself in a very relaxed state and make an affirmation to remember as much as you can. You may find that memories begin to trickle back, or that you have a dream highlighting that period.

As this stage comes into focus, you will find that as a child you were learning about the emotions you were capable of and how you handled them. You will have learnt quite early on whether displays of temper were appropriate within your family environment or whether they were frowned upon. You would have discovered whether the same ploys worked in the larger environment of the school playground or wherever. It can be a remarkable experience to watch a young lady of the age of six go through the whole gamut of feminine expressiveness in miniature from coquette to competitive woman, as she struggles to find a method of interacting with other people. Only by experimenting with her own way of expressing herself does the young girl learn what she is comfortable with and what makes others uncomfortable.

So it is that as each woman searches for an awareness of who she is, she will be able to experiment further with a full range of emotions. Where perhaps she has previously faced up to problems in a certain way (or not), she may find that her whole outlook changes and she can learn different and more appropriate ways of dealing with them. She will begin to understand why she has certain reactions and will be able to take control of and use difficult situations. No longer will she find herself feeling like a frustrated six-year-old, seemingly unable to cope with the life going on around her. Conversely, becoming aware of situations in which she received good feedback and loving care when she was a child enables her to decide that she needs more of that type of interaction and to work out how to achieve it in everyday situations.

Identifying dreams and aspirations

Ask yourself the questions:
- What did I want to be when I was six?
- Why?

Next ask yourself:
- Does this idea make me a) happy or b) sad?
- Was I encouraged in these dreams?
- Was I laughed at?

Finally:
- How closely have I succeeded?

This exercise should give you some idea of how not only you, but also your family, handled dreams and aspirations. This perception is part of developing confidence in yourself.

Self-Awareness: The Child at Eight

One of the most difficult things to be able to quantify is one's creativity. All too often, a woman, lacking belief in herself, will claim that she is not creative or has lost her creativity somewhere along the way. If she is to begin to appreciate herself and her imagination in a new way, she must go back to the beginning and rediscover her sense of wonder. This sense is an important part of growing up and is particularly apparent at around the age of eight.

Being creative does not necessarily equate with being artistic, but is more to do with learning to express an inner zest for life which can be recognized by others, often in a tangible form. It does not matter how the child expresses her creativity – writing, drawing, dancing, movement, etc. – so long as she is given an opportunity to do so. Neither does it matter whether that expression is good, bad or indifferent. The fact that she is given the opportunity to experiment with the various energies that are becoming available to her is sufficient. She has the opportunity to 'catch up with herself'.

During this time she is likely to be involved in, and experimenting with, finding out about herself. She is within what psychologists used to call the 'latency period', which is said to last about five years, from approximately the ages of six to eleven. This period is often marked by a lack of interest in boys and frankly masculine pursuits, though she may try out behaviour perceived as not specific to her femininity. Then, by imitating the behaviour of her mother and incorporating an increasing number of the beliefs and values of her culture, the girl becomes more strongly identified with her own femininity. Her way of expressing herself grows through learnt behaviour, and she is increasingly able to distinguish between right and wrong, or rather between acceptable and unacceptable behaviour.

She is likely to experiment with make-up and dressing up as

a way of finding her identity and will not appreciate being laughed at or considered ridiculous. If there is not a useful role model in the family, she may well look beyond it. A prime example of this was seen in the late 1990s with the Spice Girls' 'girl-power' phenomenon.

The views of an eight-year-old's peers are important to her and she will pay more attention to those of girls of her own age than of boys. This is probably the beginning of a skill – that of networking – that will stand her in good stead in her adult years. She is also likely to start making judgements based on her own experience rather than what she is told, and often concepts can become fixed, not to be changed until they are questioned in adulthood.

As a child continues to grow in confidence and ability and begins to explore the wider world of learning, teachers and care-workers sometimes uncover a condition that can be extremely puzzling. This is known as dyslexia and is perceived to be a major block to academic progress. It is, however, a highly creative aspect of the personality and is seen in numerous exceedingly talented original thinkers and artists. Many impediments to creativity have similarities to the condition of dyslexia, so it is worth understanding it in a little more detail.

Dyslexia is due to some flaw in the way that the sufferer's brain manages letters, word strings (how words are put together) and sometimes numbers. Largely, research has concentrated on cognitive or hearing-related causes. However, researchers have begun to broaden their approach and there is evidence suggesting that the condition might be linked to what is known as the primary reflex system. This is the name given to the earliest movements foetuses and newborns make in order to survive, assisting them firstly to move in the womb and later to find the breast and learn to suckle. According to Martin McPhillips, whose study was published in *The Lancet*: 'In normal development, we should transform [from the primary to the secondary system] at around six months after birth.' (The secondary system is that development in growth which means that the baby begins to sit up, eventually to stand up and take notice of its surroundings.) It is suggested that dyslexic children may struggle with reading and other tasks because their central nervous systems have not kept pace with their physical development. The most commonly observed reflex in infants with neurological problems is asymmetrical tonic neck reflex (ATNR). The suggestion is therefore that exercises that copy the movements of foetuses and infants could propel such children into the appropriate stage of development, reducing their reading difficulties.

McPhillips' study appears to prove that dyslexic children who had performed the primary reflex exercises showed a significant decline in their ATNR scores, improvement in reading, writing and following lines of text while others, given different tasks, did not.

There is some scepticism about the study's results. There is no reason to believe that sitting and moving your head in different ways could really change your learning ability. Yet yogic practice, which loosens tension in neck and shoulders in both adults and children, has been shown to improve creativity. If one wishes to be fanciful, one could suggest that the shoulders hold within them the 'shoulds' and 'should nots' and that these can be changed into 'I can' and 'I will'.

Expanding creativity

To get some sort of an idea of how to expand your own creativity, imagine that you are a child of approximately eight years old.

• You are sitting in a room that is nothing more than a square box. For you to feel comfortable you must furnish this room so that it both protects you and encourages you to be active.

• Make a mental list of the things you would need to furnish your own special space. Does the room have windows, one or more doors, a chimney and so on? Let your imagination run riot, for in this space you can create anything that you want.

• When you have created your room – and along with it the idea of a safe space – see whether you can remove the boundaries (the walls) and, still retaining the idea of a safe space or comfort zone, try to expand your awareness of the surrounding space.

• When you feel silly or can get no further, try looking at each block or difficulty through the eyes of the eight-year-old. Did someone tell you that you could not do this sort of thing? Did you stop using your imagination? Push your own personal boundaries a little further and take pleasure in doing so. It does not matter particularly whether you are successful – it is the attempt that is important.

The purpose of this exercise up till now has been to find a point of departure for other creative adventures. Later you will use this safe space as a reflection of your confidence in yourself and your abilities and you will find that your 'room' changes as your confidence grows.

• When you have developed your room into a safe haven to which you are happy to return at will, experiment within the room with your own talents and abilities and choose one activity to try out in your imagination. Choose something you have never done before – painting,

writing, embroidery, sculpture, fancy cooking or whatever.
• Imagine what it would be like to be an eight-year-old
trying it for the first time. What would give you pleasure?
What would frustrate you? Play with ideas until you are
confident in your imagined ability. Then, if you are very
brave, try out the activity in real life. Don't worry too much
if your first attempts seem crude and childish: you are after
all working from an eight-year-old child's perspective and
will improve with practice.

Self-Expression: The Pre-teen Group

Up until now we have been looking at the development of the
personality as it occurs through the perceptions of the child and
have tried to reach some understanding of the influences around
us in the first years of life. We now have some idea of the
profound effect that such influences have had on the way we think
and feel as adults. Most of those influences have come from the
family in which we grew up, and our schooling.

The ineffectiveness of the family as a unit, or of individual
family members in the parenting role, can have a profound
effect on other relationships and the children of the family.
Such ineffectiveness is often nobody's fault but the result of
circumstances, such as illness or teenage pregnancy. A family
unit that cannot call upon a range of resources – emotional,
financial or assistance from outside agencies – to help it cope
with problems, or to fulfil its responsibilities to the children in
the family, is often described as dysfunctional. This is not to say
that all or most families are dysfunctional. Nowadays divorce,
separation and other such family traumas are handled more
sensitively than hitherto and parents will often seek innovative
solutions to their own problems in order not to harm the
children. In other words, they are aware of the potential for

dysfunction and take steps to minimize the difficulties.

Child abuse and neglect is just one aspect of family dysfunction, and what one person sees as abuse another may accept as the norm. Naturally we are not referring to incest or sexual abuse, both of which leave emotional scars which may be very hard to deal with.

Each of us reacts in an individual way to the things that bothered us in childhood, and our responses as adults are often coloured by those childhood reactions. It is important to realize when attempting to review or instigate a growth process that our sense of self as women is reinforced by how we learnt to express ourselves in childhood. For example, if pocket money is short, one child may grumble but do nothing about it, another may steal, whereas a third may try to earn the money to buy a cherished object. By the age of ten a child is learning to express herself more openly and is beginning to experiment with ways of showing her individuality.

As adults it is often worthwhile to look back to find out what one's attitude was to those things that expressed our individuality most obviously, particularly in the pre-teen group. Did you hanker for nice clothes or was music an important part of your life and therefore a must-have? Did you tend to want something because other people had it or did you often seem to be ahead of the crowd and to set a trend? Did you feel hard done by if you were not able to achieve what you wanted? Would you voice your concerns or remain silent? There are many such questions one can ask oneself to elucidate one's attitude to self-expression. Again, many habits that developed in childhood may stay with us to the present day until we decide we have the courage to change them.

In terms of personal growth, we often need to develop enough self-discipline and confidence to carry out an intended course of action in order to make changes. Interestingly such self-discipline can find its roots in the way we widened our repertoire of responses in our pre-teen years. By learning a degree of wisdom, knowing when to speak and when to remain silent, when to act rightly and when to do nothing, we should be able to steer a careful course towards success. Ideally, a child will begin to develop these skills at around the age of ten.

The discipline and self-discipline that a child – and the adult she will become – develops will depend to a large extent on the attitude that others have to the way that she expresses herself and how she responds to them. Discipline is training through which we develop a degree of self-control and self-sufficiency. This results in conduct that follows the rules of the society in which we exist. Self-discipline is something even more subtle, allowing us to develop our own set of standards – conduct that brings us what is required for a life that we decide is successful.

A child's attitude to discipline – both her own and that of others – is often coloured by her attitude to punishment. The two terms are often confused, but the best way of drawing a distinction between them is to emphasize the positive associations of 'discipline' and the negative connotations of 'punishment'. The following differences can be highlighted:

- Discipline should arise out of respect for the child and her capabilities and allow her to develop focus, whereas punishment is based on a perception of wrong behaviour or lack of self-management.
- While in both cases there may initially be a figure of authority, discipline develops the power for the child to take control of herself and her environment while punishment implies power and dominance over the child.
- Discipline is intended to be educative and punishment is often deliberately used to inflict pain – physical or emotional

– and is often used in an attempt to vent the frustration and anger of the authority figure.

• Discipline focuses on preventing further bad behaviour by encouraging the development of internal controls; punishment, however, is a method of imposing external controls which may not alter future behaviour, unless the individual understands the reason for punishment.

• Discipline can strengthen interpersonal and family bonds provided that individual resources and a sense of value results; punishment, particularly if it is continual, devalues both the perpetrator and the sufferer and usually causes a deterioration of relationships.

Both discipline and punishment behaviour patterns may be transmitted to the next generation. A defence mechanism consisting of imitation of the antagonist can occur within the punishment scenario, while a disciplinarian may pass on a similar behaviour pattern to his or her children. In addition, where there has been excessive punishment there may be some degree of dissociation when the victim refuses to acknowledge the emotions brought on by disapproval. If a woman is not to become a victim of her own circumstances, she must discover what her attitude to discipline and punishment really is.

We have taken the time to think about the way a child of about ten years looks at life and how she is treated. This helps us to become aware of how our ability to express ourselves begins to make itself felt. Our way of expressing ourselves and our beliefs may need to be adjusted as we begin to make use of our talents and abilities.

As adults, we may now find that restrictive beliefs – such as an inability to do something – can be dropped. Where we have previously accepted our own inadequacies, we can substitute a will to succeed at our chosen venture. Where our question may have been 'Why me?' now it can become 'Why not me?' When our reply to a request has been 'Yes but ...' it can be changed to 'Yes and ...' and we can be far more creative and pro-active. We can do and be anything we wish.

Following is an exercise that may help to get rid of restrictive beliefs – those beliefs stopping us reach our full potential.

Overcoming negative beliefs

- Take a piece of paper and a pen and write down as many restrictive beliefs or excuses that you can come up with. These might range from 'I can't do X because ...' to 'I'm too stupid to do X because ...'.
- Look at each one carefully and try to remember where the belief came from. Whose voice can you hear in the statement? Is it your own or someone else's? Someone else's voice means that it was probably a figure of authority in your pre- or early teen period, in which case remind yourself that they were expressing an opinion not telling you something you needed to know. If it is your voice you can hear, then it is something you have come to believe and is something you can change.
- Now, taking each restrictive belief in turn, work with it to eradicate it. Incidentally, you should work with no more than three such beliefs in one day, otherwise there is too much negative input.

There are three or possibly four stages to the process of changing negative beliefs.

- Preface the belief with the statement 'I believe that ...'. Thus our two statements above would become 'I believe I can't do X because ...' and 'I believe I'm too stupid to ...'

• Now ask yourself if you really believe these last statements. If you do, you must set about changing that belief using the reframing technique shown below. If you don't, substitute a more accurate statement for the here and now, one that gives you the option of growth. You might try something like 'My fears are stopping me from doing X and I can overcome them.' Or 'I am capable of doing X because I have researched what I must do.'

• Finally, work out a plan of campaign to help you succeed, and decide how much discipline you will need to achieve your goal. If the idea of having to be disciplined puts you off, simply decide how much leeway you will give yourself, before you decide that you cannot succeed, i.e. you have not given up before you start.

Six-step reframing

This technique is designed to assist in personal development and helps us come to terms with behaviour or reactions in ourselves that we have not previously understood. It deals directly with several psychological issues and is a technique which, once learned, can be used to eradicate what might be termed inappropriate behaviour.

However bizarre or destructive a course of behaviour may appear, on some level of the psyche (although the purpose is often hidden from us), there must be a positive outcome, somewhere. There must always be some benefit to a particular aspect of our personality, though not always to the whole person. It does not make sense to do something that is totally contrary to our interests.

It is possible to use a 'reframing' process to learn how to change our behaviour for the better and to re-train those parts of us that are preventing progress. Take as your starting point the idea that the part of you that is misbehaving does not know that it is and will continue in ignorance until it is made aware of the consequences. You might like to think of this process as re-training a very childlike part of you. Your behaviour is modified in small steps, enabling you to judge the effect of the modification and encouraging ongoing adjustment.

By using these six steps to change behaviour, you are recreating your present and offering yourself the opportunity of enhancing any future you may decide to create. This method can be used to change both external behaviour and internal reactions. If, for instance, you perpetually get flustered when asked to perform a certain task, you can find out why you have this reaction and retrain yourself to act more appropriately.

Step 1: Identify the behaviour or response
If you listen carefully to yourself you will usually sense a reaction such as 'I want to ... but X stops me'. Or, 'I don't want to be like this, but ...'. Remember, you are seeking out the part that causes the behaviour. It is a good idea, once you have identified the behaviour, to acknowledge that aspect of your personality –perhaps just by making a simple statement – and how it has been up till now, because this reinforces the idea that it is a separate – if unconscious – part of you. This part will have had its own reasons for responding in the way it does and it is important to appreciate that reason. You do not need to understand the reasons at this stage; it is enough simply to accept that there must be a reason for that aspect to act in the way it does.

Step 2: Communicate with the part responsible
Following the idea that you are made up of many parts or facets, perceive yourself going inside your own being and asking 'Will the part responsible for this [*state the behaviour*] communicate with

me with full awareness now?' There will usually be a slight, totally spontaneous shift in awareness as you do this. Notice what response you get. Be open to subtle internal sights, sounds and feelings. Do not force it, just wait. You should receive a definite signal – often a slight body feeling. If you can consciously reproduce that exact signal you are still trying to control your responses. In that case, ask the question again until you get a 'communication' over which you have no control.

Remember that the element responsible is unconscious. If it were not, you could just stop the behaviour. When the various aspects of you are at odds with one another, this fact will communicate itself to you through some slight change in feeling or emotion. This involuntary signal can be as slight as the tightening of a muscle or a feeling of withdrawal. You have to be very aware.

Now you need to clarify and intensify that response. Perhaps the best analogy is that it is like two electrical wires making contact with one another. As you become more aware, the response will strengthen. If it does not, you have not yet gained the cooperation of the part concerned, in which case wait for a better opportunity. This response is somewhat different from an intuitive awareness, though one can enhance intuition by becoming more consciously aware of the spontaneous responses that can be experienced when using that particular tool.

Step 3: Separate the intention from the behaviour
Still thinking of this aspect as a separate entity or part of you, either thank it or acknowledge it for co-operating. Try to get the element that is responsible for your behaviour to let you know what it is trying to do – ie what its motives are. By questioning it you may receive your positive response, or you may simply 'know' what the answer is. You may be surprised at the

information that comes up. Again, thank and acknowledge the element of your personality for the information, and for doing this for you.

The reason for working in this way is that it helps you to be more objective about your behaviour rather than simply reacting instinctively. Think about whether you actually can go along with the intention or motive of that facet of your personality or whether overall it is an inappropriate response.

Always assume that this facet of your personality sees a good intention or purpose behind what it is doing and perceives some benefit. You might like to use the three questions

- What does this behaviour do to me?
- What does this behaviour do for me?
- What benefit do I get out of this behaviour?

Now go inside and ask that facet, 'If we can find a better way of doing this, would you be willing to try it?'

You may get a negative reaction based on fear initially. A straight 'No' probably means you are not totally clear as to your own intentions.

Step 4: Ask your creative aspect to generate new ways that will accomplish the same purpose

There will have been times in your life when you were creative and resourceful. Communicate your positive intention to your creative side by using positive thought or perhaps affirmation. You can then hold what is almost an internal brainstorming and come up with other ways of accomplishing the same outcome. Ask the part which has been in difficulties to choose only those behaviours it considers to be as good as, or better than, the original behaviour. These behaviours must be instantaneous and immediately feasible.

Ask it to give the 'Yes' signal each time it has another choice. Continue until you get at least three 'Yes' signals. You can take as long as you wish over this part of the process. Thank your creative aspect when you have finished.

Step 5: Ask the negative aspect if it will agree to use the new choices

You can now mentally rehearse a new behaviour for a future situation.

If you have been successful so far you will sense the permission in some way. If you get a 'No', think of it as though you were training a child. You might agree with the aspect that it has permission to use the old behaviour if the new choices do not give a satisfactory result, but you would like it to try the new choices first. If you still get a negative response then reframe again, this time focusing only on the part that objects to the new behaviour as an even smaller part of the original facet of your personality, to remove the objection. This means going back to Stage 2 to understand the objection – working with the objection first.

Step 6: Ecological check

If you think of all the various aspects of you as though they were a family living together, it will become obvious that certain members of that family might object to a change in behaviour. You need to know if there are any other 'members' that would object to your new choices. Ask the question: 'Does any other part of me object to any of my new choices?' Be sensitive to any reaction and make sure that you are very thorough in your assessment of it. If there is a signal, ask that particular aspect to intensify the signal so that you can be sure it is an objection. If you fail to ensure that the new choices meet with approval, one part of you may well sabotage your work.

If there is a difficulty you can do one of two things. Either go back to Step 2 and reframe the bit that cannot accept the new behaviour or ask the creative aspect – in consultation with the objective part – to come up with more choices. Make sure these new choices are also checked for any new objections.

By using negotiation skills between apparently separate parts of our selves, we are simultaneously able to apply logic and intuition. Anyone using a technique that accesses parts of the personality as though they were separate people by turning inwards will be in a state of altered consciousness. This altered state of consciousness enables the everyday, perhaps restrictive, personality to be bypassed.

(To help with uncovering restrictive beliefs you may have internalized and accepted during your pre-teen and teenage years, see the Workbook and specifically the exercises Vision Quest and Extracting Ideas (see pages 183 and 184), and the section Creating Space for You at the end of this chapter.)

A Glimpse of Potential: The Early Teenage Years

The transition period between the ages of eleven and about sixteen is an important one for any girl. It marks a time when she becomes aware of her own power and the potential that she will be able to develop in later years. She will want to be trying out new ways of being and new relationships. Sometimes she will have more energy than she knows what to do with, and sometimes she will be so exhausted that she does not know how to cope. Her moods will swing without rhyme or reason, and every month her body will remind her that she is a woman.

The teenager today is fortunate in that better education means that she will have the opportunity to develop a healthy respect for her own body, fostered by the attitudes around her. Those times when her body seems misshapen, will not behave itself or causes her difficulty can be treated sympathetically and openly by women who have experienced the same problems themselves. Where a teenager comes up against an old-fashioned attitude, she may later need help to understand the relationship between her own body and her sexuality, having felt that either or both were deficient in some way.

With such understanding comes new responsibility; that of recognizing that at times her first concern must be for herself and her own well-being. A woman's monthly cycle is at one and the same time a blessing and a curse, this latter word having been used by many in previous generations, almost as an acceptance of its negative implications. Known in medieval times as 'a woman's courses', representing the flow of life, this natural occurrence degenerated into something to be disliked and feared. In many patriarchal societies a woman is considered to be unclean and therefore untouchable during this time, while in pagan societies – which are based on natural rhythms – each monthly cycle is treated as an opportunity for companionship with, and nurturing by, other women.

Emotional security comes to the teenager from the recognition that her sense of self can, and will, be appreciated by others. The move from child to adult is a precarious time. The urge to prove herself as a woman can often lead to experimentation with her own physicality. Her power to attract and mystify boys and men is heady stuff and her need to be like others can often lead to her making mistakes in judgement. Family patterns are often repeated – babies being born to young mothers or, conversely, a refusal to enter into relationships with the opposite sex until they are content with the lifestyle they create for themselves. Obviously neither way is right or wrong, but if a youngster understands the sexual power that is at her command, she is more likely to treat it circumspectly.

At this stage in her life, a young woman can allow herself to daydream and fantasize, letting her imagination run riot. She can try out various scenarios and possibilities without harming anyone and can reject her constructs with equal ease. It is a time of experimentation and growth.

When a woman looks back on her teen years, she may well discover that she needs to consider very carefully the way she felt about herself at that time. Considering the way that she used her imagination then can help her to understand and change her attitudes now.

The next stage of development that all women need to understand is that of being able to create an acceptable present – a 'here and now' for herself. If we play around with the word 'present' we can break it down into pre-sent, something we have sent forward for ourselves in some way. This is not such a fanciful idea as it seems, as our 'here and now' is based on having dared to dream in the past.

All successful people have the happy facility of not only being able to dream and create aspirations, but also to make those dreams reality. If we can learn the art of being able to hold on to our visions and ideals and to manifest them in a tangible form, then whether others perceive us to be successful does not matter. In our own eyes we shall have succeeded, and life for us will have meaning. We all need to take time out to create a sense of who we are and who we want to be and to form a bridge or path that we can walk with confidence.

Ideally we should learn to dream and create our own reality during our teenage years, but all too often the pressures of the modern world and the need to achieve material success – or a change in our childhood circumstances – prevent us from accomplishing the proper art of dreaming. If we were able to step back and become more objective we would learn to create an acceptable present far more successfully. Learning how to visualize and to create visions means that we are capable of analysing our constructs and changing them according to our own wishes and desires. Being able to choose options of action that work for us means that we become more proficient at planning our lives and adopting a strategy for success. We are working at an optimum level of energy and are making wise decisions. Sometimes this can be hard work, but it is work that brings its own rewards.

Part of the planning process is learning by listening and by watching. We cover elsewhere (see Living the Labyrinth) the importance of knowing when to speak and when to remain silent. Now as never before we need to understand how to gain control of the circumstances around us; this is the time to watch and wait.

The teenager spends an inordinate amount of time trying to make sense of the information surrounding her, and so must the woman who has chosen to discover herself. She must look to others for information as to how to act appropriately, for ideas that will bring her a sense of achievement and she must practise over and over again new behaviour that achieves results. Unlike the teenager, she must be patient with herself, taking her time to get it right, but not being afraid to experiment. Just as a young person does, she must learn to handle the frustrations and anger that well up inside when her progress is blocked and she must learn to convert them into the positive usable energies of drive and enthusiasm.

For a woman to become more effective at creating her own present, she must learn, or relearn, the art of decision-making. This is the process of arranging and rearranging information into a choice of action. One difficulty for teenagers is that they have not yet developed a database of sufficient information to make rational decisions, nor have they mastered the art of categorizing the information that they do have. Many of us as adults find that we must revisit this process and find out how we actually go about making decisions.

Do you, for instance, make decisions from a safe perspective, choosing the option with the least risk or do you choose the one that can lead to the best outcome? Perhaps you try to escape the upheaval of the worst possible outcome or simply take a leap into the dark. Maybe you will not make decisions until you have more information, or will leave 'fate' to decide for you. You might leave the decision to someone else or simply let the decision come to you through some quirk of your own.

All of these methods are perfectly valid, but knowing *how* you make decisions helps you to understand your own creative style. When questioned, most women would say that they use a rational method: they define targets, study alternatives, calculate the end result and then choose the best option. They tend not to allow for their most effective tool of all, their intuition.

This is the art of being able to make a leap into the unknown without quite understanding why one has done so – it just feels right. It is also the art of being able to see the wider picture within a situation and to sense what other people's reactions are likely to be. Creating the present and dealing with the here and now becomes easy when a woman trusts her intuitive sense. She is more able to take all eventualities into account.

The more often she trusts her intuition, the more able she is to make decisions and to make them quickly. The more 'right' her decisions are, the freer she is to use the information and the imagination that she has at her disposal.

Utilizing energy
   • An effective way of learning how to utilize the energy at your disposal is to visualize yourself as a fire in the middle of

a forest clearing. (A forest is, incidentally, a symbol of femininity.)

• Perceive the frustrations and anger as pieces of wood or rubbish that must be fed into the fire to provide energy and warmth. This must be done carefully and with due consideration in case the fire goes out or burns out of control. A fire that burns too brightly needs to be controlled by careful placing of the fuel, perhaps by holding some of it back. A sluggish fire needs to be encouraged, perhaps by blowing air into the centre. Above all, however, the fire must be kept burning continuously.

• You might use the symbol of the fire to test whether your decision is correct or not. If the fire burns brightly, your decision is probably correct. If it is dull, your decision will either need some more energy expended on it or will not be correct in the circumstances. That decision must be yours.

Altruism: The 16-Year-Old

For the young woman turning sixteen, and for the woman growing in understanding of herself, the issues are very similar. Her focus on life widens to include more altruistic matters such as the state of the world in general, the community in which she lives and her feelings about her own spirituality – her relationship with the Ultimate. In many ways her own sexuality is less problematic or bothersome and is sensed more as an energy and power driving her towards her future.

Around this time our woman will become focused on 'good causes', often taking up some kind of voluntary work or crusade, such as animal welfare, as a way of using up excess energy. When they are asked, a greater proportion of girls than boys say they are involved in voluntary work. (This may, of course, be because boys did not define the tasks they undertook as being voluntary work or did not like to admit that they had such an interest.) In the 16th century such altruism was an attempt to atone for the sins of the world as women saw them. Today's woman has a wider remit in that her task is to ensure the very survival of the world in which she lives.

Perhaps because of this search for a meaningful existence, our young lady is sometimes likely to become almost obsessive in her search for idols on whom to fasten her devotion. Initially, such devotion is likely to be given to pop idols, screen or sports stars. This is fine in many ways because it gives more of a focus in the wider world. The danger arises when the young person becomes fixed on the object of her affections and refuses to allow herself to grow beyond teenage adulation, perhaps fantasizing about having a relationship with her idol or becoming jealous if that idol has a partner. This can lead to eating disorders, broken sleep patterns, anxiety, depression and relationship problems.

A more mature way of using this aspect of the personality is to look for icons of femininity, past and present, and use them as examples of how to act and react within daily life. Try choosing three women whom you admire and imagine how you would have acted in their position. You might choose the qualities of people such as Florence Nightingale for her reformation of nursing, the bravery of women during wartime, the militancy of women such as the Pankhursts in their fight for suffrage or the writings of modern poets. It does not matter who they are. Your own personal interests will decide your choice.

After you have imagined yourself in their position, turn the thought round and think of difficult situations within your own life where the techniques they used might be utilized. The section entitled Icons (pages 283–98) contains brief biographies of women who have achieved recognition in various fields of endeavour. You might like to use this as a starting point before going on to research the lives of notable women you admire.

Finally, take this concept further and for a brief period try acting in everyday life as you think these women would have done. It is more than likely that people around you will wonder what is going on – and whether you are quite yourself! – but do not let this worry you. It is more than likely that you will discover in yourself hidden qualities or ideals that have lain dormant for a long time. You can then decide whether you want to incorporate your new knowledge and behaviour into your life. Do not feel under pressure to do so. The point of this technique is to help you develop a new understanding of yourself and an awareness of how you fit into your world.

Another issue of importance to both the young woman as she steps forward into life and the woman in search of a new self is health education. In some ways this ties in with community and global issues in the present, but also focuses on the need to take responsibility for herself and others in the future she will create. For the young woman there is the need to know not just about sex and sexuality but about how to look after her own body and mind in order to give herself the best opportunities. For the older woman there is the need to recognize how she can clear away the effects of not having cared enough for the whole self in the past and to make the best use of what she has now in order to help create a sustainable future for others. Now she can take care of body, mind and spirit, looking at each part as an entity in its own right, but also looking at herself as a whole, a living, breathing, vibrant entity.

The issue of career choices is of prime importance at this stage of awareness. The teenager must make perhaps the first really major decision that will affect her life as an adult. The woman who is reassessing life must make a life-changing choice. If we appreciate that one's career is one's way of looking after the future, then the decisions become easier. There are various ways of making such major choices, but for the moment a simple question needs answering. This is: 'Does what I plan to do look after me in as many ways as possible to the best of my ability?'

Looking at the future

From this starting-point we can look to the future and make decisions that back up that original premise. We can then try to create an image that helps us to envisage the future. There are five different ways of looking at the future. How you 'see' your way forward will depend on your personality. Consider the following five scenarios:

1. Fairground ride

The future is like a huge fairground ride. Once on it, we cannot get off and are in the grip of some outside control that dictates how fast or how slowly we go. We have no idea what is to come and can only deal with the fears, doubts and emotions as they arise in response to the way the track is laid out for us.

2. Mighty river

The future is like a rushing torrent and we are shaped by what has happened to others in the past. Each individual part of the torrent can only respond to the huge power and energy surrounding it and play a very minor part in adjusting to the force in order to avoid the natural hazards within the riverbed. Only by becoming at one with the torrent can major changes be effected by the sheer force of the torrent.

3. Great ocean

The future is a vast, deep ocean, full of a multitude of currents. Those currents swirl in many directions and can be helpful or otherwise. The art of navigation is knowing which currents to use to carry you forward and which to use to avoid obstacles. Even when your destination is unclear, if you have learned to understand the currents, and you move carefully, disaster can usually be avoided.

4. *The roulette wheel*
The future is a total game of chance, and no one knows what will happen, why or how it will turn out. Everything that occurs might have happened in a different way, and it is how we deal with the randomness that is important. If we have good luck, then so be it.

5. *The croupier on a pleasure liner*
We are the croupier in life, and have a degree of control over what will happen. We spin the wheel to discover what our best chances are, while beneath us we feel the surge of the current as it carries us forward to our chosen destination. We do not know what will greet us when we finally reach it, but we look forward with anticipation to a fulfilling outcome. In the meantime, we have enjoyed our journey.

Which of them most resembles the way you think of the future? Tick your choice.

1. Fairground ride ❏

2. Mighty river ❏

3. Great ocean ❏

4. Roulette wheel ❏

5. Croupier ❏

Now answer the following questions:

Why did you make this choice?

What didn't you like about the other scenarios?

Do you believe that you can direct your future?

How much control do you honestly think you have over future events?

Now is the time to decide that perhaps you could change the way you think and feel about both your own future and the effect that your thoughts have on someone else. Your decisions in future may contain an element of awareness of your responsibility to other people, both within your immediate circle and on a wider scale. The more thought you give to decisions you have to make, the more you will clarify your ideas as to how you see the future and vice versa.

Develop your own symbol for the future, an image that resonates with you and has particular significance. Keep this symbol and play with it, changing it to suit your circumstances; your river, for example, might have within it a quiet backwater where you can rest, or your roulette wheel might have for you a particularly lucky number. The choice is yours.

Keep a note somewhere of your first attempts and make sure that you check back on a regular basis to see how you have developed and clarified your symbol. You could use creative visualization or meditation to do this. Don't worry if some of your thoughts seem to be 'over the top' or too way out: you are being asked to give your creative ability free rein. You are at the moment only experimenting after all. You are learning to give focus to your own future.

Eventually it is to be hoped that you will prefer to see yourself as the croupier since that takes in all elements of the other scenarios – but, as always, it is your choice.

Creating Space for You

So, we have traced the growth of the little girl from birth to adulthood, and in so doing have given you the opportunity to recall your own experiences as a child and hopefully to understand some of the reasons for your perceptions of yourself. More importantly, you should now be able to see how, with a little thought, the influences you have internalized and perhaps perceived as negative can be changed.

Turning positive

One easy way to start the process of turning negative feelings into positive ones is to begin a dialogue in your imagination with the child that you were. You must be prepared to listen to her and to communicate with her as fully as possible; at each stage, she must also be prepared to communicate with you. Remember that communication is not just through words but can be through touch or pictures. This may mean, for instance, that the sense of wanting to be hugged comes to the surface. Be prepared to go along with the feelings and insights that occur. If possible, keep a notebook handy to note them down. If uncomfortable feelings and emotions surface, just let them flow and be prepared to recognize that they can be changed and that you need no longer feel this way.

Create a space for yourself in your imagination where both you and the child are safe. This might be a memory from childhood or a place from your adult experience to which you can visualize introducing the child. It might be a space that neither of you knows but can be explored together. Just use your imagination and your new-found creative ability. Now, have a conversation with the child and sense her replies. You may ask questions, give information or express an opinion. Just go with whatever feels right.

When you have done this, as the child instigate a reconciliation with the adult part of you. Now switch roles and apologize to the child for the hard time, or perceived difficulty, she has experienced. Together, resolve to move away from the difficulty and not to let it affect you or her in the way it has done up until now. The two of you will form a new future, with ultimately the child you once were and the adult you now are integrating into the woman you can become.

CHAPTER 8

THE WORKBOOK

If we don't change, we don't grow.
If we don't grow, we are not really living.

– Gail Sheehey

This section of the book is a sort of pick and mix. You do not have to do all of the exercises – leave the ones that don't appeal to you – nor do you have to do them in any particular order. However, for ease of understanding they have been divided into separate sets of exercises that show a progression and a deepening of awareness. We have called these sets –

Section 1. The Process of Change
Section 2. Career Appraisal and Self-Development
Section 3. Forming the Future
Section 4. Experimenting with Life
Section 5. Integration

If you find you are having difficulty with one particular exercise (or set of exercises), try not to become frustrated, but simply put it on one side and look at it again another day. The conditions around you, the time, the place or your reason for doing it may not be right. If you constantly find that one procedure is giving you difficulty, you will need to spend some time thinking about why.

The most likely reason is that you have a resistance to that particular area and need to put in some extra effort to overcome the problem. A quiet period spent looking at it from a slightly different angle is all that may be needed. You could try seeing it from another perspective, perhaps that of a child or of an older person.

Change is not easy to accommodate, so it is always worthwhile to consider first whether you want to make changes at all. If you decide that you do, you might profitably look next at how you accommodate change – whether that change is self-instigated or forced upon you from outside. Your career and personal life then come in for consideration before looking at the possibilities for creating a new future.

Should you need encouragement to experiment, this comes next, before finally you step beyond your own boundaries and use some methods of altering your awareness to encompass the vastness which is your own potential. Finally, you bring your ordinary everyday self and all its mundane concerns into line with the wider perspective of a spiritual existence, through using the labyrinth and the spiral as tools.

Section 1. The Process of Change

The following techniques are created in order to make you think. Often when we start a process it is sensible to create some sort of structure to carry us forward and give us an ongoing sense of progression. These exercises do that by taking us through the basic processes of change.

A Challenge

This exercise is not meant to trap you but to help you decide whether you *really* want to change your lifestyle. Sometimes the more sensible – and equally valid – decision is to leave things as they are. The questions are designed to help you make a considered choice.

Ask yourself the following:

1. Do you believe in trying to be the best person you possibly can be?

2. Is it possible for you to make lifestyle changes that give you new experiences?

3. Would a more purposeful approach to life increase your efficiency, your ability to earn, and your enjoyment of life?

4. Are you the kind of person who finds time to read, listen to relaxing music or self-help tapes and deliberately follows personal development programmes?

5. Are you open to new theories and ideas that help to set goals and ideals?

6. Do you know you are adept enough to achieve much more than at present?

7. Do you have a number of good ideas but lack the ability to put them into action?

8. Are you capable of sharing your thoughts and aspirations with other people?

9. Do you welcome supportive feedback to help with your motivation?

10. How near have you come to achieving the goals that you set yourself six months ago?

Notes:

How Do You Handle Change?

This technique helps you to look at how you actually handle change both in yourself and others. Each of us has different strategies for dealing with change. If we know the way we operate we can maximize our opportunities when they come along. As with some of the other exercises, there are no right or wrong answers. This is just a way of understanding your individual style.

1. How do you instigate change in your life?

2. How do you 'psyche up'?

3. Do you make many major changes?

4. Do you make many minor changes?

5. Do you forge ahead quickly when making changes?

6. Do you wait for others to adjust?

7. Do you expect others to change at the same time?

8. How do you react to change in others?

9. Do you react or respond or both?

Coping with Change

Whereas the previous exercise was more to do with how you handle changes that you instigate, the following concentrates on changes that are forced upon you. The questions are similar and you may find yourself giving answers that are virtual repeats of your responses to Exercise 2. Don't worry about this. The purpose is to gain a better insight into the way you function in the everyday world.

Perhaps one way in which we can take responsibility is to learn how to manage change and below are some aspects of change you might like to consider. You will cope more easily with change if you can identify and gain some understanding of:

• The kinds of roles you prefer to occupy; these may range from leading or supporting others to facilitating.

• The 'security blankets' that help you cope with transition; some things in life need to stay the same to enable you to keep your feet on the ground.

• How you usually respond to fresh challenges and how you can change these responses if necessary. Do you, for instance, need a period of withdrawal to plan things through or do you jump in quickly to get it over and done with?

• How to move into a new situation with as little difficulty and disruption as possible; are you good at motivating family and friends to take responsibility for their own transition?

• How to move away from an old scenario – 'letting go'. You might like to mark a change with some kind of ceremony that helps you to move on.

• How to manage the feelings of anxiety. Understanding that any change will generate some anxiety and setting up support for yourself is of prime importance.

• How to behave in new conditions so you can make the best of your opportunities. Learn to observe customs and culture in the new scenario. Never be afraid to ask questions.

Decision-Making

Part of the change process involves understanding your decision making abilities. You must recognize that your ability to make effective decisions may be impaired during periods of stress. At such times you must learn to be gentle with yourself. There are four steps to help you do this:

1. Cut down on the information that you have to process and only make decisions that are truly important. This technique is called 'shielding'.

2. Avoid making decisions until you have all available information and the time to assess it properly. This is 'planned procrastination'.

3. Concentrate your effort on the important decisions, ignoring the less important ones. This approach, known as 'prioritizing', will help you husband your resources.

4. Plan your workload and manage your time effectively. This is 'managing'.

Managing Stress

Stress cannot be avoided when we undertake change, and learning techniques to handle it well is crucial. If we are not prepared to accommodate change we will react by trying to withdraw and avoid the problems facing us. This creates a tremendous sense of strain and leads to rigid thinking, inflexible behaviour and an inability to handle additional problems. Someone who has gained an understanding of the process of transition will use her self-knowledge to reduce strain and will be able to plan techniques for stress management. Some ways to help reduce stress are to:

• Create a personal stability zone, a space where things can remain the same. This acts as an anchor point to which you can return to regain your equilibrium.

• Understand that sometimes stress is inevitable and that you must not worry about it but learn to manage it. Use it, don't let it use you.

• Develop all the support you can – from friends, family, workmates through counselling.

Notes:

Change Checklist

Below are further questions to help clarify your strategies for change and give you an understanding of how other people manage stress.

So far you have put a great deal of effort into understanding yourself. When you have thought about the questions in this last exercise, you are ready to move into a sustainable future.

The Change Curve and Stages of Acceptance

It is now accepted that there are certain reactions and responses that everyone experiences to one degree or another when any change occurs. These are usually illustrated thus;

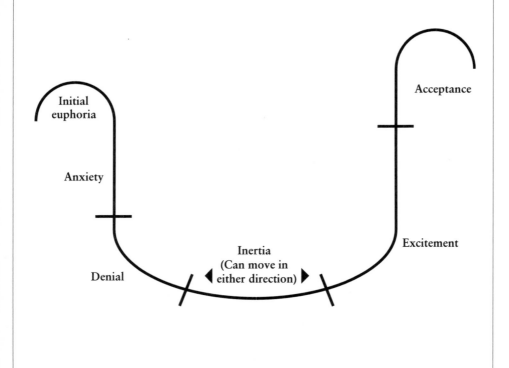

1. Identify major changes in your past life, both personal and work-related.
    a. How did you cope?
    b. How long did they take?
    c. How much stress was involved?
    d. Did they follow the general curve?
    e. What coping styles did you use?

2. Where are you at this moment, either personally or work-related, on the change curve?

3. In planning for changes in the future what are your personal methods for:
    a. managing stress?
    b. decision-making?

4. What is your method of coping?

5. What personal anchor points (points of security) do you have?

6. What support systems have you put into place?

7. How much information do you have about the new challenge?

8. What special skills or temperament do you have for coping with change?

9. What personal changes do you expect to happen in the future? Can you plan and anticipate their effects?

10. How will future changes meet your needs?

Section 2. Career Appraisal and Self-Development

The following exercises are designed to help you to find out exactly where you are in your life and help you get to where you want to be. There are no results to achieve, no right or wrong answers – the exercises are simply here to make you think more carefully about yourself.

Not everyone will consider that they have a career in the conventional sense. For the purposes of this section, think of your career as the way you take care of yourself on a daily basis. Some people will value the material rewards from what they do, while for others the satisfaction of doing something they enjoy will be more important.

Before attempting any of the exercises, first answer the following five questions. Rate each one on a scale of one to five, with five being the most important:

1. Is financial reward/security important to you?

2. Is job satisfaction important in your overall scheme of things?

3. Is doing a good job important to you?

4. How important is working with/for other people?

5. Do you like to plan for the future?

The answers to these questions will give you a fair idea of your attitude to what you do. Now imagine that the amount of effort you put in is similar to a savings bank. The rewards do not necessarily become available to you immediately, but can be drawn on later in times of need.

Lifeline

This exercise gives you an illustration of your whole life. Draw a graph which corresponds to your life.

The horizontal axis represents the length of your life. To begin with, make an assumption that you will live the conventional 'three score years and ten' – you may need longer to complete all you want to do. The vertical axis should represent the highs and lows of your life, those things you consider have had a major impact on your life. For example:

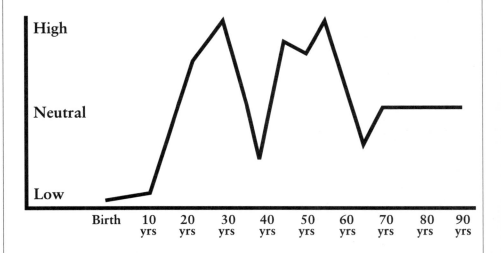

Now list those highs and lows and jot down what were they caused by. Next, draw a line showing where you are now. Think hard about how you would like to create more highs and how you might minimize the effect of the lows.

Life's Dartboard

This exercise is designed to give you a clearer idea of what you consider to be the important areas of your life. It should help you to specify achievable goals within each area.

1. List all the significant areas of your life: e.g. work, family, sport, travel, health etc.
2. Then draw a large circle and put your name in the middle.
3. Draw two smaller circles inside the circumference of the large circle. The first of these is to represent the influence each sector has on your life now.
4. Divide the circle into sectors representing your significant areas in the way you want your life to be in the future.
5. Write across the outer circumference of each sector an action to help you achieve the future you want.

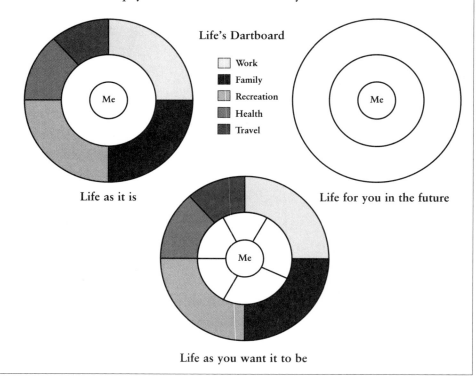

Life's Dartboard

▢ Work
▣ Family
▤ Recreation
▥ Health
▦ Travel

Life as it is

Life for you in the future

Life as you want it to be

Life-Work Time Balance

In this exercise we look at balancing out the competing claims in your life. In the first column is a specimen ideal balance between activities. In column 2 enter the values (the variance) existing in your present situation. Finally, in column 3, indicate the changes you would like to make, giving more time to one activity and less to another. Keeping the same overall balance of 168 hours (7 days x 24 hours), you may like to introduce other activities or subdivide some of the main categories.

My current life-work time balance

Activity	Hours/ week	Variance from ideal	Changes you would like +/-
Sleep	49		....
Household	35		....
Work	35		....
Travel to work	5		....
Family & friends	20		....
Leisure & fitness	20		....
Community work	4		....
Total hours per week	168		

Assessing Personal Goals

This exercise should help you to decide what is important for you personally. Below are some of the attributes that people generally consider important. Study them, then underline the ones that mean a lot to you to give you some idea of what your main focus in life might be. What do you *most* want? If there seems to be a conflict between two aspects, give careful consideration to how much time and energy you are prepared to spend on each. What are your long (5 years) and short (1 year) term life goals? What would a perfect day involve? What are your favourite dreams and your most rewarding achievements? Identify your childhood/adolescence heroes and heroines.

A Good Education	Fame	Political power
Contentment	Spiritual growth	Travel
Strength	Personal freedom	Good health
Beautiful body	Romantic love	Wealth
A devoted mate	Artistic achievement	Popularity
Respected member of the community	Satisfying sexual relationship	Attractiveness
	Companionship	

Vision Quest

This exercise is designed to help you to clarify your aims and objectives in life and to give you a goal to work towards.

- Write a summary of the meaningful events in your life, both negative and positive, then write your feelings about those events. Separate them into feelings you want more of, and those you don't want again.

- Identify the behaviour you need to get the feelings again.

- Think of yourself as a business, and then write a statement of your company aims, your business philosophy, give yourself a motto, and design a logo.

- Work on these with the aim of extracting your vision.

- Give yourself a mission statement, something that encapsulates *your* dreams and desires and sets out your objectives.

You might like to use your mission statement or your 'company aims' as a starting point for the exercise entitled 'Your Personal Undertaking' (see page 206).

Extracting Ideas

Use the following phrases to start thinking about your philosophy or the rules that you apply to life. They should help you to clarify your ideas regarding what you want out of life and what is important to you.

If ... (e.g. I had power, was happy etc.) then ... (e.g. I would feel more secure).

What I want is ....

What I need is ....

I should like to ....

What pleases me is ....

What pains me is ....

I like myself, therefore..

Unfinished Business

Most of us have left outstanding certain things which we wish we had done (or things we wish we had not). Make a list of such things, then ask yourself these questions:

What have I left outstanding?

What do I need to complete in order to move on?

What do I need to do to change things?

If your unfinished business concerns a person, try the following technique:

- Picture them in your mind.

- Say all the things you want to say to them.

- Listen to what they have to say.

- Thank them for what they have given you.

Role-Playing

Write down, on separate cards, the roles you play in life: e.g. Parent, Wife, Manager, Colleague, Friend, Lover etc.

Write down, for each role, your reactions regarding:

1. Their importance to you.

2. Their importance to others.

3. Your enjoyment of them.

4. Your skills level in performing them.

5. The time they take.

6. The priorities you must give them in your life.

7. What do you want to keep the same or change about these roles?

Now, think very carefully about these roles and decide whether you have got the balance right in your dealings with others. This exercise will help you to clarify how you carry out the various roles and should also allow you to think about whether you need to reconsider your priorities.

Working it Out

The following are some questions you might like to ask yourself as you think about your work environment. Our work is so much part of who we are that we need to be aware of how we function on a day-to-day basis. Please be aware that these questions are also relevant whether you are an employee, self-employed, do voluntary work or consider that your job is running a home and looking after children.

1. Command of basic facts

What do you know about your working place? Who is really in charge? Who knows what's going on?

2. Relevant professional knowledge

How well do you keep up with the developments in your job? If you can see the relevance of these developments, how do you go about building on that knowledge?

3. Problem-solving, analytical and decision-making skills

Do you find decision-making difficult and do you need lots of information to make those judgements? Are you open to suggestion or unyielding in the way you make decisions? Are you confident in your decision-making abilities?

4. Social skills and abilities

Are you confident in social situations? If you have difficulties, where do they occur? Recall a recent situation where you had to use your social skills. Do you know what others think of you? Do you consider that others understand you and the way you think?

5. Emotional Resilience

Think of the most stressful situation you have been in recently. Who did you turn to for advice? How do *you* usually react in extreme emotional situations? Do you sometimes experience anger, hostility or possessiveness in your work environment?

6. Creativity

How easily do you conceive new ideas? Do you only try something new when all else has failed? How creative have you been in the last year? How often do seemingly outlandish ideas of yours turn out to be successful?

7. Mental agility

Can you think quickly? How do you cope with a number of problems at the same time? Do you often get a brain-storm where everything seems to jump into place at the same time? Give some examples. How do you cope when you are given conflicting information to solve the same problem?

8. Self-knowledge

How do you increase self-knowledge? Has this affected the way you work and interact with people? Are you always aware of your goals and beliefs? How often do you consider their effect on other people and the effect that you have?

Managing Your Time

When we are able to gain some control over the time we spend on our various activities, we inevitably feel better about ourselves and the world around us. Here are a few suggestions to help you manage your time.

1. Note down at a convenient point in the day how much free time you have and things that you could be doing in that time. Restrict yourself to three things to begin with. Record, analyse and make decisions about how best to use your time both to accommodate these three things and to make the best use of your time. (You may also like to incorporate Question 3 in this.)

2. Remember that *you* make decisions about how to spend your time, so you need to know where the work comes from. You might consider the following:

   - Boss – are they assigning you enough quality work or are you there just as their personal assistant?

   - Are those who work for you too reliant on you?

   - Do you set yourself enough tasks?

   - Do your tasks come from any other source?

   Remember that running a home requires management skills of the first order and often better time management than any corporate position.

3. Whereas the previous two tasks were about using your free time and knowing what others require of you, this task is designed to give you some control over the way you structure your day. When you wake up in the morning make brief notes of what, for that particular day, you

- Must

- Should

- Would like to do

Be honest with yourself, as you are the only one who will see the list. In management terms, Parkinson's first law states that: 'Work expands to fill the time available for its completion'.

Do not give yourself a hard time if you do not get everything done. That simply creates stress.

Notes:

Section 3. Forming the Future

We take responsibility for our future the moment we decide that we can truly make things happen. The following exercises and techniques are designed to help us identify the kind of life we want.

Your Quality of Life
We need to have a very clear idea of the quality of life that we can enjoy and build upon. To clarify this in your own mind and discern what is important to you, try making a few lists under the headings below. You'll find explanations for each heading as prompts to your imagination. After reading them, list as many items as spring to mind. Don't think too hard – the more spontaneous your responses the better.

Wants
Our most urgent physical and material desires. Broadly they are the creature comforts: for example, a salary that gives us a lifestyle to which we might aspire, a nice living space, good food, etc.

Needs

Our emotional needs, such as love, security and a sense of belonging. If these are not satisfied we are likely to become isolated and perhaps alienated from others.

Requirements

Our spiritual requirements; things that round off our lives on a much deeper level. They might be to do with how we relate to the groups to which we belong, our world view, our belief system or religion – those parts of our life that make us feel complete as people.

This exercise is designed to have you look carefully at what is important to you from a personal rather than a professional point of view. (To look at decisions in your working life, see Decision-Making in Section 1.)

Event Management
Careful consideration of the way you act and have acted will give you a fairly good idea of how you are likely to act in the future. Decision-making can be used to cause change and also to adapt to change. If you know how you came to certain decisions and the thought processes you used, you can usually make an accurate prediction of what your capabilities are, or even whether you need extra resources to achieve your goal.

Look especially at events from your past, present and future.

Reviewing past, present and future
Review what has happened so far in your life, how events came about and how your past decisions influence you now. Re-evaluate your life and write down the main events that have changed your way of thinking. Work back from now.

What you remember will be important. Only think of key events and don't try to force your memory.

Is your life simply a continuation of old events or do you welcome new things? Be aware of how other people and events might affect you now and in the future you will create. Write down what you enjoy in the here and now. Even if there are only brief moments of enjoyment, write them down if they are important to you.

Finally, decide what is important to you. Look at all options and different ways of making use of those options. Allow yourself to dream. Play around with your future. Be creative with it. Take both the past and the present into account when planning your future.

Creating Your Future: Scenario scripting

Try to experience the three scenarios given below. Imagine they are your reality one year from now. Really immerse yourself in each of them – how you would feel, how you would act, what you would like and wouldn't like.

1. The best future: the most desirable future one can imagine.

2. The worst future: the most undesirable future you can imagine.

3. The probable future: the future you predict will happen.

Now examine your three visions carefully.

1. *The best future*

- Was the best future vision easy or difficult to imagine?
- Was it really the best you can possibly imagine or just the best you can expect?
- How did you feel while experiencing it?
- Was your vision distorted by excessive optimism or pessimism?
- Do you honestly believe it is unlikely to happen?

2. *The worst future*

- Did you have a clear vision of the worst future?
- Was it harder or easier to envisage than the best future?
- How did you feel while experiencing it?
- Were you unduly pessimistic or just realistic?
- Did it contain similarities with your probable future?
- What do the answers to these questions tell you about yourself?

3. *The probable future*

- Was the probable future easy to visualize?
- Could you see the details clearly or were they hazy?
- How did you feel while experiencing it?
- Was one year too far away or too near for you?
- How would you label your expectations: realistic, over the top, idealistic, etc.?
- Was what you thought would happen a truly objective assessment or based more on dreams and desires?

This kind of assessment from three different perspectives allows you to be both imaginative and objective. You have the ability to use both the tools of daydreaming and creativity to form your future. Because at this stage nothing has materialized you can change any – or all – of the scenarios as you wish: they are yours to manipulate until you are happy with them. You can then decide what you want to do – this might entail following a particular course of action, developing a mind-set or whatever to make a particular set of events occur. You can also decide whether you want to consider what effect your decisions have on other people, since almost inevitably what you do may surprise or disturb them. They may need help in understanding or coming to terms with new ideas or scenarios.

Watching and Acting: Predict and be flexible

In theory, we cannot plan for the future. People are sometimes irrational and unpredictable and often do not fit in with our ideas or plans.

Actually, we can make the future happen the way we want it to if we are flexible and remain open to possibilities. We have to find the balance between setting goals, devising strategies, predicting outcomes, learning to expect change, being able to visualize change, and actively causing it.

Without being open to whatever happens and being prepared to adjust, we will not be able to bring about a sustainable future (we give some strategies for handling change at the beginning of this Workbook, in Section 1). We need to learn to handle the dual aspects of planning and learning.

If you believe that the future does not yet exist, then it must be you that makes it happen. If you believe that it is preordained, then you will want to participate in it as fully as possible. Either way you will need to be as aware as possible and that takes two ways of working – watching and acting.

What might be called optimistic postponement suggests that decision-makers develop a balance between doing and watching; they do not rush in but they also know intuitively when to take a calculated risk.

You have two or maybe three choices, make the future happen, or watch it happen – or both.

A Personal Enquiry

If you are prepared to listen to yourself, you will almost inevitably come up with the right solution to a problem – it will float to the top of your consciousness. That is intuition, and the decision is inevitable. However, you need to establish certain criteria to test whether this is indeed the case in given situations. Whenever you are unsure whether your intended action is driven by intuition, ask yourself these questions.

Is it intuition or is it…

Fear or uncertainty? Does your solution provide you with relief from indecision or ambiguity?

Wishful thinking? Does it contain a powerful hope that you want strongly to believe?

Impulsiveness? Are you reacting rather than responding?

Emotion? Has your solution arisen out of anger, pressure, or perhaps a need to feel victimized?

Laziness? If you acted upon it, would you be taking the easy way out?

Image making? Does the solution reinforce a need to appear decisive, confident, self-assured?

Rebelliousness? Does it enhance a need to be different, fight authority, to show you've got what it takes?

The Practical and the Phenomenal

In order to make things happen we have to be able to take control of our circumstances. To do this we must be conversant with our own style of decision-making. There are several ways we can help ourselves.

- Habit hunt – Be aware of the way that you work through the information available to you. Be prepared to change the way you think in order to make the best decision possible.
- Choose your options – Learn different methods of making decisions. Learn how to assess risks or make spontaneous decisions. Know when emotion is necessary and when to be objective.
- Recognize your decision-making skills – Balance the practical and 'miraculous'. Learn to expect your universe to co-operate with you.
- Question your creative self – Ask questions of yourself so you know you are not creating illusions.
- Use right time/place/reason scenario – Make decisions only when you are ready – i.e. when you have all the facts, when you are in the right frame of mind and when you feel the time is right.
- Reason vs. intuition – question the reasoning side and the intuitive together and balance the pros and cons. Knowing that one is acting from a reasoned train of thought is very different from 'just knowing' that the action is right.
- Use your brain – Know when to be logical and when to be intuitive. Recognize that logic and intuition can be combined in different ways. Be logically intuitive and intuitively logical.

Section 4. Experimenting With Life

This exercise is to help you decide what changes you would make assuming that you could be given the gift of an ideal life. This is a life in which, all being equal, you could have anything you wish. The statements below are simply suggestions and you can, of course, add your own wishes.

If I had to live my life again ...

I'd be more relaxed and flexible.

I'd be more frivolous and spontaneous.

I would take frequent holidays.

I'd be prepared to make more mistakes next time.

I'd take more risks.

I'd eat what *I* wanted to eat.

I would concentrate on my real problems and ignore the imagined ones.

Now try to bring one of these statements into reality by living one day with it at the forefront of your mind.

Was this enjoyable or too difficult? If the latter, try again later and then see how you get on; you will find it becomes easier with practice. Make any adjustments you like to the statements as you discover more about yourself.

Identifying Personal Goals

Each of us has basic ideals that we feel are necessary to our well-being. This exercise is designed to help you decide what is important to your spiritual welfare. Prioritizing helps us to concentrate on the ideals that hold most meaning for us. Number your choices, from 1 to 11, in order of preference in the column on the left.

You may be able to think of some other ideals that are important to you. If you do, feel free to add them to the list and prioritize them.

ORDER OF PREFERENCE	IDEAL
	Organization – To organize and control others to achieve community or organizational goals. To become an influential leader.
	Know-how – To become an authority on a special subject; to persevere in order to reach a hoped-for level of skill and accomplishment.
	Status – To become well-known, to obtain recognition, awards, or high social status.
	Assistance to Others – To contribute to the satisfaction of others, to be helpful to others in need.
	Financial Gain – To earn a great deal of money.
	Independence – To have the opportunity for freedom of thought and action, to be one's own boss.
	Affection – To obtain and share companionship and affection through immediate family and friends.
	Security – To achieve a secure and stable position in financial situations and through work.
	Self-Realization – To optimize personal development; to realize one's full creative potential.
	Responsibility – To dedicate oneself totally to the pursuit of fundamental values, ideals and principles – to 'own' what one does, thinks and feels.
	Pleasure – To enjoy life, to be happy and content, to have the good things in life.

Having the Courage to Create

Often when we decide to use our own energy and power all we need is the courage to do so. Having said that, there are certain steps that we can initiate to help us develop that courage. Below are a few suggestions.

What do you want to create?

Give careful thought to what you want to create. Creativity is not necessarily purely artistic, though many find they are pleasantly surprised by their added competence in ways they did not think were possible. Some examples of these might be: painting, writing (novels, short stories, poems), an improved social life, cooking, a better job, learning a new language, gaining more qualifications, embroidering, textiles, undertaking home improvements, gardening, love-life or a baby.

Form an affirmation (a statement of intent) to help intensify the thoughts you have had. For example, 'I am determined to succeed at ...' or 'I have decided that I will ...'

How to go about it

Decide on the most appropriate way of achieving your goal. You might, for instance, decide on doing a correspondence or computer course, using self-help tapes, books, enrolling in night classes, or consulting your 'self' (through meditation or dreams). Undertake to initiate the process by:

- Making enquiries
- Making a commitment to take action within a certain time (say six weeks);
- Committing to the undertaking. It is important that this commitment is made at least to yourself, in order to keep yourself focused.

If you find yourself unable to do any of these things it means that you probably need to go back to the drawing board and find something else to which you are more committed. At least recognize your lack of commitment as something that needs to be tackled.

Focus only on one or two projects (perhaps one social and one professional)

Rather than overloading yourself with too many projects, attempt a maximum of two new projects at any one time. Try to make one of these a social project or one that requires some input from other people. This stops you from becoming isolated and is a good balance if your other project requires a high degree of concentration. This other project might be some way of enhancing your career or sphere of work.

Ascertain if you are afraid of failure or success

Never be afraid to admit failure and be prepared to move on without regrets if something has not turned out as you hoped. Within the experience you will have learnt certain lessons that will stand you in good stead for the future. If you discover that you are afraid of success, you might like to try dealing with the 'chatterbox', which is simply recognizing when this fear of failure began; often this fear forms in childhood when it is someone else's belief that you have internalized. Have the courage to try something different no matter how way-out or unusual it may seem to others.

Do you really want it or are you just 'going along' with it?

This question is somewhat difficult to answer because we often do not realize how much we have taken in childhood conditioning or the expectations of others. It is worthwhile drawing up a list of pros and cons to help you decide how best to proceed. Sometimes the negatives will outweigh the positives, but it may still be worthwhile to continue with your plans.

Are you doing it for yourself or somebody else?

As we have noted previously, childhood conditioning can affect your decisions. Therefore, you need to be very sure that you are not attempting a new project just because somebody (probably somebody whose opinion you respect) says so. Now is the time to apply the 'Three Question Technique'.

- Do I really want to do this?
- Do I need to do it?
- Do I have a driving impulse to do it?

Once you have clarified your motivation you can begin to develop your own creative energy. Here are a few suggestions:

Remember to write things down

Carry a notepad with you during the day in order to record any ideas that come to you at unexpected times. Use these ideas as the basis for your creative dreams. Focus nightly on individual aspects in the knowledge that your unconscious will eventually help to highlight recurring themes, such as characters and possible difficulties. It is important to learn and record your dreams in order to use them productively. The exercise 'Keeping a Journal' shows you how.

Try starting projects as a group

This is the time to start using your dream and creative journal (or journals). By sharing your dreams and experiences you can help and encourage one another to be creative. Whether as a group you decide to do the same project or decide on individual creativity makes no difference. The shared experience is really what matters.

Discuss aspirations and projects and learn from others
By discussing aspirations and sharing your creative projects and ideas with others you will educate yourself in what constitutes success for you. This could well be determination, discipline or drive. Whatever it is that you discover, make up your mind that you will apply it in your own projects.

Keeping a Journal
When we start recognizing how truly powerful we can be, it is as though the inner self wakes up and we become more creative. The habit of keeping a dream journal in order to record your most important dreams can be very beneficial. Each individual must make the choice as to whether they are also going to keep a journal of their creative pursuits and/or a journal of their progress on the journey towards self-realization.

The suggestion here is that you decide to keep only one journal which, according to personal preference, can be divided into three or can simply be used to keep a record of all relevant or exciting experiences.

- For something as private and personal as this journal it is important that it gives you a great deal of pleasure. For those of you for whom texture is important, choose a good textured paper and a suitable writing implement. If colour is important, choose one that appeals to you.
- Always keep your recording materials at hand.
- Write the account of your dream, thoughts or experience as soon as you possibly can. This helps to fix the experience as a memory so that it can be worked on later.

- Use as much detail as possible on this first writing down so that later you can add more detail as you think about it more deeply.
- Try to review your journal at least once a week. This will help you to see where dreams and your day-to-day reality are corresponding and where your daily experiences are helping in the creative abilities you are developing.

The nice thing about this personal journal is that you do not have to show it to anyone unless you so choose. However, the method given allows you to quantify the entries and ideas in any way you please. You can come back at any time, often years later, to follow up a concept or project. The mind has a way of presenting what it needs you to know over and over again – and in different ways – until you have internalized the message.

Recording a Dream/Experience

Always be consistent in the way you record your dreams and experiences. The following is a simple method that has been used effectively in scientific experiments:

Name: ....

Age:...... Gender: .... Date of dream/experience: ....

- Write down the main points of your dream or experience:
- Write down anything out of the ordinary about the dream (e.g. animals, bizarre situations, etc) or experience; e.g. someone acting out of character or using bad language.
- How do you feel about the dream/experience?

Your Personal Undertaking

Finally, as a way of keeping you focused on the activities and creativity, you need to create a personal undertaking This is a statement which is probably best kept very private. You may feel that by telling someone else about your personal undertaking this lessens its value or makes it less attainable. Similar to an affirmation, the statement you choose for your personal undertaking needs to be short and succinct so that it has meaning for your every time you think about it.

• When thinking about your personal undertaking, take a piece of paper and write down the things that you want to do, would like to do or feel you ought to do. This need not be in the form of an organized list but can be scribbled down at random.

• Look carefully at each of your statements and group together any that seem similar.

• On a separate clean sheet of paper formulate a sentence which, for you, is powerful, meaningful and expresses the recurring sentiment properly. Do this for each of your basic ideals that become apparent.

• Keep both pieces of paper in a safe place for future reference.

• Now, with your second sheet of paper, try to reduce the sentences to one very powerful and relevant description of your mission or task in life. Keep it as short and incisive as you can.

The second stage of this exercise is to write out this short statement on two postcards.

• Place one of these by your mirror or on your bedside table where you will see it when you first wake up. This is so that it is almost the first and last thing that you think about every day.

• Remember to repeat the statement three times as often as you can during the day, preferably on at least three occasions every day. This helps to focus your mind and also allows the subconscious to 'hear' the intent and to internalize it.

• Place the other postcard where you can see it in your work area. It is important to move this postcard around about once a week to avoid its becoming just part of the scenery. Moving the postcard forces you to think about the statement, reinforcing the intent behind it and giving you the opportunity to change it should you so wish.

Your main personal undertaking will contain within it the germ of many sub-statements. You can if you wish concentrate as well on these sub-statements or can change the focus of your main statement when it feels right to do so in order to include another aspect. Your personal undertaking is yours to do with as you will; the only thing you must do is make it work for you.

Section 5. Integration

Having given you some idea of how to change, we can now bring the various strands of information together at a slightly higher level of awareness. To begin this process we will use two simple creative visualization exercises involving the spiral, an archetypal image of feminine awareness that demonstrates the raising of vibration towards more spiritual goals.

Restoring Your Equilibrium
Think of the three different parts of yourself – body, mind and spirit – as components of a child's plaything that need to be fitted together to make it work. You could use the image of a jigsaw or of a toddler's toy requiring you to place three different coloured rings onto a central pole. Each ring is a different colour:

- Red for the body
- Green for the mind
- Violet for the spirit

Play with the various colours, making them darker or brighter as the fancy takes you, changing them and experimenting with how each change makes you feel.

You may find that the changes make you feel happier, more sad, more angry, more peaceful and so on. When you are pleased with the result and the overall feeling, memorize the best feeling so that you can recall it at times of need to rebalance yourself when you are under pressure. Do remember, however, that each day will be different and there will be highs and lows as you find the correct technique. Try to finish each practice session on a high.

The Simple Spiral

When you become more proficient at this simple exercise, you might like to extend it. By using the seven colours of the rainbow, you can encompass all aspects of the human psyche as well as the spiritual centres in the body (the chakras) and integrate them into a coherent whole. This exercise forms the basis of the next one, involving the spiral.

Wait until you sense yourself to be calm before embarking on this exercise. Again, take the image of the child's toy as your starting point, only this time using the seven colours of the rainbow: red, orange, yellow, green, blue, indigo, violet. Imagine each ring blending into the next so that you 'see' a spiral of seven different colours; thus red will blend into orange, orange will blend into yellow, yellow into green and so on.

You may find that one colour is more pronounced than the others. If this is the case, you will need to check out the personal significance of that colour. Certain personal issues are associated with each colour, and you may need to consider these – study the following table:

Colour	Issue
Red	Self-image
Orange	Relationships
Yellow	Emotional issues
Green	Self-awareness
Blue	Self-expression
Indigo	Creativity
Violet	Future responsibility

The better you become at creating your spiral, the more proficient you will be at dealing with the issues that present themselves on a day-to-day basis.

Eventually you may well find that all of the colours are of equal intensity but that the 'blending' becomes difficult. This would indicate conflict. For instance, if the difficulty is in blending orange and yellow, there may be a problem in balancing your needs for relationship with the unresolved emotional issues you may have. Again, if the difficulty is in blending blue and indigo, you might have to look at the way you express your creativity.

A woman's journey towards self-discovery and the changes she must make are epitomized by the symbols of both the spiral and the labyrinth. In the next chapter we shall be looking at how these can be used in conjunction.

CHAPTER 9

Living the Labyrinth

'The wise man bridges the gap
by laying out the path by means of which he can
get from where he is to where he wants to go.'

– J. P. Morgan

The preceding chapter might be regarded as a Learning Place, whereas this chapter is the Doing Place or living out of our awareness. Here you will be putting into practice what you have learnt and applying it throughout your life – living responsibly and applying the checks and balances that you will find very quickly become a natural part of existence. The labyrinth with its seven-fold path and the spiral of attainment then become woven into the fabric of the journey we take.

We referred earlier in the book to the meaning of the labyrinth and the spiral in relation to the mystery and magic of women (Chapter 3). Now we learn how to appreciate, and walk, the labyrinth in the physical plane, before moving towards a more spiritual appreciation.

The Complex Spiral – The Double Helix

First, try thinking of your physical self and your spiritual self as being represented by two spirals, which may or may not be coloured, as you wish. Envisage the spirals as interconnected and becoming intertwined, like the fundamental strands of life, DNA, of which these are a representation. You may find it easier to think of the physical spiral as rising from below and the spiritual dropping from above.

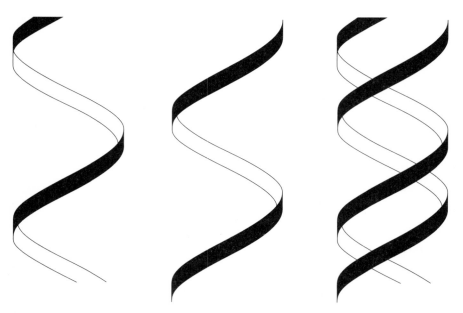

This exercise is a very personal one and you may well surprise yourself as you work through it. Pay attention to any random thoughts that arise for consideration later. Because you are using one of the oldest images known to man and also one of the simplest, you may find yourself contemplating the spirals with a fair degree of detachment. Enjoy the sensation as you put yourself closer and closer in touch with your own essential being.

Remember that any result you achieve is right for you and

that practice makes perfect. Once you have succeeded, you will be able to build on that result. Ideally, success will bring with it a strong sense of additional energy being available to you.

Walking the Labyrinth

Many people nowadays are rediscovering some of the knowledge of the Ancients, and in this context specifically that walking a labyrinth can alter awareness of the external world. Modern designs of labyrinths are usually based on the old designs, which were deliberately complex in order to achieve maximum effect.

When you physically walk a labyrinth, you wander backwards and forwards, turning 180 degrees each time you enter a different circuit. The effect of this, which you can heighten if you wish, is to change activity from the right side of the brain to the left side as you shift direction, altering your awareness from a logical thinking process to an intuitive contemplative one and inducing a heightened state of consciousness. It can also help to balance the chakras or spiritual centres of the body, something we looked at earlier with the Restoring the Equilibrium exercise (see page 208).

If you can find a real labyrinth to walk, so much the better, but, failing that, the illustrations in this book should suffice. Try the next exercise and its accompanying design.

Quick 'walking' the labyrinth

Think of a question or concern, clear your mind of conscious thought, and, using a pencil or other pointed instrument, trace around the design below, starting at the entrance to the labyrinth. As you follow the path, sense the power in the design; take especial note of how you feel when you reach the centre and later when you come out of the labyrinth. When you reach the centre, wait while you sense an answer to your question, then come out.

Visualization

If we are to live with awareness, then a suitable visualization using what we have learnt can help us to keep to our chosen path in life. Having understood and appreciated the archetypes, we now have the opportunity to take seven steps towards a more successful future. One of the simplest forms of labyrinth can help us to achieve this goal.

There are many types of labyrinth; the classical or seven-circuit labyrinth refers directly to the seven circular paths – or states of awareness – that lead eventually to any centre or goal. Each path is complete in itself, but also leads to the next level of understanding. As we have seen, this ancient design is found in most cultures and is thought to date back more than 4000 years. Also known as the Cretan Labyrinth, it is associated with the myth of Theseus and the Minotaur (see page 54). The design shown above has been found on Cretan coins.

Labyrinths have probably always been used in a spiritual manner. The sense of disorientation they can produce creates a heightened perception of what it means to be human. It is therefore of assistance in psychological and spiritual growth. When we build or even envisage a labyrinth we are creating a sacred space. The more we understand the concept of a labyrinth, the more powerful it becomes as a symbol of transformation. To physically walk a labyrinth imbues both the construction and its use as a symbol with power and meaning.

Sometimes called the Greek or balanced-arm cross, this representation, in which the arms are equidistant along the length of the upright, is said to represent femininity.

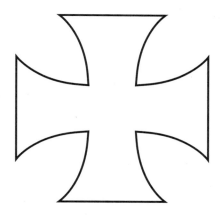

This cross is generally accepted as the starting point for the construction of the labyrinth. Within ourselves it represents the still, calm centre. Whether one chooses to work initially towards or away from the centre, the cross can become a focus for meditation and also a point of contemplation to enable us to benefit from the experience of traversing the labyrinth.

The balanced-arm cross can also be the starting point for the beginning of the spiral, which is a very simple way of representing the search for spirituality. Here we have the opportunity of taking everything to a higher level. The archetypes of the Wise Old Man and the Great Mother are not only part of the psychological manifestation of spirituality on Earth, but are also reflections of a greater energy with which each of us may choose to be in contact. Using the spiral as an image we are able to reach this energy. There is a sense of awe in the idea that we are able to access such a tremendous source of power. The spiral – with its movement both upwards and downwards – can help us to make links between the physical and the spiritual realms and weave the various strands of our lives together.

The Journey of Life

The most basic metaphor for walking a labyrinth is that of life's journey. 'Walk' the labyrinth while thinking of your own life, paying attention to your Personal Undertaking (see page 206). Visualize yourself moving into your future and think about what you learn.

- If you have the opportunity to walk a real labyrinth, be aware of everything that happens. Notice any synchronicity with your thoughts or feelings.
- Do you like one part of the labyrinth more than another? Why?
- What do the turns represent in your life? Do you resist some turns and instinctively like others?
- Do you feel lost at any time? If so, at what point in the labyrinth did it occur?
- What does that mean to you?
- What does the labyrinth teach you about your life?
- Consider all of your experiences in the labyrinth in relation to your life's journey.

• Walk alone and then record your experience. Walk with a group and then share your experiences.

The purpose of this exercise is to turn your awareness inwards so that you are engaged in an active meditation. Gradually all extraneous considerations should fall away and your mind should become quiet and relaxed. If you are so inclined, you may like to include the ritual of walking the labyrinth in your regular regime of spiritual exercises.

The Dance of the Labyrinth

If you are able physically to walk a constructed labyrinth, or to construct one of your own, you will almost inevitably find yourself captivated by the flow of energy within it. Children will often run or dance as they traverse it, linking with the instinctive movement felt as one connects with the energies of the earth. It is for this reason that many societies used this dance as part of their basic rituals. If you choose to use your labyrinth for such a purpose, be sure to develop your own personal rhythm in the dance. Any music can be used as accompaniment. It is a matter of personal choice.

Seven Levels of Contentment

The seven levels of self-awareness with which we started our journey in the labyrinth can now be allowed within the spiral to take on a more spiritual connotation. We become more aware of both how small we are in relation to the greater energy but also how vast is the power available to us. As we become more confident of our own ability to handle everything life offers, we are also able to love and enjoy our relationships for what they are and not for what we hope they may be.

These new insights enable us to be truthful about ourselves but also to be tolerant of others, treating them with the dignity they deserve. We then know how to use the qualities of wisdom, to know when to speak and when to remain silent. The creation of a world in which we can live and a world in which we would want to live then potentially becomes much easier. We are truly using our potential and knowledge to create a sustainable future.

Self-Discovery

The first circuit of the labyrinth, and therefore the first aspect of our journey towards the still calm centre, is one of self-discovery. Apparently we human beings have not got a very efficient memory and most of us forget much more than we remember. However, our experiences form the basis of our reactions and our beliefs, sometimes in a major way, sometimes in a minor.

For instance, a child who is badly frightened by a dog may not necessarily grow up with a fear of dogs but may have difficulty with them. In later life, when perhaps her children want a dog as a pet, she may need to address that difficulty. When an individual starts out on the road to self-discovery she needs to rediscover 'lost' memories and also to recognize that childhood perception may give memories that are not entirely accurate.

Often there is the necessity to put bad memories where they belong – in the past – and to recognize the effect they have had on us. We need to know that they can be accommodated and form part of the more effective person who is now moving into the future. It is also necessary to recognize that working at remembering and forgetting things that are no longer appropriate can leave a great deal of space for new things. (Included at the back of the book are affirmations that might help you to come to terms with the past.) Below is a technique in learning how to remember.

Learning how to remember

Select a memory with which you wish to work. Start with something fairly innocuous, either in the recent past or in your early years – perhaps something you did well or a childhood holiday. As a preliminary, try to assess why you particularly remember this occasion and what relevance it has in the here and now.

- Remember how you felt and see whether, using something in your life today, you can reproduce the same feeling.
- Are you now aware of what gives you good feelings and what does not?
- Resolve to reproduce more of the good feelings in life.
- Then, if you wish, repeat the exercise, taking yourself back in easy stages, no longer than five years at a time, looking for times in your life when you felt really good about something.
- Identify other occasions when you felt similarly. Was the situation comparable or was it something totally different?

You may well find that working in this way your memory takes you back further than you first thought. Now repeat the exercise, this time trying to remember times when you felt most intensely about yourself. Take pleasure in those feelings.

Only when you have practised the exercise sufficiently, working with the positive, should you attempt to come to terms with the negative. When you are confident of treating these negatives dispassionately, repeat the exercise and work with these more negative times.

Good memories need to be brought to the forefront of one's mind. The Six-step reframing technique (see page 148) should help you to appreciate positivity and reframe or reassess the way that you experience negativity. As one matures one is able to appreciate experiences that were meaningful but perhaps did not appear to have much relevance at the time. (Often word association helps us to get hold of memories that would otherwise remain buried.) You might also like to try the 'If I had to live my life again' exercise in the Workbook (see page 199). Remember, you are not only looking for bad memories to eradicate but also for good memories on which to base the new you.

It is interesting to discover what is your earliest memory. Is it good, bad or indifferent? Learning to recall your memories helps you to deal with the effects of your experiences. It can often be enlightening to discover why you are the person you are and why your reactions can sometimes surprise you. The way you feel about yourself is the cornerstone of how others see you and the impression that you give on first meeting people is what they will first remember about you. If you have a good self-image, this will come across.

You may feel that you have a very poor self-image, probably because of the way your family regarded you (and perhaps still do). Practising remembering and forgetting helps you to adjust your perception of the way they see you.

Your new journey of self-discovery can give you a whole new self-image, with your newly emerging personality retaining the best of the old you and discarding the worst.

Earlier in the book we looked at the need for partnership. Self-image and sexuality are very strongly bound up with one another. The ability to make successful relationships is part of a process of self-confirmation. We seek a 'fit' with our sexual partners that encompasses much more than just the sexual act – we want to relate to them emotionally. We also hope that they have minds like our own and we would like them to have similar spiritual values. Behind all this, however, we want them to like us and to find us sexually attractive. If we have not learnt to like ourselves and to appreciate our own attractiveness, we are not able to form a good image of ourselves. Being prepared to retrace our steps and find out perhaps how or at what stage we lost the ability to like ourselves means that we can work to repair the damage. We can then move on to creating confidence and the ability to be ourselves.

Confidence

The second circuit of the labyrinth is to do with gaining confidence and our ability to handle any situation. It is not only teenagers who need to develop confidence in their own abilities. When we are reassessing our lives, we often have to go back and develop – or redevelop – our confidence. Here is an easy way to do so:

Developing confidence

• Make a list of all of the things that you are, or have been, good at. When you first try this you will probably not be able to think of anything in particular. Even if you are feeling particularly negative, think back to something that gave you a real sense of achievement and remember how it felt. It can be something quite small, such as learning to tie your shoelaces, or the first time you ever did your own buttons up. It is not important what it was, only how you felt. What you need to do is to reproduce more of the good feelings and less of the bad.

• Try to reproduce the same feeling in something that you are doing now, whether that is, for instance, putting on make-up, solving a management problem or not arguing with your relatives. The more prepared you are to feel better about things – in other words, the more practice you give yourself – the easier it will become. Try practising one particular new way of thinking and being for a week to ten days. Only then assess how much better you feel about yourself. The sheer fact that you have persevered will give you another plus, because along with the new skill you are developing determination.

• Keep your original list of achievements handy and always within easy reach. Each time you think of something new that you would like to become better at, add it to your list and resolve to make time to try it out.

• As you become more proficient at remembering how good you have been, use your list to assist you in working out a strategy to improve your days and make them more interesting. Before you go to sleep, choose three things from your list that you will try the next day. Then go to sleep with those three things on your mind. On waking up the next morning remind yourself of your intention.

This will have the effect of jogging your unconscious and reminding you that you are capable of success. When we work with the talents that really interest us, we minimize the chance of failure, and can live in a more upbeat manner.

Accepting Compliments

Another way of gaining confidence is to learn to accept compliments. Most women initially find this very difficult, possibly because during puberty their rapidly changing body image does not really give them time to get used to the way they look. When they themselves cannot get a feeling either of how they come across to other people or of how they feel about themselves, it can be very confusing to be told they are beautiful, dress nicely and so on. The usual response is utter embarrassment and an inability to respond appropriately in the right way. This can give rise to an awkwardness that often does not go away until a woman begins to gain confidence.

The easiest way to break this cycle of confusion is to respond with a simple 'thank you'. You can wonder later about what had prompted the compliment! Just be glad that you have made a 'connection' with the person concerned and enjoy their approval. Once you experience the 'feel good' factor this brings, you will find yourself wanting more of it. As you continue to take the trouble to respond – to believe that you deserve it – the more people will compliment you. Remember that you can be complimented not only for your looks but also for your actions and the way you are. You may always wonder what people are perceiving. True humility is recognizing that your public persona may be very different from the private one. Robbie Burns put this quite succinctly:

> *'Oh would some power the giftie gi'e us*
> *To see ourselves as others see us'*

It would indeed be good to be able to stand outside ourselves, be totally objective and not need the reassurance of positive feedback.

To get fairly close to this, without being at all arrogant, you might try imagining that you are meeting yourself for the first time. Do you like this new person? How is he or she coming across? Are they someone who is super-confident or very shy? What qualities do you admire and what do you dislike? The acid test is whether you might have the confidence to tell this person that you admire them or dislike them. By being able to do this, you are opening yourself – that is, the real you – to the potential for confident change and the next circuit of the labyrinth.

Emotional Maturity

When we develop confidence in ourselves we can then have the emotional maturity to recognize where our power lies. We can begin to take risks. We also learn how not to be victims – we become victims of circumstance when we allow feelings of futility and powerlessness to develop. The root cause of the victim mentality is often a blockage in our childhood which has rendered us unable to develop a sense of responsibility for what happens to us. The child's perception may have been that only authority figures have power over circumstances. Conversely, the child may have adopted a family attitude of life being a struggle and everyone else being out to 'get them'. If such attitudes are constantly being reinforced there is no impetus for change and often enormous effort and perhaps outside help are needed to break free of them. Part of the problem is that the so-called victim often requires some kind of 'negative reinforcement' of her bad feelings and continually finds herself in situations that seem to emphasize how bad/naughty/difficult she is. This sets up a truly vicious circle with each new difficulty becoming confirmation of her negative view of herself.

The woman who is still in this circle needs to be reminded that she is not a helpless child but a mature adult who can take responsibility for what she sees and feels. She needs to be reassured that her thoughts and feelings are valid. Only when she believes that they are will she be able to accept herself in a new and emotionally mature way. There is a belief that if this sense of responsibility is not developed at the right time in childhood it will never manifest. However, there is also evidence that the adult can learn to 'grow up' in the effective way denied to her earlier by making connections with the feelings and awareness of her childhood. This repair work should be taken slowly and small, manageable changes in attitude attempted rather than huge changes with a potential for failure.

The first step in dealing with the victim syndrome is to question yourself whenever you have a sense of being victimized. Ask yourself whether this is really so or are you simply following an old pattern? Secondly, you should try to become aware of the overriding feeling and become conscious of what has brought on your response. You might find yourself thinking any of the following:

- What have I done to deserve this?
- It wasn't my fault.
- But I didn't do anything.
- Why has this happened to me?

The tone of these statements or questions often triggers a memory and allows us to trace back to the childhood experience on which the prevailing bad feeling is based. By reassuring yourself you, the adult, can eradicate the childhood difficulty.

One method of reassurance is to use the 'mirror technique'. Sit yourself in front of a mirror and treat the person looking at you as someone who needs reassurance. Try giving that person as much emotional support as you can to overcome their difficulty. Initially you will probably feel somewhat silly, but if you persevere you will begin to sense what kind of support you really need. By allowing yourself to have the support you need, you are allowing the adult fuller expression.

Emotional maturity means not constantly being dependent on other people for feedback. We do have to allow ourselves to be supported but we also need to be aware that we can stand on our own two feet and can take risks. It is worthwhile finding out what our greatest area of risk is in order to deal with it correctly.

Personal risk taking

In life we can all expect to be faced with many challenges, both professionally and socially; the more difficult these are, the greater the personal risk involved in meeting them. Below is a series of situations that could be described as potentially 'risky'. Score points for each situation according to the scale given. Make a note of your scores to the right of the questions.

Scale:

1 point   If the situation would be comfortable for you and present little challenge

2 points   If the situation would present some challenge

3 points   If the situation would present quite a lot of challenge

4 points   If the situation would be very challenging or threatening to you

Questionnaire:

1. You have to separate two people who are fighting at work.
2. You have to tell someone their services are no longer needed.
3. You have to attend an important dinner requiring evening dress.
4. You have to make a high level of contribution to a management meeting.

5. You are asked to write an article for a newsletter.
6. You are asked to prepare a detailed budget.
7. You have to jump into a river to rescue someone who is drowning.
8. You have to break the news to a colleague or friend that their partner was taken ill at work and died suddenly.
9. You are asked to sing at a social event.
10. You have to tell your boss that his/her pet scheme is not going to work.
11. You have to read a poem in public.
12. You have to read a thick manual dealing with a subject you don't know much about.
13. You have to make up the number for a sports team.
14. You have to tell someone they haven't got the promotion you promised them.
15. You have to be Father Christmas at a children's party.
16. You are to act as host or chairman for an important meeting.
17. You are asked to paint a picture.
18. You have to take an examination on a technical topic.
19. You have to free someone who is trapped in dangerous conditions.
20. You have to attend the funeral of a close friend.
21. You are asked to role play on a training course.
22. You have to give an official vote of thanks to an honoured guest.
23. You have to tell someone how much you admire them.
24. You are enrolled for a course of study at the local college.
25. You have to go to the help of someone being mugged.
26. You have to discipline two of your staff because their illicit love affair is interfering with their work.
27. You have to attend a fancy dress party.
28. You are to be Master of Ceremonies at a social event.
29. You have to prepare, and give, a speech.
30. You have to write a detailed proposal about ways to improve production.

Scoring and interpretation

The number in each box in the table below refers to the question number and not the number of points. Enter your scores in the appropriate boxes.

A	B	C	D	E	F
1	2	3	4	5	6
7	8	9	10	11	12
13	14	15	16	17	18
19	20	21	22	23	24
25	26	27	28	29	30

Add up the scores for each column. Enter the total points scored for each letter in the empty boxes below.

A	B	C	D	E	F

The letters represent the following:

A. The ability to accept physical challenge.

B. The ability to deal with emotional situations

C. The ability to cope with unconventional social situations

D. The preparedness to be 'visible', i.e. to stand out

E. The ability to use creative expression

F. The ability to cope with detailed or academic work.

The higher the score in each column the less comfortable you are in those types of situation and the more personal risk there is involved in meeting the challenges they pose. Reflecting on these and relating them to personal and work experiences will enable you to anticipate and prepare – to take the calculated risks upon which being effective depends.

The Co-dependency Conundrum

Emotional maturity also means being able to act appropriately even though we may be upset or under pressure. An easy way of understanding how we may move within an emotional framework is to use a version of the co-dependency triangle. Here three roles are played out. One is that of victim, the second that of persecutor and the third of helper. In this context victim also means underdog – someone who has a tendency to put themselves in a subordinate position. The persecutor might be called the authoritarian figure. The helper is that part of us which insists on being 'good' and making the best of any situation.

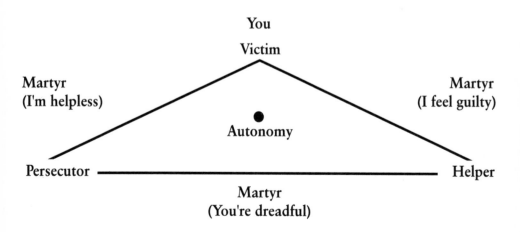

When we have enough confidence in ourselves, we are able to choose which role we wish to adopt and not have one or another forced upon us. Thus, rather than trying to escape from being victim by becoming persecutor or helper, we can stand in our own 'centre' and act with integrity and honesty from that centre.

Self-awareness and Honesty

If we are to act with self-awareness and honesty in our lives, we must become aware of our capabilities. This is our goal on the next circuit of the labyrinth. At the outset we must be realistic about what we can and cannot do and about what we will and will not do. These are not necessarily the same – you may not have the skills to enable you to be a first-class musician or linguist, for instance, but you may have the determination to take lessons until you are as good at it as you can be. Should other priorities take precedence, however, you might have to be honest enough to admit that your lessons are not sufficiently important to warrant you dropping everything else to devote yourself to them.

Too many women sabotage themselves when it comes to their capabilities, and will too easily give up their own pursuits if family or other duties require them to do so. Unless a woman reconciles the resentments or negative feelings with the 'feel good' or positive feelings, she will not be at peace with herself and her decisions. A woman may reach the conclusion that she has to put duty first. In the case of the example given above the woman may be honest enough to admit that she is dreadfully disappointed at not being able to continue with her lessons, but can at least feel, and draw consolation from the knowledge, that she has acted with integrity.

She may, though, be glad of the excuse to drop her course because it is becoming too difficult. In this case she can be honest enough to admit, if only to herself, that there is good enough reason to stop. The self-awareness lies in the woman's admission to herself. Either way, she can still finish up liking herself for what she has done.

In many ways this liking (or loving) of oneself is the simplest form of self-awareness required. If we are continually doing something of which a part of us does not approve or like, then we are not giving ourselves the correct feedback for living with awareness. We may choose to ignore the 'off balance' feeling, but eventually it will have repercussions somewhere in our existence and we will suffer in some way or another, be it physically, mentally or spiritually. If we are out of integrity with ourselves, we cannot be in integrity with everyone else.

The second awareness that women need is that of understanding another's capabilities. Too often when we are in a relationship with someone – whether that is family, friends or a partner – we want to change them into what we think they should be. This almost inevitably leads to a sense of disappointment and letdown. If we can let them be themselves and understand that there are some things of which they are capable and others of which they are not, then there is no stress on either side. Tolerance – a much talked about concept – is really just the ability to accept people for what they are.

It is difficult not to develop expectations of someone, but if we do we must be honest and share these with the person concerned. Provided it is made plain that such hopes are our responsibility, it is likely that the other person will try to co-operate and collaborate rather than meet our desires with a blank stare or a flat refusal. 'It would be nice if …' or 'What do you think of doing …?' will give better feedback than giving an order or producing a grumble.

The third way in which we can operate with honesty and awareness is to recognize our limitations and then – paradoxically

– reject them. This can really be seen as a development of the previous two points. If we know what our present capabilities are, and we also accept others as they are, then any change that occurs must be triggered by us. Circumstances may change around us, either because we have done something to make them or because we have gone along with a change that is occurring to, or because of, someone else. Ultimately we have to accept the need for change and, taking negative and positive together, accept the best options. If we wish, we can then change a seemingly negative occurrence into a positive one.

This used to be called the Pollyanna effect or the 'Glad Game' as immortalized in Eleanor Hodgman Porter's books. In this game, one is required to look for the good in any situation and make the best of it. You can be glad that, for instance, some awful disaster has not occurred. Admittedly, trying to do this can be highly irritating initially, but as a way of training yourself not to accept the limitations of a situation it is an excellent learning tool.

An extension of this is the acceptance that there is some deeper reason behind what occurs and each occurrence holds within it a lesson to be learnt. Such an awareness then allows the opportunity to look at one's limitations and work out possible ways of overcoming perhaps fears and doubts or lack of skill. The final extension of this is the recognition that each situation – no matter what it may be – is a miniature Hero's Journey with its own task, Dragon and reward. We then truly begin to discover and express our own story and creativity on our path towards our own centre.

Creativity

By now you will probably have a fair idea of the sort of person you are and be prepared to try new ways of expressing yourself. In the context of this book, creativity is about using the talents and gifts you have developed over the years. It is not to do with artistic ability. To be truly creative we need to have an interest in what we are doing, or at least be curious about it.

Creativity is putting yourself in touch with an energy within. When we first try tapping into this energy it is very diffuse and scattered. As we work with it we learn to shape it into something that will give expression to our innermost feelings, emotions and beliefs. One of the biggest problems is that in its passage from the very diffuse – and the way that we experience this – through to its realization, our original idea or project becomes distorted. The finished creation, therefore, is never as 'pure' and wonderful as our original vision of it. This naturally results in a degree of frustration that can stop us from going any further with what we have decided to do. There are two principal causes – among many – of this distortion: a spiritual difficulty in translating what we experience on an inner level to the physical, or sheer lack of ability to create something new.

So very often we are inhibited by the old beliefs and projections of family members. If, when trying something new, you come up against such a belief, ask yourself whose voice you 'hear' when you decide you are, for instance, inept or uncreative. It may be that of a parent, a former teacher or a family member. Once you have identified the origin of the false belief it should be possible to confront the offending thought and convince yourself – as you have done so often in the journey you have undertaken – that you are capable of anything you choose to put your mind to. You might like to use the Six-step reframing technique (see page 148), the affirmations or to return to the section entitled Confidence (page 221) to reinforce the good feelings you are developing about yourself.

Knowing your strengths and weaknesses will enable you to develop a plan of campaign to increase your skills to the point where you can tackle new projects and ideas with equanimity.

Often at this stage of the process you may not be able to think of anything in particular that you want to do, or you may feel too inhibited to tackle something different. You might like to try the exercise below to help to remove those strictures and inhibitions.

Creating a new reality

For this exercise you will be putting to one side your logical, restrictive mind and allowing the child within to create a new reality to deal with any problem, apparent difficulty or challenge. Just as each of us has a frightened child within us, so also we still have the happy carefree youngster we once were. Don't be concerned how you are going to bring the new reality into effect, or even if you ever will. This is just a game to get your creativity flowing properly. Give yourself the opportunity to play freely and intuitively with it.

Whatever the challenge you are currently facing, select one of the three following statements, whichever seems most suitable:

- It would be wonderful if ...
- It's easy for me to ...
- It's simple for me to ...

Now, say to yourself –

- The way to achieve this is to ...

And jot down as many ways as you can think of.

This step of the exercise is called 'thinking outside the box' – that is, not allowing your fears and doubts to restrict you. You are giving the child you once were permission to be as spontaneous, ridiculous or courageous as he/she wants.

Let all sorts of ideas come to the fore, no matter how outlandish they may seem – this is your 'personal' brainstorming session. You may find some valuable courses of action emerging. Make a note of any that strike you as particularly relevant, even if you are unable to make use of them now; they may prove invaluable later.

Below are some questions that you might like to ask yourself:

- What improvements can I make to my present situation?
- What priorities – physical, mental or spiritual – are most important to me?
- Within that framework, have I prioritized my time and energy properly?
- Am I already making the best use of my time?
- What is stopping me from making radical changes to my way of life?
- What is my perfect day?
- What do I need to do to achieve more?
- How can I enhance my meaningful relationships?
- Can I work better/harder in any way?
- What parts of my day give me the greatest satisfaction?
- How can I improve my management of time?
- Whose help and support can I call on in making changes in my life?
- How can I eradicate bad habits I have developed?
- What other questions do I need to ask?

The other part of creativity is the ability to know when to communicate with others and when to remain silent. Some creative people work best when they are able to communicate their ideas, while others prefer to remain alone until the project is fully formulated. Exploring your creativity should enable you to discover your optimum way of working. Do remember, though, that what works for one project may not necessarily work for another.

Wisdom

Speaking of communication, it is worthwhile remembering that wisdom can also be defined as the ability to know when to speak and when to say nothing. The inner wisdom that we have is part of our creativity and is a gift to be treated with dignity and sensitivity. It enables us to apply our knowledge and experience on behalf of others and to tap into the spiritual wisdom available to us. Many women of past generations chose a contemplative life in order to make a link with God. Today's woman is often less able to withdraw from the world in this way and must express her wisdom through her career, mothering and creativity. Applying wisdom or being creative is one of the finest forms of self-expression there is.

Often our dreams prove fertile ground for creative projects, although you could also simply use your own ideas. As a starting point for developing creative projects, you may wish to try the following:

- Deliberately choose an activity that takes you beyond your everyday life. Preferably it should be something that you have never tried before.
- Keep a notebook in which to write down anything striking that is connected with your project. This will help you to develop the self-expression that is part of this process.
- You will probably experience several different stages of awareness, ranging from sheer pleasure at your new perceptions to a real sense of achievement when you succeed at something you have not done before.

You will learn to recognize the times when your fears and doubts are preventing you from being creative. When things are working out for you, however, you will experience a strong physical, emotional or spiritual sensation, perhaps all three. This 'locking on' is itself part of the creative process and is linking you to the inner wisdom that is uniquely yours. The more you tap into the wisdom, the more you tap into the creativity, and vice versa.

You might also like to try expressing your ideas through more than one activity. For instance, if cookery is your chosen activity, you might like to develop an illustrated recipe file using photographs you have taken of your creations. None of the projects need be world-beating or especially innovative. Simply concentrate on things in which you take pleasure. They are steps along the path.

Clarity of Vision
As you grow in wisdom and begin to appreciate your own creativity, your attention will turn quite naturally to the community in which you live. Whereas previously your attention will more than likely have been focused on children, family or career, sooner or later there will come a time when you will realize that you have something to offer the rest of the world. Almost inevitably you will find yourself taking an interest in matters that hitherto have not had much meaning for you. This may take the form of wanting to study and learn about community issues such as local politics, global issues such as conservation or spiritual issues, such as the meaning of religion.

One way of giving focus to the concerns that arise is to develop what might be called 'clarity of vision', an ability enabling you to step back from a situation and be objective about it. You are then able to see things as they really are and not as you or anyone else would like them to be. It also means that you are able to assess fairly accurately what needs to be done to improve a situation and what might happen if the worst came to the worst.

Developing this ability ensures that you live more fully in the present – the here and now. It becomes necessary to be observant in your everyday life so that you become aware of the small changes occurring around you. The first sense involved is, of course, sight. It is worthwhile 'tuning up' the other senses as well so that you learn to trust them to back up your impressions.

There are two ways in which you can begin to train yourself to do this. Both are based on childhood games that you may already have learnt.

- Ask someone to place several small objects on a tray. Then observe their positions carefully. Try to name them and remember where they were. Have an object removed from the tray and the other articles moved around. Track those movements and make a note of them. Repeat the exercise until you are proficient at it.
- Next blindfold yourself and pick up an object. Try to identify it by using your other senses. Judge how sensitive your fingertips can become in feeling the physical qualities of the article you are holding – its texture, shape and so on. Repeat the exercise until you are satisfied with your progress.
- Now try an extension to the childhood exercise. If the object you have picked were to have a sound associated with it, what would it be? Would it be sharp/dull, pleasant/unpleasant, low/high, etc.? This sound is a very personal awareness and does not have to correspond with anyone else's perception. Note your findings. Train your memory by remembering what you thought and felt. Later

come back to your various objects and practise again.

The second exercise is very similar, except that it is carried out away from home.

• Choose an activity that you perform fairly regularly, such as a bus ride or a walk to the shops, a trip down the corridor at work. During this activity try to remember everything you can – maybe the colours of the front doors on your route, the position of plants, whether doors are open or closed. By doing this you are learning to live with awareness and to note changes; so each time you carry out the activity, note what is different and what remains the same.

• When you have enough confidence in your powers of observation, concentrate also on your sense of touch, noting textures, shapes, etc. Then, in addition, listen to the various sounds that occur. Which sounds are always present and which ones change?

• Finally, shift your observation from inanimate objects to people and the way they interact with their environment. Try to be aware of how people are feeling as you pass them by. Without intruding on their privacy, see whether you can sense if they are happy, sad, in pain and so on. There is no need for you to do anything at this stage other than be aware.

As you improve your observation and your sensory input, you may become aware of aspects of life that need improving around you. For instance, you may notice that graffiti are a problem. Perhaps you can do something about it by contacting the authorities. Maybe a youth club or similar organization might get involved.

This does not involve turning into a busybody, as it may at

first appear. By being prepared to do something you are beginning to take responsibility for yourself and the way you live. You can acknowledge your own idiosyncrasies without allowing them to get in your way. You may find, for instance, that you have an aversion to any kind of authority figure. That is fine; it is the acknowledgment of the fact which is the important thing.

The development of clarity of vision allows you to live your life more intensely and will enable you to decide how you need to be within any situation. Just as you have learned to use your wisdom and to know when to speak and when to remain silent, now you can learn to appreciate when to take action and when not to. Sometimes it is better to take no action in the knowledge that there is a more appropriate time ahead.

This knowing grows out of trusting yourself. First, you will recognize the feeling of doing the right thing – for you – in any given situation. This is simply an awareness of everything being as it should be at a particular moment. The situation might contain negatives or even develop a negative outcome. If this is the case, it is simply an inevitability that such a state of affairs would develop given the actions of the people concerned.

Secondly, you will, with your new-found objectivity, be able to stand back and believe that your further course of action, or that of others around you, will become obvious to you. You will have assessed the various aspects of what is going on and will have a fair idea of what each person is capable. When you become aware of the various courses of action that might be appropriate, you will gradually find that your decisions are made in the light of this knowledge and in the light of what seems best in the long run. You will also be aware of why other people have decided to act in the way they have.

Finally, you will become aware, with great clarity, of the

outcome of your own course of action. Initially, imponderables, such as spontaneous action by others, may throw your perception out of kilter. Gradually, however, you will learn to incorporate these into your assessment and be able to predict the outcome of most situations.

The next step is to recognize that you are now in control of your life and, using the past and present you are now creating – you can begin to lay down the basis for a future for yourself.

Creating A Sustainable Future

As women, one of the aspects of life that we must inevitably be intimately involved in as we progress towards our own centre is the creation of a sustainable future for ourselves and those we love. Whether as young women with careers, mothers with children or women who have developed and cultivated wisdom, we cannot help but be aware of our responsibility towards the world in which we live. Inherent in every woman – despite what others would have us believe – is an awareness of a wider picture belonging to a greater world beyond our immediate horizons.

With this awareness we will look further than our own community and will seek out others who feel as passionately as we do to confirm our validity. We will attempt to point out to our children the mistakes we have made. We will perceive the question of women's issues – whether matters of health or the right to freedom – as being our concern.

When we have clarified our vision and recognized our ability to think clearly about such issues, we are ready to commit ourselves to the making real of all those things that arouse our passion. We do not merely react in anger against the injustices of which we learn; we question ourselves as to what we can do about them. We need no longer believe nothing can be done, though we may be unable to take immediate action. We are becoming aware of the power of positive thought and that there is something magical and encouraging in being able to use the perception we have developed. We can link with others to make changes in the world we love.

This ability to unite with others is perhaps the most reassuring part of being a woman in today's society. Modern technology means we are no longer isolated within our own small world but can be in contact with others who share our interests. Not everyone will wish to mount campaigns and not everyone will want to be perpetually conversing with people on the other side of the world. However, with the realization that there is a network of concerned people around the world comes awareness of how our combined energy and strength can be used to the benefit of all. We can make the world a better place by learning to use the power of our minds and our compassion to great effect, both as individuals and jointly.

To be able to experiment with this way of thinking you need to assume that you can make a difference within the world. You must also realize that it is quite likely you will never be sure you have done so – it is a matter of trust. For the purposes of the exercise below, and to train you to work within a wider framework, choose something about which you feel particularly passionate. Let us suppose that you are aware of the issues to do with women's health in other countries. The steps you might take are:

• Start by reminding yourself that things are as they have to be but that they can change.
• Select your particular issue and spend some time thinking about it. You will probably find that you need to know more about your subject and can do some research.
• With this gathering of information you are initiating change within yourself, and moving simply from feeling passionately to knowing more.

• Now spare a little thought for your particular issue every day and believe that things must change for the better.

• Before long, often as soon as 72 hours from the time you started thinking about your issue, information and knowledge will come your way. You may find, for instance, that you meet someone who has special knowledge of interest or something that is useful to you. This phenomenon is called synchronicity, when the universe starts co-operating with you.

• Such synchronicity (the coming together of events) is your signal to intensify your efforts should you so choose. You may wish to become more deeply involved practically or you may feel that you can do more by being aware, and that positive thought or prayer adds its own vibration.

• Finally, you can rest easy in the knowledge that you have adopted responsibility for a little bit of your future world and that that in itself brings its own reward.

Each one of us has accountability for the world as we experience it, but perhaps now we are also aware of our ability to create magic for ourselves and others. If you have tried the exercise above, you will already have used that magic on a wider scale, and hopefully will have had a degree of faith in the right outcome. It is time, therefore, to bring your awareness closer to home and begin to take responsibility for making things happen within your own environment and in your community.

Now your agenda can be unselfish and much more geared towards what might be called the Greater Good. Really this is living mindfully, knowing that our thoughts and actions can have a greater effect on others around us than we can necessarily comprehend. We can also see that our present actions can have an effect on our future and that of others.

One word of caution, however. What *we* perceive as the Greater Good is not always so in the overall scheme of things. Someone may benefit by what is happening to them – though in some instances this can be hard to believe – and, as we have seen, it may be wiser for us to take no active part in what is going on. This does not mean that we must not have feelings or emotions, but does mean that we must not let our emotions get in the way.

We must try, insofar as we are capable, to cultivate absence of desire. This means having no expectation of a particular outcome. We simply learn to hold the intent for the best outcome. That way, while we have put an effort in to make things right in accordance with the Greater Good we have not personally skewed the result in a way that might be inappropriate. This particular aspect is often difficult to understand and even more difficult to carry out when those we love may be suffering. Truly, we need to call on the wisdom of Sophia to be able to hold to that intent.

Future woman can choose whether to be militant, to work quietly in the background, to find her own individual self-expression – whether that be as an entrepreneur, working for somebody else or as a member of a corporate body. She now has the right to make decisions in the light of her own experiences and to do what she thinks is right, not what someone else has told her to do. She can learn to trust her own intuition and to take responsibility for it, without feeling that she is thought mad, sad or bad. She can reach for the stars and achieve her dreams.

Now is the time to take up that challenge, and to put everything that this stands for into operation. You will no doubt have got cross, frustrated or upset at various times as you have tried some of the suggestions in the book. Hopefully you will have smiled a little, agreed with some things and treated others with a great deal of scepticism.

Now it is time to make a promise to yourself. Take a piece of paper and write or draw on it the sort of woman you wish to become. Include as much or as little detail as you need to really be able to feel how this woman will be. Put in all your dreams, your 'Wouldn't it be wonderful if ...', 'If I could I would ...' How does she dress? How does she react to challenges? What has changed? What does she now know? Project yourself forward and feel within yourself the potential for the changes you will choose to make.

When you have the vision and the feeling in place, make a dedication to this woman as she stands in the future and promise her that you will do everything in your power to make her life possible. If need be write her a letter, setting out how you yourself think and feel at this moment. Commit your thoughts to paper for both your sake and hers, because as you perform your transformation you may well lose sight of the person you are at this particular moment and it will be good to look back. Hopefully, you will be able to use other parts of this book as you travel towards your future.

Then put the letter away for this Future Woman to read at her leisure. As she does so, we hope that she will look at herself with pride and give herself the accolade she deserves – 21st-century Woman.

CHAPTER 10

Women through the Ages

'She is like a stone on the hilltop,
difficult to be moved.
Yet when she is once started she goeth fast and far;
no man knoweth her end.'

When we delve into our rich heritage, we can find examples of women who used the prevailing attitudes and conditions of their time to move through to their own sense of themselves. In this chapter we shall be considering some of these women, taking representatives from each strata of society, to highlight how they learned to push aside boundaries that were either self-inflicted or imposed upon them.

You may like to use this section to see how the journey that we encourage you to take was also taken – in their own way – by these women. You will then indeed have explored the labyrinth. After reading about each period in history presented here, you might find it interesting to imagine yourself as you might have been if you had been living then. Would you have shown similar courage? How would you have handled the problems that faced our examples? Would you have been able to handle them as well?

Each period builds upon the experience of its predecessor and can only sense within itself the potential of the next. Looking back, from our perspective, it is a salutary lesson to realize how difficult it must have been for those women to make sense of feelings and thoughts that appeared to be out of step with prevailing beliefs.

If we are to have any concept of what being a woman really

means, and to understand our own sexuality and gender, we need to trace the path of women through history right from the proverbial cave woman through to women of the present day.

Traditionally, cave woman was captured from her own tribe and dragged kicking and screaming to her man's lair. In fact, our perception of Neolithic man has had to change recently when it was discovered through archeological excavations that he already possessed knowledge of medical matters and had developed sophisticated relationship structures far in advance of that formerly attributed to him. Since woman has by and large always taken care of the softer skills of nurturing and caring, one must assume that she will have played her part in developing healing and caring within those communities.

It would be fascinating to be able to travel back in time for ourselves to find out what life was like. We do have some information on women who lived and died for their principles within their own period. Women such as Boudicca, Hypatia and the Trung sisters – whose stories are included in the Icon section following – had faith in themselves and were prepared to make sacrifices for their beliefs. To demonstrate how woman began to recognize her own autonomy, and to enable us to make an appraisal of her journey through the ages, we shall start with the medieval period. The most extensively documented aspect of woman's history at this time is her relationship with her spirituality.

Spiritual Women: the Middle Ages

In the Middle Ages the position of women who found themselves alone without the protection of a family or husband was precarious. Often they took refuge in the convent. There was still quite a sharp divide in treatment between noblewomen and women from the broad lower band of society, even within the protection of the Church. Much depended on education and finance. Many women totally accepted the extreme moral purity demanded of them, either because they knew no other life – having been entrusted to a religious order at an early age – or because they had already been married and entered the convent as widows and no longer needed to think of procreation or wifely duty.

Ironically, the restrictions and harsh rules imposed in the enclosed orders, coupled with the difficulty – due to the sheer weight of numbers – in being accepted into other less stringent religious houses meant that many women with a leaning towards chastity were left with no choice but to accept – against their better instincts – the protection of a man within marriage. It is unlikely that women opted for 'spiritual marriage' – an arrangement whereby sexual abstinence by both partners within the marriage was acceptable – as an *ideal* vocation. Such a marriage remained a last resort and a viable alternative for the devout woman who, for whatever reason, was forced into marriage.

This type of arrangement would have suited both parties equally well. For men spiritual marriage was often simply a stage of transition to a formal renunciation of the world, once they had fulfilled their procreative duties. Women, on the other hand, were better able to accept a looser, more fluid arrangement and did not need totally to withdraw into seclusion. Many women, even after their husbands died, having discovered a way of fulfilling their spiritual inclinations, chose not to join formal religious orders but continued to live within the world in a way that fitted in with the prevalent idea of living a life of atonement for the world's sins. They served their God by remaining in the world but living a life of prayer.

There was also another way in which women's perception of spirituality was markedly different from that of men's. Dependent on male priests as they supposedly were for their connection to God, women did not see the sexes as anything other than complementary. Men, though, saw the need to be removed from the temptations of the flesh and to live a life completely separate from women. Their spirituality seemed to operate best within the more formal, regimented framework of the monastery. Women even then perceived the need for freedom of choice and the right to have control over their bodies.

Preference and belief are vitally important components in the spirituality of a woman. It is still possible for a woman to perceive herself capable of sacrificing the pleasures of the flesh in favour of the greater principle of spiritual love. In the concept of the 'spiritual marriage' as it was practised in medieval times, we see one way that a woman could handle the two aspects of herself, with the sexual urge being subsumed under the spiritual one.

From the 12th century onwards there were many cases of trances, seizures and ecstatic nosebleeds reported by women in search of mysticism. Some of these women became what today would be called anorexic, taking only the 'bread of Christ' – the holy Eucharist – as sustenance. It does seem that women tended to accept suffering and illness as something of religious significance and a gift from God rather than a hysterical reaction to their own perception of themselves. Ecstatic experiences were often accompanied by various 'miraculous' bodily secretions, demonstrating a particular state of grace. Such occurrences as stigmata, echoing the wounds and trials of Christ or other holy figures, were relatively common, as were phantom pregnancies, which were thought to be evidence of a mystical union with Christ. There is also evidence that some women secreted a lactiferous fluid when they experienced a pure maternal love for the Christ figure. In a simple society these occurrences would not have been seen as psychosomatic but must have seemed truly miraculous.

Surprisingly perhaps, in this period, strong-minded and self-sufficient women could survive within the confines of a contemplative life. Religious orders have, in fact, since time immemorial been places of sanctuary for such mavericks – today such women would probably have risen to positions of prominence in business. We consider three examples of such mavericks here.

In their day – between the 11th and 14th centuries – these women were mystics and subsequently have become regarded as icons of spirituality. (A mystic may be defined as someone who has a spiritual appreciation of truths that are beyond the understanding of the normal person.) Each of our examples expressed her mysticism in very different ways.

Hildegard of Bingen (1098–1179) was a 'first' in many fields. At a time when few women wrote, Hildegard, known as the 'sibyl of the Rhine', produced major works of theology, visionary writings and music. She was consulted by bishops, popes and kings. She used the curative powers of natural objects for healing and wrote treatises about natural history and the medicinal uses of plants, animals, trees and stones. The all-female 'family' she formed was initially attached to a Benedictine monastery and later was established in a convent of its own.

Mechthild of Magdeburg (13th century) became a béguine (see below) at the age of 23. She wrote a treatise called *The Flowing Light of the Godhead*, which was considered highly erotic and a dangerous influence. Consistently hounded by the Church authorities for her views, which were regarded as heretical, she eventually found refuge in the Cistercian convent at Helfta which was renowned as a place of women's learning.

Julian of Norwich was a 14th-century mystic whose cell was attached to the church of St Julian in Norwich. She was often visited by troubled souls in search of spiritual reassurance. She completed her *Revelation of a Divine Love*, a rewriting of her *Book of Shewings* (interesting too for being the earliest English text attributable to a woman), some 20 years after first making notes of her mystical experiences.

All three women committed themselves to some form of religious life, thereby deliberately cutting themselves off from the opportunity of becoming wives and mothers. All based their mystical accounts on a series of personal spiritual experiences. These they considered important enough to record for others, thereby breaking several taboos imposed on their sex: silence, submissiveness and a sense of inferiority.

The fact that these women rejected marriage meant that they chose to express other aspects of womanhood in different ways. All three women show themselves to have been intensely feminine, each expressing herself through her basic nature.

Hildegard, for instance, did not see the dominant, active role as being the exclusive property of the male sex. One of her most startling representations of the Divine is a huge star-filled, fiery cosmic egg – a grandly all-encompassing female image. She saw the women who joined her convent as her 'daughters', who were brides of Christ. She celebrated the fulfilment they would find in that relationship.

Mechtild's most prominent imagery is, however, erotic. As a béguine, she showed divine union as a consummation between two lovers, whereby the soul is transported in ecstasy to a secret and blissful place that it is upsetting to leave. Her high regard for the maternal ideal is her representation of the Virgin Mary.

Julian reveals her femininity through her understanding of

the motherhood of God. She stated that the Trinity actually includes a female component and that Jesus, as well as being the Son of God, is our mother who feeds and nurtures us during our lifetime.

Of the three, Julian's character is the most serene and self-contained. The quiet life of privacy allowed her the freedom to achieve a deep tranquillity. None of these women was prepared to accept the restrictive practices of their religion and, in refusing to submit – indeed, disobeying when necessary – they achieved a transcendent or inspirational viewpoint which still has relevance today.

New forms of spiritual life did emerge in the Middle Ages, both in the family and in free communities that were unconstrained by the rules of a religious order. The béguine movement, for instance, which was founded in the 12th century by Lambert le Bègue, arose because of the need for some kind of organization of the 'sisters between' – women who saw themselves as belonging neither to family life nor to the religious houses. They perceived themselves as the brides of Christ. Their particular form of mysticism gave them spiritual power and gifts of wisdom and therefore direct access to the heavenly realm. Their asceticism allowed them to transcend their earthly bodies, forming female identities uncorrupted by the 'female sins' that so frightened the menfolk. The béguines demanded – and took – freedom of expression as their right and therefore created for themselves an area which was in effect a third gender, untainted by their femininity and yet owing allegiance to no man. Not constrained by the teachings of the Church and its priests – as were the formal religious orders – the béguines were able to express a passionate religious devotion in their lives and writings which, at the time, were often seen as heretical. This was self-authorization of a kind not previously perceived in women.

There was no way that a béguine could be called a nun; she was part of the movement towards community through her own conviction. She did not take a vow of obedience; if she chose, she could return to the world and marry, and she did not renounce her right to property. If she had no means of support, she did not ask for alms but worked to support herself by using what skills she had. A community of like-minded women tended to grow up around a Grand Mistress, initially living with her but later moving into their own dwellings with servants if they could afford to do so. Every community was complete within itself; it was the community of worship and similar aims in life that held the community together.

Such communities were a genuine attempt at sisterhood, supportive of their members as a semi-respectable group through to a degree of institutionalism followed by certain persecution due to lack of understanding of their motives. Seeking only to follow their own path to self-expression and worship as 'instruments of God', they suffered extreme suppression in the 16th and 18th centuries. Today a few such communities survive in Belgium. An interesting parallel might be drawn between this movement and the Missionaries of Charity begun by Mother Teresa out of pure personal conviction.

There were, of course, those – like Julian of Norwich – who chose solitude instead of community as a means by which to forge a singular relationship with God. The life of simplicity and devotion undertaken by a solitary or anchoress was not easy. Their living quarters consisted of a cell no larger than twelve feet square, attached to a church or convent. This structure had three windows, but no door. The first was open to the church to enable the recluse to receive the Sacraments, speak with a confessor and also hear Mass. The second window was a portal by which necessities such as food could be received. The third must be covered so that the light was allowed in but outside activity did not distract the occupier or occupiers. After enclosure they remained, normally for life, in the same restricted quarters, having held what amounted to a funeral service to signify that they were dead to their previous lives. In an instruction to young anchoresses, the *Ancrene Riwle*, they are enjoined to remember the following:

'Now, you ask what rules you anchoresses should have. You shall always with all might and strength keep well the inner, and for her sake the outer. The inner is ever same; the outer is variable. For each one shall maintain the outer according to how she may best serve the inner with her.'

This solitary calling drew many untrained people who sought seclusion for various reasons. There were poor as well as aristocratic; monks and nuns who required a wholly contemplative life and those who had dedicated their lives to service and saw a life of prayer as supreme. The vow – the commitment to God – of most anchoresses was stability and an unchanging focus, rather than the wandering life of the hermit, and many grew to love their tiny homes.

Away from the religious life in the late Middle Ages, society was still divided into estates, but distinction at all levels could now be won by achievement as well as birth. There was a largely sympathetic attitude towards widows, unmarried women who were living in their fathers' houses – presumably as mistress of the household – and, oddly, maiden aunts. (There were many poor women in the towns, mostly widows and maidservants.) A society had come into being in the towns which was particularly dominated by the principle of achievement and was very mixed in terms of its members' origins.

Unmarried women, widows and even a significant number of wealthy married women were engaged in commercial work, often in the family business. There are many such examples. In a Regensburg trading house, a Margarete Runtinger kept the books and managed the money-changing over a long period, enabling her husband the freedom to take up many honorary posts. In the silk industry of Florence, the women were engaged in silk-making while their husbands were often porters of raw silk or were responsible for selling silk. Blacksmiths' wives were usually responsible for the commercial side of the business. Work and home thus came together.

Further away from the towns, the peasant husband was entitled to one cart of wood from his lord if his wife gave birth to a daughter and two if the baby was a son. There does not seem to have been any rational reason for the preferential treatment; it was simply custom to acknowledge that a daughter was of less economic value than a son since she had to be provided with a dowry whether she married or entered a convent. It seems to have made little difference to the division of labour between the sexes, however. Life was hard for both sexes, with women working just as hard as men.

The woman at the head of the household, whatever its size or importance, had the responsibility for the health of those around her, mostly dealing with wounds, broken bones and illnesses caused by occupational hazards. Women in households that did not have access to a medical practitioner – these latter being usually fairly down to earth, relying on experience rather than training – turned to traditional folklore and herbalism. Healthcare was viewed as a craft rather than an art, and until the rise of the universities even surgery continued to be the province of the barber.

From the 15th century onwards there was a discrepancy between the levels of education given to boys and girls. 'Scholars'

– mostly men – were now able to force their way onto municipal councils. Doctors, notaries and licentiates all had to study at university and so women were forced into subordinate positions because of their lack of academic training, a situation that would continue until the 20th century.

Emotional Tenacity: late Renaissance

There are two women who deserve attention in our search for icons of this period. Both made their mark through sheer strength of character and tenacity, and may be said to have altered the course of history. They amply demonstrate the emotional commitment to their own faith in themselves which we explore as part of woman's knowledge of herself. The first, Anne Askew, was persecuted for her religious beliefs and dared to challenge the authority of the Bishop of London. The second was Bess of Hardwick, initially a commoner, who rose through the social ranks by virtue of her marriages, becoming almost as rich as Elizabeth I, and founded a dynasty that has close connections to the Royal family, even today.

Anne Askew (1521–46) has become known for her stance against persecution. She converted to Protestantism in defiance of her Catholic husband. Petitioning for a divorce, which was refused, she joined the group of women associated with the sixth wife of Henry VIII, Catherine Parr, a Protestant sympathizer, who protected from persecution those who dissented from Catholic doctrine. In 1545 Anne was suspected of heresy but was released through lack of evidence. Examined and released a second time, she was finally imprisoned in the Tower of London and was put on the rack and tortured because she would not reveal who her associates in Parr's group had been.

She carefully chronicled what she called her 'Examinacions'

and the resulting document is partly a diary and partly the story of her spiritual trials, complete with her prayers and meditations. When questioned by the Chancellor of the Bishop of London – and others – as to her right to speak, write and defend herself, she said:

I answered hym that I knewe Pauls meaninge so well as he, which is I Corothians xiiii, that a woman ought not to speake in the congregacyon by the waye of teachinge. And then I asked hym, how many women he had seane, go into the pulpett and preach. He sayde, he never saw none. Then I sayd, he ought to find no faulte in poore women, except they had offended the lawe.

Her argument is very reminiscent of that made much later by the women who defended the Levellers and by Catherine Booth of the Salvation Army who in the 19th century challenged her husband over her right to preach.

Anne records her terrible ordeal by torture totally dispassionately and shows great fortitude in the face of cruelty. Askew knocks on the head any long-held idea of woman's 'frailty' – physical, ethical or intellectual.

Bess of Hardwick showed no insufficiency either in her rise to prominence. She began life as the daughter of parents of moderate means. Her father died while she was still young, leaving her and her sisters a small dowry each. She went into service with Sir John and Lady Zouche and at 13 married Robert Barlow. He died shortly afterwards and Bess, in accordance with the law of the time, inherited one third of his income.

This seems to have set a pattern, for she was to marry three times more, nursing her husbands and inheriting progressively larger estates. Her second husband was Sir William Cavendish, 22 years her senior, with whom she had six surviving children. He died in 1557 and in 1559 she married Sir William St Loe, who seems to have been much in love with her and settled her debts from the previous period. She was, by this time, lady-in-waiting to Queen Elizabeth I and became unwillingly embroiled in the marriage plans of Lady Catherine Grey and the Earl of Hertford. For this she was imprisoned in the Tower in 1561 for seven months for not supporting the monarch.

On her husband's death she again inherited lands and property, including Chatsworth House. On marrying the 6th Earl of Shrewsbury, George Talbot – said to be the richest man in England – Bess cemented her place in history, for the two families were also united by the marriages of their respective children.

During the time that the Earl of Shrewsbury was custodian of Mary, Queen of Scots, Bess became associated with the royal families of both England and Scotland. Her daughter by William Cavendish, Elizabeth, fell in love with and married, against Queen Elizabeth's wishes, Charles, 6th Earl of Lennox. He was the brother of Mary, Queen of Scots' murdered husband and his lineage stretched back to Princess Margaret Tudor, sister of Henry VIII.

Their daughter, Arabella Stuart, born in 1575, was thus in line for the throne, since any children that Elizabeth and Charles had, stood in opposition to James VI (of Scotland) and I (of England) – Elizabeth I's cousin. However, Arabella's father died in 1576, her paternal grandmother, Countess Lennox, in 1578 and her mother in 1582, which meant that Bess of Hardwick (her maternal grandmother) had full responsibility for her. There was much scheming to bring about Arabella's succession to the throne and unite the royal families of England and Scotland. But these efforts were doomed to failure, although Bess's many stratagems ensure that her blood still flows in aristocratic families today. As was said of her at the time:

'She was a builder, a buyer and seller of estates, a money lender, a farmer, a merchant of lead, coals and timber.'

We have chosen these two women as examples of their time in order to show how women of principle – whether right or wrong – were prepared to work towards a deeply cherished aim. Anne Askew found a spirituality that worked for her and allowed her to challenge the official system of religious integrity. Bess's belief in herself permitted her to ride roughshod over the obstacles in her path. Such beliefs did not prevent her from making use of everything she had to enable her to achieve her goal. There were, of course, many such women about whom we know very little. By comparison, the struggles of these two women are particularly well documented.

Claiming their Power: Jacobean women

Had Arabella Stuart been a boy, her bid to secure the throne of England would have met with greater success. Seen as a traitor because of her marriage to the Earl of Hertford, she was sent to the Tower and died in 1615. These were dangerous times for many women.

In the reign of James I women were increasingly prepared to step out of the shadows and declare competence in areas previously regarded as inappropriate. Women writers, for example, wanted the acknowledgement they felt they deserved. (Up until this time there had not really been the need to acknowledge the right to express themselves more fully since women had chosen not to make an issue of such expression.) One such writer was Rachel Speght, who interpreted the Creation story in Genesis as evidence of woman's natural and spiritual equality with man. She wisely claimed that her ultimate consent to write came from God, who wished all humankind to utilize the whole of their potential.

Largely the classics and other such intellectual studies were thought not only to be superfluous in a woman's education, but very likely to harm both her mind – presumably because it was not equipped to deal with such high-flown studies – and her marriage prospects. Women from the higher ranks of society were taught to read and often to write in English, and in addition they often studied French, needlework, geography, music and dancing. Opinion varied greatly as to the value of even this type of education. The father of the noblewoman Anne Clifford forbade her to learn Latin. However, her education was still unusual for a woman, thanks largely to her tutor, Samuel Daniel, who taught her philosophy, history and literature.

Both Clifford and Speght therefore benefited from the enlightened attitudes of the men around them. Male enlightenment on the subject of women only extended so far, however. When she challenged the laws of inheritance, the same Anne Clifford was ostracized by society, although she would be ultimately successful in her claim, which she pursued over an inordinately lengthy period.

Lucy Hutchinson – who would later chronicle the English Civil War – wrote of herself: 'My mother, while she was with child with me, dreamed that she was walking in the garden with my father, and that a star came down into her hand, with other circumstances ... only my father told her, her dream signified she should have a daughter of some extraordinary eminency.' She was therefore encouraged to develop her innate abilities to a high degree, believing implicitly in her right to be a powerful woman, as had Bess of Hardwick.

By and large the attitude to women was somewhat ambivalent at this time. This is particularly highlighted in the contemporary fashion of cross-dressing. It began among the lower class 'roaring girls' and was later adopted by both noblewomen and the wives of citizens, causing consternation both at court and in the Church. This practice was seen as a challenge to the division between the genders, though it was pointed out at the time that men were adopting more feminine styles of dress, such as ruffles and buckles. King James' attitude to, and fears regarding, the rights of women seems to have been a reaction to the various shifts in their power and the possibility that men might be emasculated and women might assume masculine roles and privileges.

James was also fearful of the widespread belief in the power of the supernatural, having had to confront it already in his time as King of Scotland. He also saw the necessity for a new translation of The Bible which made its teachings available to everyone.) Alchemy (a largely male-oriented profession) did have a degree of respectability, as also did astrology, yet witchcraft was perceived as being destructive and its exponents more easily seduced to practise evil intent. It was this perception of such women being weak and easily led which gave others problems.

Traditionally, witches were perceived as being able to change their shape; to fly, albeit at night; create magical charms; have a 'familiar' – usually an animal that would carry out her magical commands – and be capable of enhancing her power by communication with others like herself. Many of these same qualities can be developed from a psychological standpoint by the woman who understands and has come to terms with her own power, as we have seen earlier in the book, when we looked at the archetype of the witch.

The fear engendered in men by women who had found this power within themselves would naturally have caused a need for suppression, and also the creation of the myth of the need for submission. This fear and its effects were most evident in the Puritan era. Thus in the 17th century we can again see two strands in the development of women: the need for self-expression and the instinctive use of natural powers, this time perhaps more magical than spiritual.

During the English Civil War there was a strong reaction to the perceived excesses of the preceding period. The new Puritan government purified the Church of what it saw as secular practices and those not based on strict adherence to the Scriptures. Many people found they were unable to handle the problems associated with following their beliefs and left for the New World. The courage that many women required to uproot themselves and start a new life, not knowing whether or not they would survive, is outstanding.

Those women who followed the soldiers as they went into battle also required a kind of courage – albeit a slightly different one. Camp followers, as they were known, have been perceived as being prostitutes but this was not necessarily always the case. They were often women who had been left destitute or dispossessed with nowhere else to go. Throughout time there have been women who followed soldiers, but during the Civil War the position was unusual in that women followed their men through their own conviction and in order to contribute to the war effort.

This feminine support was seen when several leaders of the Leveller movement were imprisoned after agitating for a new political compact, an Agreement of the People. Their women chose to assist them by presenting a petition claiming that, in the same way as the women waited at the Crucifixion of Christ, they also had the right to wait for and support their men.

The petition very carefully turned the usual line of argument about women's piety on its head and asked if it was not right that they as women should offer their support to those who had been imprisoned. Was it wrong to feel a sense of compassion? Just because they were weak women, it was 'a usual thing with God, by weak means to work mighty effect.' Did they not also have the right to watch and wait and demand justice now? As a matter of interest, this was the first time that women had joined together to protest against injustice. In the 19th century the Chartists, perceived as the Levellers of their time, did not make use of the support of their women.

In considering two groups of women in these times we have reflected the growing concerns of the period. Women began to challenge perceived masculine supremacy, both privately and publicly. They saw the need for a movement towards grouping together those of like mind and for communities which had women at their centre. Some confronted patriarchy and dictatorship as they were manifested, both in the family and in the state, while others rewrote cultural and literary discourses regarding courtiership and patronage.

In other areas of life it was difficult for the English to accommodate to the idea of absolute monarchy as embodied by the Scot who became their king, James I. His style of rulership was very different from that of his predecessor, Elizabeth. In many ways the whole of the 17th century, and the beginning of the 18th, was a period of turbulence as the Scots and English learned to live together. James's favouritism and profligate spending did not endear him to the English, while the Scots felt they were being short-changed. This situation exacerbated the existing bad feeling between the two nations.

In the Jacobite Rebellions of 1715 and 1745 women were once again required to use their resources to carry out whatever tasks were necessary in support of their menfolk, whether that was nursing them back to health, acting as stewards for their lands and possessions or using their commercial acumen. In Scotland particularly women came into their own just as women at the time of the Crusades had had to do when their men were required to enter combat far from their native soil. By the 1745 Rebellion in Britain many people were financially, mentally and physically exhausted. At the same time, exploration overseas of the New World was gathering pace. New ways of trading such as those seen in the Spice Wars – the fight for supremacy of commodities such as nutmeg – meant that women from all countries were beginning to broaden their horizons and have a new sense of what boundaries they might transcend.

Marking the Difference: the late 18th century

In 1750, a young marine got to his feet in a London pub and astounded his fellow soldiers. He told them that 'he' was really a she. Hannah Snell had hidden her true sex, had sailed to India and fought at the siege of Pondicherry while serving in a regiment of the Royal Marines. She was encouraged to make the most of her story, and applied for a pension from the head of the British army, which she received eventually for a period of about forty years. During that time she married twice and raised two sons.

There would always be women like Hannah who would feel the need to challenge the existing system. Such women would not do this from a sense, necessarily, of needing to change that system, but just to see whether it actually could be challenged. This was obviously a further extension of the 'roaring girls' phenomenon of the previous century, but does demonstrate how far some women were prepared to go. Other women, such as Mary Woolstonecraft, did feel strongly about the existing system and through their writings made their opinions felt. She wrote:

'After considering the historic page, and viewing the living world with anxious solicitude, the most melancholy emotions of sorrowful indignation have depressed my spirits, and I have sighed when obliged to confess that either Nature has made a great difference between man and man, or that the civilisation which has hitherto taken place in the world has been very partial.'

Her belief was also that men were capable of minimalizing women by their attitude. Women were not simply objects to be cosseted and adored, they actually had brains they were capable of using. She wrote:

'... *the understanding of the sex has been so bubbled by this specious homage, that the civilised women of the present century, with a few exceptions, are only anxious to inspire love, when they ought to cherish a nobler ambition, and by their abilities and virtues exact respect.*'

Woolstonecraft was well aware of the potential for women to be enervated by men's treatment of them, but equally aware that women of her class were their own worst enemies. The Restoration of 1660 had released society's pent-up desire for fun after the strictures of Puritanism and the party mood had not yet died. Women of quality became perhaps overly concerned with their appearance and would run up huge bills on entertainment of various sorts. At the other end of the scale, the poor had a hard time in managing to keep body and soul together. There was certainly no equality among women, let alone between the sexes. This is well demonstrated in the writings of the time, for many women wrote about what they knew.

One interesting outcome of this divide was, however, that as new scientific interest emerged in 'the plurality of worlds' (those worlds that existed beyond the range of normal sight and thus investigation), ladies were encouraged to take an interest in peering through the new scientific 'toys' of the microscope and the telescope. Some people believed that women, because of their natural curiosity and detachment from the business of making a living, could be better than men at scientific pursuits. The difference between the professional scientist and the gifted amateur became very blurred, which meant that those women with the resources and the intelligence could pursue their interest quietly and without fuss. A tradition of patient research developed which was later to reap its reward in the many women world-wide who have made their mark in modern science.

The Age of Enlightenment gave rise to visions of Utopia – a perfect society – and cast fresh light on ideas of property-holding, community and social and political reform movements, including those for the extension of rights to women, slaves and animals. Women writers such as Fanny Burney, who was also a diarist, Maria Edgeworth and later Jane Austen were sharp observers of the human condition and used humour and irony to expose prejudice against women.

Not all well-bred women, though, were content with merely being pampered and patronized. The Bluestocking group, as it became known, was set up by some ladies who decided that they preferred good conversation to interminable card playing. The group held meetings at which learned men and those with radical or novel ideas were invited to speak. (The term 'bluestocking' – which would later be used to ridicule women with intellectual pretensions – was coined after it became known that one of the speakers, Benjamin Stillingfleet, unable to afford the black silk stockings which were then part of every gentleman's wardrobe, attended meetings in blue stockings.) Only with hindsight is it possible to appreciate the part the original 'bluestockings' played in the movement towards the eventual emancipation of women, and their acceptance of radical ideas.

Bearing Witness: the 19th century
In the 19th century we pick up again two of the themes we have been following in our history of women – self-expression, and the determination not to be thwarted from following their own

inclinations, especially by an authoritarian viewpoint. These two strands draw together in two women who, although having very different beliefs, expressed their spirituality through a passionate concern for their fellow beings. The women are Catherine Booth and Annie Besant.

There were still strictures against the right of women to express themselves by preaching from the pulpit and it is obvious this was a bone of contention among many. Catherine Mumford Booth, wife of the founder of the Salvation Army, ably defended her right to think, speak and preach in the pamphlets she circulated, thereby challenging the wishes of her husband.

In one of her pamphlets she shows her appreciation of her own sex:

'God has given to woman a graceful form and attitude, winning manners, persuasive speech, and, above all, a finely-toned emotional nature, all of which appear to us eminent natural qualifications for public speaking.'

She cited the argument used previously when the Quakers, or Society of Friends as they are known, had allowed their women to bear witness if the Spirit moved them. She stated that if women were moved to speak they were shielded from all coarse and unrefined influences and that their vocation would lead to them to commend 'all the tenderest and most womanly instincts.' She believed passionately in this ability of women, and in her pamphlet states that if this were not so, she would not have dared to put forward the argument. To quote her again:

'Believing however that they will bear the strictest investigation, and that their importance cannot easily be over-estimated, we feel bound to propagate them to the utmost of our ability.'

Catherine also based her arguments on the correct translation of the word *lalein* in the Bible, pointing out that it could be translated as 'I answer, I return a reason, I give rule or precept, I order, decree.' Normally taken to forbid women to prophesy, in fact it gave them permission to speak. Catherine shows the same grasp of the inherent meaning of the Scriptures as shown by Anne Askew earlier. Her understanding was not based on pure Christian belief, but was instinctual, although backed up by hard study and thought.

Annie Besant's story was a sad one in some ways. After enduring an unhappy marriage to a somewhat cruel and authoritarian clergyman, she left him and secured a legal separation, but was forced to lose contact with her son, whilst retaining custody of her daughter.

A contemporary of Catherine, Annie was initially concerned with the social conditions of the times. She had a penchant for challenging authority. With Charles Bradlaugh, leader of the Secular Movement in Britain, she published a book by Charles Knowlton entitled *The Fruits of Philosophy*, which advocated birth control. The pair published in the full knowledge that the book would cause controversy and probably lead to prosecution, which it duly did. The conviction was subsequently quashed, however, and Annie's own writings were then published.

Of this episode she would later write:

'I wrote a pamphlet entitled The Law of Population *giving the arguments which had convinced me of its truth, the terrible distress and degradation entailed on families by overcrowding and the lack of necessaries of life, pleading for early marriages that prostitution might be destroyed, and limitation of the family that pauperism might be avoided, finally giving the information which rendered early marriage without these evils possible. This pamphlet was put in circulation as representing our views on the subject.'*

Annie became interested in the fate of women in the East End of London, as indeed Catherine had been, and in 1888 she helped to lead a protest against low wages and the use of phosphorus in the Bryant & May match factory. This led to the formation of the first trade union for women, the Match Girls' Union which, after a three-week strike, forced major concessions from the factory owners.

In the 1890s Annie joined the Theosophy movement, begun by a Russian émigrée called Madame Blavatsky, and later took over as its leader. Her spiritual quest would take her to India, where she would campaign for home rule. She also continued to campaign for the rights of women, and as late as 1911 spoke at an important National Union of Women's Suffrage Societies (NUWSS) rally in London.

If we are to appreciate the problems these two women faced as they tried to find their own autonomy and help others, we need to be aware of circumstances elsewhere, and to recognize that across Europe and America similar conditions prevailed.

In Britain it was not only in the East End of London that poverty and poor working conditions were rife. In gathering information in the 1840s on conditions within the mines, enquirers found that girls as young as eight years old told of how frightened they were of working without lights. Others aged between fourteen and seventeen worked in only their chemises alongside naked men, since it was so hot in the mines. Their education was almost non-existent, though some learned their letters in Sunday school. They often showed only a rudimentary knowledge of the scriptures. Many of the older women could not read or write either, because there was never the time to pay attention to 'learning'. Some had become de-skilled as a result of working as long as thirty years down the mine.

The colliery owners were well aware of the problems of employing women, as the following quote shows:

'The employment of females of any age in and about the mines is most objectionable, and I should rejoice to see it put an end to; but in the present feeling of the colliers, no individual would succeed in stopping it in a neighbourhood where it prevailed, because the men would immediately go to those pits where their daughters would be employed.'

It was fully recognized that women worked through economic necessity, and as is seen today in many third-world countries children were perceived not wholly as an economic burden, but as a resource, the number of births amply replacing the numbers lost through death. It would be some years before improved working conditions could make inroads into the health problems experienced by the poor, though it was recognized that the two went hand in hand.

Mill working was considered a better option than the colliery, though conditions were just as difficult in their own way. Accidents, death and the changing face of Britain, as it moved from an economy based on agriculture to one based on industry, reduced many families to penury. There were considerable discrepancies between the wages paid to men and to women. Because they were cheap labour and supposedly more dexterous, more women were recruited into the textile and other such industries. A good illustration of this is the table given on the following page, showing the weekly earnings of the Courtauld silk mill workforce in 1860.

As a matter of interest, and comparison, the Huguenot silk weavers of the 16th and 17th centuries were considered to be skilled artisans and were far more highly paid pro rata than these workers, who were thought of as mere factory fodder.

Wage bill of the work force at the Courtauld silk mill, 1860

Number	Weekly wages	MALES
26	15s–32s	Overseers and clerks
6	17s–25s	Mechanics and engine drivers
3	14s–21s	Carpenters and blacksmiths
1	15s	Lodgekeeper
16	14s–15s	Power loom machinery attendants and steamers
18	10s–15s	Mill machinery attendants and loom cleaners
5	5s–12s	Spindle cleaners, bobbin stampers and packers, messengers, sweepers
-	7s–10s	Watchmen
-	5s–10s	Coachmen, grooms and van driver
38	2s–4s	Winders

(The Mill Manager received £1,000 per annum plus 3 per cent of the profits)

114		Total Males

Number	Weekly wages	FEMALES
4	10s–11s	Gauze examiners
4	9s–10s	Female assistant overseers
16	7s–10s	Warpers
9	7s–10s	Twisters
4	6s–9s	Wasters
589	5s–8s	Weavers
2	6s–7s	Plugwinders
83	4s–6s	Drawers and doublers
188	2s–4s	Winders
899		Total Females

1013		TOTAL WORK FORCE

NB: The wages are shown in shillings (1 shilling = 5 pence in today's money).

Increasingly in Britain in the 19th century, women were beginning to recognize that they would have to find a group voice in order to change their situation for the better. Trade union activity was often barred to them, so they would have to develop this for themselves. This need to do something for themselves crystallized eventually for many women into the Suffragette movement. Not everybody, however, approved of the more violent actions of some of their members.

There were three Acts of Parliament important to women prior to the formation of the militant wing of the Suffragette movement. In 1857 the Divorce and Matrimonial Causes Act denied a husband a right to the earnings of a wife he had deserted, and gave back the property rights of a single woman to a woman who was divorced or legally separated. The Married Woman's Property Act of 1870 allowed women to keep earnings or property acquired after marriage; a further Married Woman's Property Act in 1882 allowed women to retain what they owned at the time of marriage. These political moves instigated a series of changes across Europe, particularly in northern Europe, where there had been widespread demand for similar reforms. Alterations in the economic structure as it continued to shift away from agriculture towards commerce and manufacturing industry gave rise to a growing number of middle-class women entering the work force.

In 1868 the Amendment to the Reform Act, which aimed to give votes to women, failed and the Kensington Society – one of its prime movers – formed the London Society for Women's Suffrage. There were many such small groups of women who later joined together to form the National Union of Women's Suffrage Societies, led by Millicent Fawcett. This was a largely moderate group, dedicated to using political propaganda, rallies and persuasion, all within the bounds of the law.

When moderate action did not succeed, a more radical wing, called the Women's Social and Political Union (WSPU), was formed at the beginning of the 20th century by Emmeline Pankhurst. The goal of these 'suffragettes', as they became known, was also to obtain the vote for women but by a strategy of direct action and militancy. The essential difference between these two groups is identified by a male supporter quoted in one of the WSPU's pamphlets: the suffragists, he declared, 'just wanted the vote but suffragettes went out to get it.'

As a result of this radical approach, prison terms, hunger strikes and force-feeding became commonplace experiences for those women who felt strongly enough to act in the face of what was growing oppression by the Establishment.

This more strident note actually has an echo in the radicalism of part of the Women's Liberation movement of the late 20th century. Before that, however, there were to be two world wars which, by their very nature, considerably enhanced woman's ability to both express herself and develop her own creativity.

Women of Spirit: the 20th century

In many ways the 20th century is a microcosm of the journey that every woman undertakes as she searches for clarity and her own place in the larger scheme, as her focus changes from her own concerns to those associated with the wider world. This century encapsulates all the changes that women have chosen to make as they moved from Victorian values towards a greater equality and also into a new appreciation of their own values, spiritual and otherwise.

The inter-war years of the 20th century provide a vantage-point from which to view the end of one era and the dawning of the so-called technological age. It allows us to get a perspective on the way women have continued to develop their potential since the end of the 19th century. This is the most immediate of the ages we have been assessing, for many of us have not only photographs spanning much of the era but the memories of older relatives to draw on.

While women had got the vote and had proved that they could do men's jobs, they were nevertheless still pushed into certain roles. The First World War had decimated a whole generation of men; many women had been left single, by bereavement, a shortage of suitable male partners or – having recognized their own abilities – by choice. There was a tendency to ridicule single women who chose any kind of unconventional path, and to disparage women's issues, such as feminism, pacifism and woman's need for intellectual pursuits. Many women who were unsupported in any way by men lived in fear of being labelled abnormal. This was simply a different twist on the idea that women were a burden on society; in medieval times this had resulted in women entering convents. At the same time the art of motherhood was highly praised in an effort to raise the birth rate.

Unemployment was rife in the time of the Great Depression of the 1920s and 30s. During the First World War many women through necessity had taken over – or were accused of taking over – men's roles. In reality there was a general lowering of status and jobs for men *and* women, and there was still a great deal of deprivation even in the Western world. Women were considered yet again to be more suitable for employment in the new industries where 'tiny fingers' were necessary, as they had been in the mills of the 19th century. Such skills, however, did not warrant better pay. This still remains evident today in that many women's salaries, except at the highest levels, work out at approximately only two-thirds those of men, despite legislation bringing in equal pay and equal opportunities.

Anyone who looks to the inter-war years to understand how women's minds were working must be struck by the realization that, although some now had the vote, the main issue was no longer equal rights for women. The focus had shifted and now the welfare of women as wives and mothers had to be taken into account. Childbirth was still dangerous, there being no adequate healthcare for any but the wealthy and the provision of contraception was still patchy. Working-class women generally accepted a poor level of health.

By the 1930s those women who had a mind to campaign began to busy themselves with wider issues, such as the movement for peace. The election of a small number of women MPs gave feminists much hope but still politics continually clashed with the interests of women. Many British women felt strongly enough to campaign not just against unemployment at home, but also on wider issues such as on behalf of Spanish refugees and for peace in Europe.

With the arrival of the Second World War, women were once again put in the position of having to draw on their own resources and take their place alongside the men in defence of their country. Women were welcomed not only in the caring professions but for the first time also in roles requiring mechanical and technological competence. In the armed forces many drivers and radio operators were women, and in one specialist branch, the Special Operations Executive, everyday skills allied to great courage and resourcefulness were put to good use. Civilian women were used in many ways, such as to work on the land. Obviously, those women who were left behind when their men went to war coped as admirably as they had done for centuries, indeed since the Crusades.

Such women found that they were capable of doing most of the jobs previously considered the responsibility of men. It was inevitable that women's feelings about themselves and their competence therefore had to change. Previously, where men had worked in dangerous occupations or those requiring long absences from home, women had been used to coping alone. They had often developed ways of surviving that did not necessarily include their men. Long absences by servicemen meant that for everyone a much greater adjustment had to be made when they returned. Women had to get used to having men around again and often the men were uncertain as to their position within the family. It seemed that life had moved on without them and family life would never be the same again.

There were, in fact, so many changes in the aftermath of the Second World War affecting everybody that it is perhaps easiest to put them into the context of how those changes affected women and the way they thought about themselves. In Britain, the creation of the Welfare State meant that mothers could address their own and their children's health concerns. Throughout the Western world new education laws meant that better and higher education was more readily available to all, and girls and women were fully prepared to take full advantage of the increased opportunities. Economically, young people had more money available and, along with this, wanted more control of their lives. The word 'teenager', heard first in America, was coined to describe young people who were on the threshold of adulthood.

This aspect of control of one's life was also highlighted by the arrival of the birth control pill in the 1960s. It now meant that Annie Besant's dream from the previous century was realized – women could now choose whether to become pregnant or not. Inevitably, the focus on the issue of a woman's right to decide how others would use her body also altered. In the present day the young girls (and otherwise) who sell themselves on the street corner for a rock of crack cocaine do so ultimately from an informed choice. They follow in the footsteps of women down the ages who were driven through desperation to work the streets, from the camp followers of the Civil War through to those in the Victorian era who would sell themselves for a bed and a drink of gin.

In the sixties this freedom of decision widened out into what a woman would, or could, do with her own life, never mind others for whom she might be responsible. If she wished to delay pregnancy, she could do so. Later, she would be faced with further choices: for example, having become pregnant, whether she would choose to have the baby. The abortion laws of the 1970s gave her even more choices. Later yet, with the medical advances made, issues of fertility came further under her control.

As women perceived that they had more rights, they refused to condone behaviour which had previously caused them difficulty and they realised they need no longer put up with – for instance, authoritarian conduct and cruelty. Divorce, which had previously been very much frowned upon by society, became easier and by the 1970s grounds for divorce were completely revised, though Catholic countries lagged behind on this somewhat. John Milton's belief in the 1600s of the right to separate if there was not mutual support was finally given credence. There was no longer the legal need to remain in a relationship or to be trapped within an untenable situation. More promiscuous behaviour led to a questioning of issues to do with sexuality, of what was or was not acceptable, and of differences between the genders and how to satisfy needs that were considered deviant by many.

All these new freedoms naturally led to the idea that women needed liberating – though this was in fact precisely what had been happening to some extent for the last five centuries. This desire for freedom could now be called the Women's Liberation Movement and women writers in the western world could show a new frankness in setting out their needs, their desires and their requirements. Just as different rhythms could be heard in the popular music of the time, so a new sound was emerging in the voice of women, and this could not be gainsaid. Initially, women wanted freedom from the constraints placed on them by men, but gradually they came to realize that they needed liberating too from their own narrow viewpoint and that their inner drive could be used to carry them forward. The consciousness-raising exercises of the 1970s gave way to an awareness that women could reclaim their much-maligned intuitive and spiritual heritage.

There was – and still is – a distinct danger, however, that women in their need for autonomy would 'throw the baby out with the bath water' in more ways than one and that men would become emasculated in the process. Men recognized that as women became stronger, they themselves might become more sensitive. This was a very frightening process for them because it meant they would have to accommodate a change in their own perspective – something to be resisted by the majority at all costs. Women, on the other hand, needed to be aware that it was unwise to expect their menfolk to understand what was happening.

Ideally gentle persuasion should have worked, whereas in fact it took determination and sometimes a rigidity of purpose to effect the changes just in themselves, without having a great deal of energy to spare for those niceties of feeling that were important to their men. Nowadays, fortunately, there is a movement back towards a state of balance between the sexes with shared responsibility, understanding and an additional mutual respect among young people.

This is most clearly demonstrated in the new technological industries and the lifestyles required. In some ways this is giving a new definition to poverty, and a sharper division between the haves and the have-nots as the Third World lags behind in technological competence. Looking back to the arrival of the computer in business, which is after all only twenty or so years ago, it was natural and necessary for secretaries to have to learn the new technologies in order to offer the best support to their employers. (This is one of the reasons that the old QWERTY keyboard originating with the manual typewriter is still in use today and has been adopted by most computer manufacturers.)

Now, however, the computer is used for so many tasks in the business environment that more skills than simple word processing are needed – everything from graphic design to accounting to marketing. The young woman of today not only is able, but by and large is encouraged, to widen her skill profile until she is as competent as her male counterpart, and vice versa.

To bring this historical revue of women and their issues of power and principle to a close, we cannot do better than cite three examples of women who combine leadership and compassion and who belong to the 20th century; all three, too, share the characteristics discovered in our medieval women of note. These are Mother Teresa of Calcutta, Anita Roddick, founder of the Body Shop, and Aung San Suu Kyi, Burmese opposition leader. These women have felt sufficiently strongly about their various causes that they have risked displeasure and opprobrium from authority or their own peers in order to bring about the changes they saw as necessary.

Mother Teresa, who became a nun in 1937, was initially refused permission to set up a ministry in Calcutta to tend the sick and dying, an undertaking she regarded as a necessity. She persevered, though, and later her Order of the Missionaries of Charity would be recognized as a pontifical congregation under the jurisdiction of Rome. Members of the Order take four vows – poverty, chastity, obedience and service to the poor – which are, as Mother Teresa described them, the embodiment of Christ. She later extended her ministry to all five continents of the world and was awarded the Nobel Peace Prize in 1979. On her death in 1997 she left behind a truly universal organization dedicated to relieving suffering.

Anita Roddick was brought up in a small British coastal town. She trained as a teacher and in the 1960s became interested in the customs and rituals of different peoples around the world. Working on her own original ideas and beliefs, she and her husband developed what was at the time a unique philosophy for a commercial company. The Body Shop, they decided, would trade on the basis of profits with principle, and one of its aims would be to create social and environmental change worldwide. Now the company is committed to helping empower communities in the Third World, to fair trading, AIDS awareness, recycling and the ending of animal testing. Anita has received many awards for her innovative approach and business acumen. In the United States she has become involved with social activism and joined other companies in forming Business for Social Responsibility. Her particular strength is in being able to enthuse others.

Aung San Suu Kyi is internationally regarded as a symbol of heroic and peaceful resistance to oppression. Born in Burma, the daughter of a prominent politician, she studied in Britain, where she met and married Michael Aris, an Oxford University academic. He knew where her loyalties lay, and said: 'Before we were married I promised my wife that I would never stand between her and her country.' This love of her country led to the military dictatorship in Burma ordering her to be held under house arrest for six years, separating her from her husband and young children. She has said of the National League for Democracy in Burma, an organization that she was instrumental in forming: 'We are always ready to work together with the authorities to achieve national reconciliation and we would like to think that the strength of our good will and the very strong desire of the people for democracy will bring positive results.' She was awarded the Nobel Peace Prize in 1991, and even today is not allowed to move freely around her own country.

These three women demonstrate very clearly the qualities that it is possible for women to develop within themselves when they reach for the best there can be. The characteristics of compassion, caring and concern beyond their own personal world are qualities that can be developed more fully by each and every woman. Each century's women have learnt from the experiences and examples of the past. We now have a rich heritage of knowledge and information that we can use to carry us forward into the new century and a new life. Available to us as examples are spiritual writings, the creativity that women have developed, the nurturing that is so natural to many women and the wonderful crusading spirit that guards and enhances the rights of people.

In this chapter we have traced the fortunes of women through many centuries and have seen, within each century, recognition of a specific aspect of femininity. Woman's journey has been a gradual self-realization of her power, talents and abilities. In medieval times she recognized that spirituality and a relationship with God was a way of 'being herself'; throughout the middle of the millennium she learnt to bow her head in submission yet still maintain her integrity. Later still, despite obstacles, she learnt to express herself more fully through her creativity. As time went on she allowed herself to become more militant and to fight against injustice. Finally, she claimed for herself the right to be man's equal, and yet have her own autonomy. Now she can decide for herself that she can be whole woman and express each facet of her personality in the way that is appropriate for her. Fortunately, we have in those women who have gone before many icons to whom we can look for inspiration.

Icons

We have previously mentioned various women achievers who even today could be adopted as role models. In this section we have included many more, of different nationalities and from various fields of endeavour. Most of these women have one overriding quality in common: a particular kind of courage. They were and are women who dared to question the system and were prepared to do something about it. In that sense it says something about my own personal predisposition, because such women have fascinated me since childhood. You will have your own preferences and will find it worthwhile, for your own development, to take careful note of those women who intrigue and impress you.

ARTS

Hepworth, Barbara (1903–75)

One of the first British abstract sculptors, Hepworth studied at Leeds College of Art and at the Royal College of Art, London, where she met and became friends with Henry Moore, who would become the first British major contemporary sculptor of international standing. Hepworth's interest in abstract form was awakened by her second husband, the abstract painter Ben Nicholson. Initially her work was allied to his and that of Moore, but she quickly found her own unique means of expression, moving further towards non-objective expression than Moore, often using the concept of 'negative space'- space surrounded by material. One commentator has observed that whereas Moore's abstracted forms seem to move towards organic life, 'Hepworth's may be thought to be departing for more speculative regions of the mind'. She was made a Dame Commander of the British Empire in 1965, and at the time of her death was recognized as a major figure in the international art world.

Sappho (c. 625 BCE)

Often referred to as the 'tenth muse', Sappho is one of the great lyrical poets of Western civilization. She also invented a 21-string lyre to accompany herself when she sang. Her verse is characterized by simplicity, a control over rhythm, a lively use of description, directness and intensity. Her poems were collected into nine books around the third century BCE, but much of this has been lost as a result of opposition by the Church authorities, who labelled it obscene. She also founded a *thiasos*, a society of women bound by religious and secular oaths. The feminist movement has adopted Sappho as one of their most powerful icons.

Valois, Dame Ninette de (1898–)

Born in Ireland, as Edris Stannus, de Valois moved to England at the age of 7 and started studying dance. By the age of 14, she was performing in musichall revues – there were no professional ballet companies in England at that time. Inspired by a performance given by Diaghilev's famed Ballet Russes, she went abroad to train, later changed her name and joined that company in 1923. When she returned to England, she opened a ballet school in Kensington, suggesting to the director of the Old Vic that the theatre needed a ballet company. She founded the Sadlers Wells company in 1931, became its first ballet director and fostered the talents, amongst others, of choreographer Frederick Ashton (working with him for many years), and dancers George Balanchine, Margot Fonteyn and Rudolf Nureyev. She is credited with the creation of a national tradition of classical ballet in Britain.

Woolf, Virginia (1882–1941)

Virginia Woolf is best remembered for the original contribution she made to the form of the novel, developing innovative literary techniques in order to reveal women's experience and present an alternative to male-dominated views of reality. She was also a distinguished feminist essayist, critic in *The Times Literary Supplement* and a central figure in the Bloomsbury group, a group of modernists dedicated to unifying artistic concerns of the time. Suffering mentally since the death of her brother when she was 24, Woolf eventually committed suicide – a fact which has led people to believe that her work was an exploration of her own traumas. In actuality, its themes are relevant to all women.

HUMANITARIANISM

Brittain, Vera (1893–1970)

After initial opposition from her industrialist father, Brittain eventually attended Somerville College, Oxford. She broke off her studies to serve as a nurse in the First World War, later returning to Somerville where she met and made friends with the writer Winifred Holtby who was to be her companion until the latter's death. Vera later wrote frankly about their relationship in her book *Testament of Friendship*. A prolific writer and campaigner, in 1957 she helped to form the Campaign for Nuclear Disarmament, in which she remained active until her death.

Brittain's daughter, by political scientist and philosopher Sir George Catlin, Shirley (Williams), entered Parliament in 1964 as a member of the British Labour Party. Subsequently (1981) she became a founder and president of the Social Democratic Party, the first British woman to found a mainstream political party. In 1993 she was created Baroness Williams of Crosby.

Butler, Josephine (1828–1906)

Josephine Butler became involved in charity work (primarily in workhouses and with young prostitutes) after the death of her daughter in an accident. She believed that women should have the vote because they had different concerns from men, a view unpopular with many of the suffragettes. She argued that women's special role was to protect and care for the weak and that women's suffrage was of vital importance to the morality and welfare of the nation. She is perhaps best remembered for her stance against the Contagious Diseases Act – a move to control prostitution but which violated the rights of women.

Corbett Sisters

Cicely (1885–1959) and her older sister, Margery (1882–1981), were initially educated at home and became involved in women's suffrage at a very early age. Later, at Somerville College, Oxford, the sisters broke away from the Women's Liberal Federation to form The Liberal Woman's Suffrage Group.

Cicely organized several conferences on the problem of sweated labour and women's working conditions. In 1913 she married the radical journalist, Chalmers Fisher; both took the surname of Corbett Fisher. After the First World War she was an active member of the Labour Party and the Women's International League.

Margery became one of seventeen women who stood for Parliament after the Qualification of Women Act in 1918, the first of her seven unsuccessful attempts to get elected. Her political involvement spanned almost a complete century – in the 1970s she was involved in the Women's Liberation Movement.

Hamilton, Cicely Mary (1872–1952)

In 1909 Hamilton's most important contribution to the women's movement, *Marriage as a Trade*, was published. In this Hamilton argued that women were brought up to look for success only in the marriage market and that this damaged their intellectual development. After the First World War Cicely became a freelance journalist and a regular contributor to the feminist journal *Time and Tide* in which she advocated free birth control advice for women and the legalization of abortion.

Martineau, Harriet (1802–76)

The parents of Harriet Martineau and her three brothers and two sisters held advanced views on education and ensured that their children received the same schooling. Harriet, pushing the boundaries of women's writing of the time, identified her audience as 'ordinary' readers. Martineau believed in the improvement of women's education, so that 'marriage need not be their only object in life'. Later in life she involved herself in the campaign against The Contagious Diseases Act and was credited by Josephine Butler with being the motivating force behind her own campaign. Martineau continued to write pamphlets and articles on women's rights until her death.

Marx, Eleanor (1855–98)

The youngest daughter of the political philosopher, Karl Marx, Eleanor acted as her father's secretary from 1871. In 1876 she became involved in the campaign for female equality, eventually forming the Socialist League with William Morris. In the same year she met Edward Aveling and lived with him as his common-law wife. She began working with the Woman's Trade Union League and in 1888 helped Annie Besant organize the Bryant & May match-girls' strike. The following year she was involved in the Dockers' Strike and in setting up the National Union of Gas Workers and General Labourers. She committed suicide on learning of Aveling's infidelity.

Murphy, Emily (1868–1933)

Born Emily Ferguson, Murphy became a judge in Edmonton, Canada, in 1916, the first woman appointed to the bench in the British Empire. A male lawyer objected to her authority on the grounds that, as a woman, she was not a 'person' in law. Later, when attempting to be appointed to the Senate, she was told women were not considered qualified persons under the British North America Act. She appealed to the Privy Council in Britain and in a landmark ruling in 1929, it was ruled that women were in fact persons. She was married to Arthur Murphy, a preacher and missionary. She also wrote under the pen-name, Janey Canuck.

Sanger, Margaret (1883–1966)

Birth-control pioneer Margaret Sanger first worked as a nurse where she witnessed first-hand the health hazards of unwanted pregnancy. She published numerous pamphlets and magazines on contraception. Her 50-year crusade to educate women in birth-control methods resulted in numerous arrests on charges of obscenity and also to the founding of what was to become the Planned Parenthood Federation. By the time of her death, birth control had been established as every woman's right, if she so chose. She was an inspiration to many, including Marie Stopes.

Sanger's books include *Women, Morality and Birth Control; My Fight for Birth Control*, and *Margaret Sanger: An Autobiography*.

Stopes, Marie (1880–1958)

Born in Edinburgh, Stopes won a science scholarship to University College, London, and in 1905 became Britain's youngest Doctor of Science. Her radical beliefs on marriage led to an interest in birth control and the founding, with financial help from her rich second husband, of the first of her birth-control clinics in Holloway, North London. On first publication, in 1918, her books caused a furore, were declared obscene and she was reviled by both the Church of England and the Catholic Church. She was instrumental in bringing about massive changes in the management of issues pertinent to women and marriage.

Trung Sisters (died 42 AD)

The Trung sisters, daughters of a powerful Vietnamese lord, became symbols of the first Vietnamese resistance to the Chinese occupation of their land.

Vietnamese women then still retained many rights and privileges which their Chinese sisters had lost due to the teachings of Confucius, which required women to be subservient.

In about 39AD the Trung sisters organized a rebellion and with the support of various tribal lords formed an army of some 80,000. Many of the generals of this force were women, and included the sisters' mother. The Vietnamese troops were eventually defeated. According to popular belief, the Trung sisters elected to take their own lives by jumping into a river and drowning. Temples were later built in their honour and the people of Vietnam still celebrate their memory every year with a national holiday.

Webb, Beatrice (1858–1943)

Born Beatrice Potter, granddaughter of the radical MP for Wigan, Richard Potter, this most famous of British social reformers first became interested in the achievements of the co-operative societies that existed in many industrial towns. The causes of poverty had to be tackled at their roots and communally, she believed, declaring that 'self-sacrifice for the good of the community is the greatest of all human characteristics'. She and her husband, Sidney Webb, campaigned for Poor Law reform. Always active politically, she and her husband were willing to work with any party which they believed could help achieve their aims. When the Fabian Society, of which they were early influential members, was left a large sum of money they founded the London School of Economics and later launched the radical political magazine *New Statesman*, which still exists today.

Yarros, Rachelle Slobodinsky (1869–1946)

Forced to flee Russia because of her political beliefs, Rachelle Yarros became closely identified with social hygiene and birth control. The first woman admitted to the College of Physicians and Surgeons in Boston, USA, in 1897 she was appointed instructor in clinical obstetrics there. Her efforts to promote social hygiene and eradicate prostitution and venereal disease through education and legislation won her enthusiastic support. In 1914 she founded the American Social Hygiene Association and became closely associated with similar initiatives. Unlike other Russian émigrés, she admired the Soviet Union, to which she and her husband made several visits. She was particularly impressed with the Venerealogical Institute in Moscow and with the measures taken by the Bolsheviks which had 'practically done away with commercialised prostitution.'

POLITICS

Akiko, Yosano (1868–1939)

This woman of modern ideas, a 'bluestocking', was born near Osaka, Japan just as the country was restoring the emperor to power. After graduating from the Sakai School for Women she evolved into a social critic and became something of a rebel, living openly with Yosano Tekkan, a married man, whom she would ultimately marry.

Despite much criticism, she influenced many women to become more open to change. Akiko used *Myojo*, a poetry publication, as a platform to criticize the government and to foster social change and rights for women. Although others were imprisoned for their beliefs, Akiko was not. She continued to publish her views concerning politics, economics and women's rights until her death.

Astor, Nancy Witcher Langhorne (1879–1964)

American-born Nancy Witcher Langhorne was the first woman to take her seat as a Member of Parliament in Britain. In 1919 she ran for her husband, Waldorf Astor's, safe seat of Plymouth when he was elevated to the House of Lords. She once said of her fellow women, 'We are not asking for superiority for we have always had that; all we ask is equality'. Her main concerns were temperance and issues affecting women and children, though she did not always toe the Conservative party line. She was the first woman to introduce a bill into Parliament. This prohibited the sale of alcohol in bars to people under the age of eighteen.

Bondfield, Margaret (1873–1953)

Bondfield became politically active largely as a result of her experience of the conditions of shop-workers. Her first success was to persuade the Liberal government to include maternity benefits in its Health Insurance Bill in 1910. In 1923 she was elected as Labour MP for Northampton. She served twice under Prime Minister Ramsey MacDonald and became the first woman to gain a place in the British Cabinet, as Minister of Labour. Controversially, she later supported the government policy of depriving some married women of their unemployment benefit. After losing her seat in Parliament she continued to be interested in social issues and between 1939 and 1945 was chairperson of the Women's Group on Public Welfare.

Breshkovsky, Catherine (1844–1934)

Born into a wealthy Russian family, Catherine embraced the cause of revolution some decades before the advent of the Bolsheviks who would emerge victorious in 1917. Breshkovsky would become a thorn in the side of the tsarist government, and in 1878 the Little Grandmother (Babushka), as she was known, was exiled to Siberia. After her return she formed a political party, the Social Revolutionists, in 1896, and once again became a target of repression. Later she was again imprisoned and exiled. Freed by Kerensky, she became a member of his government and had to flee to Czechoslovakia in 1919 after the Bolsheviks had seized power in 1917.

Gandhi, Indira (1917–1984)

The only child of Jawaharlal Nehru, later the first prime minister of India,

Indira would become the first woman leader of her country. In 1938 she joined the National Congress Party and became active in the independence movement. In the early 1940s she was imprisoned by the British for subversion. Gandhi became Nehru's official hostess, and in 1959 was made president of the Congress Party for one year. In 1966, after the death of her father's successor (Shastri), she was elected prime minister, later leading her party to a landslide victory. She kept a rigid control on all aspects of the country's way of life, sometimes making herself unpopular in the process, and did her best to ensure a Gandhi succession. She was shot by one of her own guards after trying to suppress an uprising of Sikh militants.

Markiewicz, Constance (1868–1927)
Born into an Irish landowning family, the Gore-Booths, Constance drew on radical influences close to home. Her father's example of fair trading led to her developing a deep concern for the poor. Her sister, Eve Gore-Booth, a poet and trade unionist, was active in the suffrage movement, which Constance also joined, becoming a member of the radical NUWSS. She married Count Casimir Markiewicz, a Polish painter, in 1900. She later committed herself to the cause of Irish Republicanism. She was arrested and sentenced to death for her part in the Easter Rising of 1916 but was reprieved in the general amnesty of 1917. She was the first woman to be elected to Parliament in the United Kingdom, when in 1918 she stood for the Republican Sinn Fein party. Her refusal to take the Oath of Allegiance, however, prevented her from attending the House of Commons.

Meir, Golda (1898–1978)
Born Golda Mabovitch in the Ukraine, she moved first to the United States, where she married, and then, in 1921, to Palestine, where she dedicated herself to building a homeland for Jews and became active in the labour movement. In 1948, by this time separated from her husband, Morris Meyerson (or Myerson), she was a signatory to the proclamation of the new state of Israel. A year later she was made Minister of Labour in the first government of Israel. She held this post until 1956, when she was made Minister of Foreign Affairs and also changed her name to the Hebrew form Meir. In 1966 she resigned because of ill health. Three years later the 'grand old woman of Israeli politics' was back, this time as Prime Minister. She held office until April 1974, when she resigned after being criticized for Israel's lack of preparedness in the 1973 Yom Kippur War.

Peron, Evita (1919–52)
Maria Eva Duarte was born into poverty, the youngest child of five. Her ambition to become an actress took her to Buenos Aires, where she met Colonel Juan Domingo Peron and, in 1945, became his second wife. Since the overthrow of dictator Ramon Castillo in 1943, Peron had built a following among workers, clerics, landowners and industrialists. After he was elected

president in 1946, with a huge majority, Eva virtually ran the ministries of health and labour, holding an ambition to be vice-president. She championed women's rights, getting women the vote and the right to divorce, organized the women's branch of the Peronista party and formed the Eva Peron Foundation, which enabled people to get help with housing as well as providing them with clothing and money. She also built a number of orphanages. Juan Peron's support among the industrial working class weakened after Eva's premature death from cancer, and in 1955 he was removed from power, being re-elected in 1973 with his third wife as vice-president.

Qiu Jin (1875–1907)
This Chinese poet and revolutionary became a symbol of women's financial and intellectual freedom. Born into a moderately wealthy family, she encouraged women to resist familial and governmental oppression and to seek their independence through education and training. The practice of foot binding, which she saw as signifying female submission, was especially abhorrent to her. With her cousin she worked to unite many secret revolutionary societies with the aim of overthrowing the ruling Manchu dynasty. In July 1907, shortly before a planned uprising, she was arrested and beheaded.

Roosevelt, Anna Eleanor (1884–1962)
Born in New York City, Eleanor lost both parents when very young. She married her fifth cousin, Democrat politician Franklin Delano Roosevelt, and after he was stricken with polio in 1921, became active in politics herself. She travelled the length and breadth of the nation, reporting her observations to the President. She also exercised her own political and social influence; she became an advocate of the rights and needs of the poor, of minorities, and of the disadvantaged. In World War II, she visited England and the South Pacific to foster goodwill among the Allies and boost the morale of US servicemen overseas. After her husband's death, in 1945, she continued her activities. In 1946 she was made Chairman of the UN Commission for Human Rights, and throughout the 1950s led the liberal wing of the Democratic Party. She was highly regarded by several presidents for her pragmatic and down-to-earth approach.

Thatcher, Margaret Hilda (1925–)
Margaret Thatcher was the first woman to become Prime Minister of Great Britain – a post she held from1979 to1990. In the early 1970s, as Minister of Education and Science, she had been notorious for abolishing free milk in schools, a decision disliked by many. Later in the decade she challenged the Conservative leadership and won. She vowed to reverse Britain's economic decline and proved implacable in some of her decisions. She took the country into war with Argentina in 1982 when that country attempted to annex the Falkland Islands, which they felt were theirs by right. She became the first Prime Minister to serve three consecutive terms of office in the 20th century but was ousted from office in 1990 after some difficult decisions mainly over questions

of policy in Europe. Her way of working was given its own name and was dubbed Thatcherism.

RELIGION

Eddy, Mary Baker (1821–1910)
The Discoverer and Founder of Christian Science is widely recognized as one of the most remarkable religious figures of modern times. Born a sickly child to a family in New England, she later spent many years looking for healing in the many remedial methods then available. In 1866 she was healed of a serious injury as she read the account of one of Jesus' healings in the New Testament. This led her to discover what she came to understand as the Science of Christianity, which she named Christian Science. Before her death in 1910, the religion she established had spread around much of the world.

Fry, Elizabeth (1780–1845)
The death of her mother when Elizabeth Gurney was twelve left her with responsibility for several younger siblings. She married Joseph Fry in 1800 and gave birth to eight children in quick succession. In 1811 she became a preacher for the Society of Friends. She also became heavily involved in prison reform, with particular reference to the way women were treated. Later she campaigned for the homeless and in 1840 started a training school for nurses at Guy's Hospital, which heavily influenced the work of Florence Nightingale.

Joan of Arc (1412–31)
Jeanne d'Arc, also called the Maid of Orleans, led the resistance to the English invasion of France in the Hundred Years War. When Joan was about 12 years old, she began hearing 'voices' of those she thought were St Michael, St Catherine, and St Margaret, believing them to have been sent by God. She knew it was her divine mission to free her country from the English and help the dauphin gain the French throne. After achieving this aim, she was betrayed by the Burgundians and sold to the English. They handed her over to the ecclesiastical court at Rouen to be tried for witchcraft and heresy. Refusing to be tried in women's clothing, she was burned at the stake in 1431. In 1456 a second trial was held and she was pronounced innocent of the charges against her. She was beatified in 1909 and in 1920 canonized by Pope Benedict XV.

Lange, Elizabeth Clovis (1784–1882)
Lange was born in the French colony of Saint Domingue. Later, as Mother Mary Elizabeth, she founded and was the initial 'Superior-General' of the Oblate Sisters of Providence Order, the first black Roman Catholic order to operate in the United States. Refugees from the Haitian Revolution could not learn their catechism so Lange began the mission school which later grew into a primarily educational order, although it was also involved in community

programmes. In setting up a religious order dedicated to the improvement of disadvantaged Blacks, she upset many white people but still held to her faith. She was the first African-American woman to be put forward for canonization.

Lee, Mother Ann (1736–84)

Originally inspired by a vision which convinced her she was the human incarnation of Christ's femininity, Lee drew thousands to the Shaker movement by the strength of her personality and the appeal of Shaker convictions – chastity, morality and equality for all. The style of communal living fashioned by Mother Ann at Watervliet became the social pattern for other Shaker settlements throughout the United States. The Watervliet community divided into four separate 'families' as a way to expand both the material output and communal spirituality of this self-reliant movement.

ROYALTY

Anne (1665–1714), Queen of England, Scotland and Ireland (1702–7); later Queen of Great Britain and Ireland (1707–14)

Anne was the second daughter of King James II and, unlike him, was staunchly Protestant. In 1683 she married Prince George of Denmark. The anti-Roman Catholic Glorious Revolution of 1688 brought her sister Mary and Mary's husband, William of Orange, to the throne. Becoming queen on William's death in 1702, Anne restored to favour John Churchill, who had been disgraced by her predecessor, making him Duke of Marlborough and captain-general of the army. During Queen Anne's reign the parliaments of England and Scotland were united (1707), and she showed considerable political acumen in fostering the growth of parliamentary government. On her death she was succeeded by her German cousin, George, who was crowned King George I.

Boudicca (died 62 AD)

Boudicca (or Boadicea) was the wife of Prasutagus, king of the Iceni, a British tribe, at a time when Britain was a Roman province. Seizing the opportunity of Prasutagus' death, the Romans annexed his whole kingdom when they were only entitled to half. Boudicca joined forces with a neighbouring tribe and in a series of ferocious battles at what are now Colchester, London and St Albans defied – and beat – the Roman legions. The superior strategy of the Romans told in the end, however, and her army was crushed. Boudicca and her daughters poisoned themselves rather than face capture.

Catherine de' Medici (1519–89)

This daughter of Lorenzo de' Medici, Duke of Urbino, became queen-consort of Henry II of France (1547–59) and mother of the last three Valois kings of France. Catherine's main focus in life was the preservation of Royal power, and her manipulations of her children's marriages in order to bring this about and preserve the balance of power are legendary. She ruled as regent for her second son, Charles IX, until he reached his majority in 1563, and continued to dominate him thereafter. Reluctantly he agreed to her plan for a general massacre of French Protestants, the infamous St Bartholomew's Day massacre of 1572 which claimed the lives of some 50,000, including Gaspard de Coligny, the Huguenot leader and a favourite advisor of the king.

Catherine the Great (1729–96)
Born Princess Sophie of Anhalt-Zerbst, in 1745 she married Grand Duke Peter of Holstein, who became Tsar in 1762. His elevation was short-lived, however, and he was deposed in favour of Catherine. Now Empress of Russia, Catherine continued the process of Westernization begun by Peter the Great and made Russia a European power. Characteristic of Catherine's reign was the role played by her lovers, or favourites. Ten men occupied this semi-official position, and of these at least two influenced her policies. Among Catherine's more caring achievements were the foundation of the first Russian schools for girls and of a medical college to provide health care for her subjects.

Cleopatra VII (c. 69–30 BC) Queen of Egypt (51–30 BC)
On her father's death in 51 BC Cleopatra, and her brother, Ptolemy XII, succeeded jointly to the throne of Egypt with the provision that they should marry. In the third year of their reign Ptolemy assumed sole control of the government and drove Cleopatra into exile. Cleopatra was unable to assert her claim until the arrival at Alexandria of Julius Caesar, who became her lover, espoused her cause, and eventually proclaimed her Queen of Egypt. After his death, when Cleopatra hesitated to take sides in the ensuing civil war, Mark Antony summoned her to meet him to explain her conduct and fell in love with her. They were married in 36 BC. The Romans were hostile, though, and in 31 BC they were defeated by Octavian (Julius Caesar's heir) at the decisive battle of Actium. On their return to Egypt Antony committed suicide and Cleopatra poisoned herself rather than face capture.

Margaret I (1353–1412), Queen of Denmark and Norway (1387–97) and of Sweden (1389–97)
Margaret I was also founder of the Kalmar Union, the first time the Scandinavian lands were joined under one ruler. She was the youngest child of King Waldemar IV Atterdag, and as a child she was married in 1363 to King Håkon VI of Norway. After her father's death, she had her young son elected King of Denmark, in 1376, and governed in his stead, as she also did in Norway after her husband's death in 1380. Margaret faced opposition abroad from King Albert of Sweden and the Count of Holstein. Albert was finally defeated and deposed in 1389; the Swedes then accepted Margaret as their queen. As head of three realms, she had her son Eric crowned King of Denmark and Sweden in 1397 (he had been accepted as King of Norway in 1389) and had a treaty signed at Kalmar that created a union of all three countries.

Victoria (1819–1901), Queen of Great Britain and Ireland (1837–1901) and from 1867 Empress of India

Victoria was the only child of Edward, Duke of Kent (fourth son of George III) and Princess Mary Louise Victoria of Saxe-Coburg-Saalfeld. In 1837 she ascended to the throne on the death of her uncle William IV, who had failed to produce an heir. She was only 18 at this time and the Prime Minister, Lord Melbourne, served as her educator, mentor and friend in political decision-making. However, Victoria soon exhibited considerable decisiveness, which was unexpected at the time in one so young. In June of 1840 the Queen married Prince Albert of Saxe-Coburg-Gotha. They happily raised nine children, who married and intermarried with the royal families of the rest of Europe. The Queen's loss of the Prince-Consort in December 1861 drove her into prolonged mourning and depression. She was not always popular with her people, nor did she always see eye to eye with her Prime Ministers. However, she gradually became one of Great Britain's most popular monarchs, and an icon of motherhood for her people.

SCIENCE/MEDICINE

Anderson, Elizabeth Garrett (1836–1917)

Garrett Anderson studied medicine privately and was the first woman to qualify as a doctor in the United Kingdom. In 1859 she met Elizabeth Blackwell (see next entry), the first woman in America to gain a medical degree. In achieving her ambition Garrett Anderson had to fight deeply ingrained prejudice against the notion of a woman becoming a doctor, and it was largely due to her continuing efforts that the British examining boards eventually allowed women to sit their examinations. After gaining her medical degree at the University of Paris, she had to go to the Society of Apothecaries in Scotland to get the necessary accreditation to practise. In 1866, she founded a dispensary which became the New Hospital for Women, London. This was later renamed the Elizabeth Garrett Anderson Hospital in her honour. She conflicted with Josephine Butler over the Contagious Diseases Act. Josephine believed this act discriminated against women – Elizabeth Garrett Anderson took the view that the measures provided the only means of protecting innocent women and children. Garrett Anderson was a sister of Millicent Fawcett (see her entry, under Women's Suffrage Movement).

Blackwell, Elizabeth and Emily

British-born Elizabeth Blackwell (1821–1910) was the first woman in America to gain a medical degree and was also included in the first British Medical Register in 1859. She graduated from New York's Geneva Medical College at the top of her class in 1849. Her younger sister, Emily (1826–1910), followed in her footsteps and enrolled at Rush Medical College, Illinois. However, pressure applied on the college authorities by some physicians resulted in her being refused entry to study for a second year. Emily would find her niche later, though, as a very capable administrator and fundraiser when, in 1857, helped by a friend and fellow student Marie Zakrzewska, the two sisters opened The New York Infirmary for Indigent Women and Children. In 1868 the Blackwells opened the Women's Medical College, New York, which remained open under Emily's direction until 1899, when women were first admitted to Cornell University Medical School.

The influence of Elizabeth Blackwell extended beyond the United States, and in 1875 she was appointed professor of gynaecology and obstetrics at the London School of Medicine for Women. She was an active proponent of education for women.

Cavell, Edith Louisa (1865–1915)

At the outbreak of World War I, British nurse Edith Cavell was matron of a nursing school in Brussels, a position she had held since 1906. She continued to treat the soldiers of both sides at the school, which became a Red Cross hospital during the German occupation. On 5 August 1915 she was arrested by the Germans and charged with sheltering 200 British, French, and Belgian soldiers and assisting their escape from Belgium. She was shot by firing squad on 12 October 1915 after unsuccessful appeals for postponement of her execution were made by the United States and Spain. The execution aroused widespread indignation. A commemorative statue to Cavell was erected in Saint Martin's Place, Trafalgar Square, London.

Curie, Marie Sklodowska- (1867–1934)

Born in Warsaw, Poland, Marie Curie was one of the first woman scientists to win worldwide fame. She won two Nobel Prizes, the first, in 1903, for Physics, which she shared with her husband, Pierre, and Henri Becquerel, who, like the Curies, had been investigating the phenomenon of radioactivity, a term coined by Curie during the course of her work. In 1911 she was awarded the prize for Chemistry for discovering radium and polonium. Her husband died in 1906, weakened by their work. Marie suffered similarly and in 1934 she died of leukaemia.

Fossey, Dian (1932–85)

The work of this American zoologist has helped to dispel many myths about the violent and aggressive nature of gorillas in the wild. Fossey was encouraged by the British anthropologist Louis Leakey to make use of her degree in occupational therapy and undertake a long-term field study of gorillas that would shed light on human evolution. This she did for 22 years. Due largely to her research and conservation work, mountain gorillas are now protected by international conservation and scientific communities. Fossey was found murdered at her campsite, it is believed because of her stance against animal poaching.

Hodgkin, Dorothy Crowfoot (1910–94)

After being awarded an honorary doctorate in chemistry by Cambridge University in the 1930s, Hodgkin began work on the structural analysis of penicillin, through a relatively new science, crystallography. Her tenacity resulted in the deciphering of the structure of insulin and a breakthrough in understanding the molecular structure of vitamin B12. Among her many honours, Dr Hodgkin received the Nobel Prize for Chemistry in 1964. In 1965 she received the Order of Merit, the first woman to be given this accolade since Florence Nightingale. Her humanitarian principles led to her being remembered as 'a great chemist, a saintly, gentle and tolerant lover of people and a devoted protagonist of peace'.

Hypatia (370?–415)

Mathematician, scientist and philosopher, Hypatia was raised in the world of education. She was taught by her father, who developed a physical routine which ensured she had a healthy body as well as a highly efficient mind. Hypatia was the first woman to have a profound impact on the survival of early philosophical thought in mathematics, initially making it more easily understood. Christians, though, regarded her learning and science as pagan and she became caught in the middle of arguments between them and the civil authorities. She died a horrible death at the hands of fanatics (probably Nitrian monks), who used broken shards of pottery or, some say, oyster shells, to strip her of her flesh.

Kingsley, Mary Henrietta (1862–1900)

Kingsley first visited Africa in 1893, following the deaths of her parents, and spent the trip studying African religious practice. She returned to England in 1894, but went back to West Africa later that year, this time exploring territory (Gabon) that was seldom visited by Europeans. After studying the life and culture of the region's Fang people, she returned to the Cameroon coast and climbed Mount Cameroon (4095 m/14,435 ft), the area's highest peak. She died after contracting typhoid while nursing prisoners during the Boer War.

Nightingale, Florence (1820–1910)

At the age of seventeen Florence felt herself to be called by God to some unnamed great cause but when some years later she told her parents she wanted to become a nurse, they were totally opposed to the idea, although later they relented. In 1854 she was given permission to take a group of 38 nurses to look after British soldiers fighting in the Crimea. Appalled at the conditions and lack of medical facilities, she got to work and by the war's end had secured her place in history. On returning to Britain she instigated massive changes in the training of nurses in both military and general hospitals. In 1860 she established a nursing school at St Thomas's Hospital, London. Three years before her death, and by this time in bad health, she was given the British Order of Merit, the first woman to achieve this distinction.

Tereshkova, Valentina Vladimirovna Nikolayeva (1937–)

Tereshkova was a textile worker and amateur parachutist at the time of her recruitment into the Soviet cosmonaut training programme in 1961. She was the first woman in space and between 16 and 19 June 1963 orbited the earth 48 times in Vostok 6. She then worked as a goodwill ambassador, and later entered politics. Following pressure from Khrushchev, she married another cosmonaut, Andrian Nikolayev in November 1963. Their child, born in 1964, aroused interest as the first offspring of parents who had both been exposed to the space environment before their child's conception.

WOMEN'S SUFFRAGE MOVEMENT

Davison, Emily (1872–1913)

Although many suffragettes endangered their lives by hunger strikes, Emily was unique in deliberately risking death, more than once. At the time of her protest at the Epsom Derby in 1913, when she was killed trying to stop King George V's horse, Anmer, she had in fact been prepared to make the ultimate sacrifice twice previously, believing that the suffragette cause needed a martyr. However, even her ultimate sacrifice – fed by a mixture of fanaticism and, probably, mental instability – did not have the desired impact on public opinion.

Fawcett, Millicent Garrett (1847–1929)

Introduced by her sisters to leading social reformers, such as John Stuart-Mill, she became interested in the campaign for women's rights; it was through Stuart-Mill that she met her future husband, Henry. By the 1880s she had become one of the leaders of the suffragette movement, heading the NUWSS, which, she believed, should campaign for other causes. Politically a supporter of the Liberal Party, she became increasingly angry at its unwillingness to acknowledge the importance of women's suffrage. She remained, however, committed to using constitutional methods to gain votes for women, disliking the tactics of the more militant suffragists. Millicent Fawcett is commemorated by Britain's national women's library, based in London, which is named after her. Also see entry for Elizabeth (Garrett) Anderson.

Lytton, Constance (1869–1923)

The daughter of Robert, first Earl of Lytton, and Edith Villiers, Constance joined the Women's Social and Political Union after being denied the right to marry the man she loved. Always frail, in 1909 Constance took part in a demonstration at the House of Commons and was arrested. In 1910, having disguised herself as a working-class woman and given a false name, she was imprisoned in Walton jail and force-fed. When her true identity was discovered, Constance was released – she would have been too easy a martyr. Arrested again in 1911 and released because of her obvious ill health, she suffered a stroke shortly afterwards and was paralysed until her death.

Pankhursts

Emmeline (1858–1928) was born to a passionate feminist mother who started taking her daughter to women's suffrage meetings in the early 1870s. In 1878, Emmeline met and married a lawyer, Richard Pankhurst, by whom she had four children: **Christabel (1880), Sylvia (1882),** Frank (1884) and Adela (1885). Disillusioned with the existing women's political organizations, in 1903 she founded the Women's Social and Political Union (WSPU). In 1907 Emmeline moved to London from her home town, Manchester, and joined her two elder daughters, Christabel and Sylvia, in the militant struggle for the vote. For the next seven years she was imprisoned repeatedly. Emmeline inspired many other women to follow her example of committing acts of civil disobedience.

The militancy of the WSPU was exemplified by Christabel and a fellow member of the movement, Annie Kenney. After deliberately disrupting a Liberal Party meeting in Manchester, they were arrested and elected to go to prison rather than pay the fine. Their action brought a dramatic increase in the membership of the WPSU. Christabel favoured limited suffrage, by which the vote would only be given to women with money and property. Sylvia disagreed with her mother and sister on several counts, not least Christabel's wish for a militant campaign. Sylvia was also a pacifist and could not support British involvement in the 1914–18 War, as had the WSPU.

In 1917 Christabel and Emmeline formed the Women's Party, which proposed 'equal pay for equal work, equal marriage and divorce laws, the same rights over children for both parents, equality of rights and opportunities in public service, and a system of maternity benefits.' Christabel, having previously fled the country, stood for Parliament twice and was unsuccessful both times. She died in 1958.

Sylvia's defiance of her mother was evident on a personal level too, notably in her refusal to marry the father of her child. She remained politically active, becoming involved with global issues such as the Russian Revolution, the status of refugees and the Spanish Civil War. She died in 1960 in Ethiopia.

Pethick-Lawrence, Emmeline (1867–1954)

In 1891 Emmeline became a voluntary social worker at the West London Methodist Mission. Shocked by the poverty she witnessed, she became a convert to socialism and formed the Esperance Club, set up to help a group of young women establish a co-operative dressmaking business. Emmeline was heavily involved in various other social campaigns, including suffrage. She was nevertheless against the 'Toffee hammer campaign', or ritualized smashing of shop windows, and was expelled from the WPSU for her stance against it. Despite this ejection, she and her husband continued to work for the suffrage movement.

Spiritual Connections

In these few pages are included some aspects of personal support which we hope may be of help to the reader. For many the idea of petitioning aspects of the feminine in Bridget and Hecate will seem strange and perhaps beyond understanding, as may moving away from the conventional funeral service. Sometimes, however, concentrating on these aspects helps to crystallize the qualities and energies that they represent, as do the affirmations. They are yours to use (or not) as you will.

Ceremonies and Readings for the Dying

For those who would like to feel that they do not wish to say goodbye to their loved ones with a conventional funeral service, a simple ceremony may suffice. One suggestion is to offer everyone when they are gathered together the opportunity to light a candle in memory of the one who has passed away. Provide enough candles for those present and keep a few in reserve for those who cannot join in at that particular time. Remember also to provide a stable sand-filled tray or flat non-flammable surface so people may place their candles securely to burn for the duration of the ceremony. As each candle is lit, each person can quietly remember their friend in their own way.

Try to arrange that friends or relatives honour the deceased appropriately, perhaps in the choice of music which they all shared or in a suitable reading or poem. Below are some suggestions:

Readings

Death is nothing at all.
I have only slipped away into the next room.
I am I, and you are you.
Whatever we were to each other,
that we still are.
Call me by my old familiar name,
speak to me in the easy way
which you always used.
Put no difference in your tone,
wear no forced air of solemnity or sorrow.
Laugh as we always laughed
at the little jokes we enjoyed together.
Let my name be ever the household word
that it always was,
Let it be spoken without effect,
without the trace of shadow on it.
Life means all that it ever meant.
It is the same as it ever was;
there is unbroken continuity.
Why should I be out of mind
because I am out of sight?
I am waiting for you, for an interval,
somewhere very near,
just around the corner.
All is well.

('Death is Nothing at All', Henry Scott Holland)

'I honour the place in you in which the entire universe dwells. I honour the place in you which is of love, of truth, of light, and of peace. When you are in that place in you and I am in that place in me, we are one.' (Nemaste)

'Then Almitra spoke, saying, We would ask now of death.

'And he said:

' "You would know the secret of death. But how shall you find it unless you seek it in the heath of life? The owl whose night-bound eyes are blind unto the day cannot unveil the mystery of light. If you would indeed behold the spirit of death, open your heart wide unto the body of life. For life and death are one, even as the river and sea are one.

' "In the depth of your hopes and desires lies your silent knowledge of the beyond; and like seeds dreaming beneath the snow your heart dreams of spring. Trust the dreams, for in them is hidden the gate to eternity.

' "Your fear of death is but the trembling of the shepherd when he stands before the king whose hand is to be laid upon him in honor. Is the shepherd not joyful beneath his trembling, that he shall wear the mark of the king? Yet is he not more mindful of his trembling?

' "For what is it to die but to stand naked in the wind and to melt

---

Indira would become the first woman leader of her country. In 1938 she joined the National Congress Party and became active in the independence movement. In the early 1940s she was imprisoned by the British for subversion. Gandhi became Nehru's official hostess, and in 1959 was made president of the Congress Party for one year. In 1966, after the death of her father's successor (Shastri), she was elected prime minister, later leading her party to a landslide victory. She kept a rigid control on all aspects of the country's way of life, sometimes making herself unpopular in the process, and did her best to ensure a Gandhi succession. She was shot by one of her own guards after trying to suppress an uprising of Sikh militants.

Markiewicz, Constance (1868–1927)
Born into an Irish landowning family, the Gore-Booths, Constance drew on radical influences close to home. Her father's example of fair trading led to her developing a deep concern for the poor. Her sister, Eve Gore-Booth, a poet and trade unionist, was active in the suffrage movement, which Constance also joined, becoming a member of the radical NUWSS. She married Count Casimir Markiewicz, a Polish painter, in 1900. She later committed herself to the cause of Irish Republicanism. She was arrested and sentenced to death for her part in the Easter Rising of 1916 but was reprieved in the general amnesty of 1917. She was the first woman to be elected to Parliament in the United Kingdom, when in 1918 she stood for the Republican Sinn Fein party. Her refusal to take the Oath of Allegiance, however, prevented her from attending the House of Commons.

Meir, Golda (1898–1978)
Born Golda Mabovitch in the Ukraine, she moved first to the United States, where she married, and then, in 1921, to Palestine, where she dedicated herself to building a homeland for Jews and became active in the labour movement. In 1948, by this time separated from her husband, Morris Meyerson (or Myerson), she was a signatory to the proclamation of the new state of Israel. A year later she was made Minister of Labour in the first government of Israel. She held this post until 1956, when she was made Minister of Foreign Affairs and also changed her name to the Hebrew form Meir. In 1966 she resigned because of ill health. Three years later the 'grand old woman of Israeli politics' was back, this time as Prime Minister. She held office until April 1974, when she resigned after being criticized for Israel's lack of preparedness in the 1973 Yom Kippur War.

Peron, Evita (1919–52)
Maria Eva Duarte was born into poverty, the youngest child of five. Her ambition to become an actress took her to Buenos Aires, where she met Colonel Juan Domingo Peron and, in 1945, became his second wife. Since the overthrow of dictator Ramon Castillo in 1943, Peron had built a following among workers, clerics, landowners and industrialists. After he was elected

' *"Only when you drink from the river of silence shall you indeed sing. And when you have reached the mountain top, then you shall begin to climb. And when the earth shall claim your limbs, then shall you truly dance."* ' (From *The Prophet*, Kahlil Gibran)

'*I have no idea where I am going. I do not see the road ahead of me. I cannot know for certain where it will end. Nor do I really know myself, and the fact that I think that I am following your will does not mean that I am actually doing so. But I believe that the desire to please you does in fact please you. And I hope I have that desire in all that I am doing. I hope that I will never do anything apart from that desire. And I know that if I do this you will lead me by the right road though I may know nothing about it. Therefore will I trust you always though I may seem to be lost and in the shadow of death. I will not fear, for you are ever with me, and you will never leave me to face my perils alone.*'
('Thoughts In Solitude', Thomas Merton)

Do not stand at my grave and weep,
I am not there. I do not sleep.
I am a thousand winds that blow,
I am the snow on the mountain's rim,
I am the laughter in children's eyes,
I am the sand at the water's edge,
I am the sunlight on ripened grain,
I am the gentle Autumn rain,
When you awaken in the morning's hush,
I am the swift uplifting rush of quiet birds in circled flight,

which enabled people to get help with housing as well as providing them with clothing and money. She also built a number of orphanages. Juan Peron's support among the industrial working class weakened after Eva's premature death from cancer, and in 1955 he was removed from power, being re-elected in 1973 with his third wife as vice-president.

Qiu Jin (1875–1907)
This Chinese poet and revolutionary became a symbol of women's financial and intellectual freedom. Born into a moderately wealthy family, she encouraged women to resist familial and governmental oppression and to seek their independence through education and training. The practice of foot binding, which she saw as signifying female submission, was especially abhorrent to her. With her cousin she worked to unite many secret revolutionary societies with the aim of overthrowing the ruling Manchu dynasty. In July 1907, shortly before a planned uprising, she was arrested and beheaded.

Roosevelt, Anna Eleanor (1884–1962)
Born in New York City, Eleanor lost both parents when very young. She married her fifth cousin, Democrat politician Franklin Delano Roosevelt, and after he was stricken with polio in 1921, became active in politics herself. She travelled the length and breadth of the nation, reporting her observations to the President. She also exercised her own political and social influence; she became an advocate of the rights and needs of the poor, of minorities, and of the disadvantaged. In World War II, she visited England and the South Pacific to foster goodwill among the Allies and boost the morale of US servicemen overseas. After her husband's death, in 1945, she continued her activities. In 1946 she was made Chairman of the UN Commission for Human Rights, and throughout the 1950s led the liberal wing of the Democratic Party. She was highly regarded by several presidents for her pragmatic and down-to-earth approach.

Thatcher, Margaret Hilda (1925–)
Margaret Thatcher was the first woman to become Prime Minister of Great Britain – a post she held from1979 to1990. In the early 1970s, as Minister of Education and Science, she had been notorious for abolishing free milk in schools, a decision disliked by many. Later in the decade she challenged the Conservative leadership and won. She vowed to reverse Britain's economic decline and proved implacable in some of her decisions. She took the country into war with Argentina in 1982 when that country attempted to annex the Falkland Islands, which they felt were theirs by right. She became the first Prime Minister to serve three consecutive terms of office in the 20th century but was ousted from office in 1990 after some difficult decisions mainly over questions

I am the star that shines at night,
Do not stand at my grave and cry,
I am not there, I did not die. (Unknown)

'*Your essence was not born and will not die. It is neither being nor*
nonbeing. It is not a void nor does it have form. It experiences
neither pleasure nor pain. If you ponder what it is in you that feels
the pain of this sickness, and beyond that you do not think or desire
to ask anything, and if your mind dissolves like vapour in the sky,
then the path to rebirth is blocked and the moment of instant
release has come.' (Bassui (1327–87), Zen Buddhist)

O Divine Master, grant that I may not so much seek
to be consoled as to console;
to be understood as to understand;
to be loved as to love.

For it is in giving that we receive;
it is in pardoning that we are pardoned;
and it is in dying that we are born to Eternal Life.
(Saint Francis of Assisi)

'*We do not want to know life, which includes death, but we want*
to know how to continue and not come to an end. We do not want
to know life and death, we only want to know how to continue
without ending. That which continues has no renewal.... It is only
when continuity ends that there is a possibility of that which is ever
new.' (Krishnamurti)

Prayers to the Goddesses

Brighid

The following rituals and offerings are to entreat Brighid's blessing whether you think of her in her more pagan form or of the later St Bridget. Traditionally Brighid is honoured on 1 February, which is also the feast of Candlemass. Brighid Crosses, woven from rushes, are hung over the door in the home, and a light is sometimes left to burn in the window through the night in commemoration of her eternal flame. A piece of cloth known as Brighid's Mantle is put outside overnight. Should you wish to honour her directly, a suitable form of words – which should come from your heart – might be something like the following –

Brighid of the holy flame,
Send me your grace
Let me use my talents as you did
And be the best that I can be.

If you prefer to think of her more Christian aspect then try sitting quietly just thinking of St Bridget and her qualities in order to help you in what you have to do.

Virgin Mary

The traditional prayer of supplication used in the Roman Catholic church is of course as follows:

Hail, Mary, full of grace, the Lord is with thee;
Blessed art thou among women and blessed is the fruit of thy
womb, Jesus.
Holy Mary, Mother of God, pray for us sinners now,
and at the hour of our death. Amen

You may like to spend some time considering the life of Mary and how it compares and contrasts with your own before using your own form of words to honour her.

Hecate

Acknowledging Hecate in the form of the Dark Mother is traditionally used to help banish negativity from the immediate environment. A suitable form of words might be:

Dark Mother help me now
Banish negativity from this place
and understand those dark places in me which I recognize

If you prefer to use Christian prayer, you might simply say:

Lord help me to understand the side of myself that is negative and capricious
And to use my wisdom and experience for the good of mankind.

Do remember that these are simply suggestions and can be used according to your own beliefs.

Affirmations

Affirmations are positive statements intended to have an effect on the way you think and feel about yourself. Your affirmation must be something you are able to relate to and preferably feel passionately about. You should want it to take effect immediately, not in the future, so always use the present tense. The outcome you are seeking should always be positive, so use only positive language.

Points to Remember:

- Affirm only the desired result, otherwise you may inadvertently strike a negative. Affirm what you want, rather than what you want to get rid of. For example, if you have come through a rocky patch in a love relationship, affirm the improvement by saying 'My relationship is giving me pleasure' rather than 'My relationship is no longer difficult'.
- Use the first person if the affirmation is a statement. Try to include your name in every affirmative sentence.
- Practise only one or two affirmations at a time, initially for a period of at least ten days to give them a chance of working. Affirmations work by affecting the subconscious, so you must give your instruction time to sink in. Recognize that the results may be unexpected.
- Affirmations must be concentrated on fully every day. Only through repetition will they have a chance of taking effect. Use every opportunity to practise your affirmation and reinforce the positive thought it engenders.
- Don't stop making your affirmations if difficulties arise from them. Work with the difficulty. For example, you may find yourself reacting against your chosen affirmation and experiencing negative feelings or thoughts. This indicates that the affirmations are highlighting your block to progress and are stirring up unresolved conflicts. Work with these reactions by talking things over with someone you can trust, writing in your creative or personal journal, or by meditation. You may find that simply rephrasing the affirmation makes it easier for you.

Getting Started

Here are a few suggestions to help you get started, but do remember your statement must reflect your own concerns.

- I have a basic trust that my affirmations will work.
- My efforts will be rewarded appropriately.
- My mind is constantly creating optimistic and positive thoughts.
- I was born with a limitless capacity for well-being and growth.
- I like myself and acknowledge my uniqueness.
- I am enthusiastic in everything I undertake.
- I concentrate properly upon any subject at any time.
- I am efficient in everything that I do.
- I face all problems with courage and tenacity.
- I am confident of myself in all situations and with all people.
- I complete any task that I undertake.
- I am honest with myself, and with everyone else.
- I treat all difficulties as opportunities to be creative.
- I possess an abundant supply of energy and draw upon it at will.
- I am well organized in every phase of my life.
- I have an excellent memory that is growing better and better every day.
- I read quickly and easily and understand the subject matter.
- I contact, feel, and easily show my emotions to myself and to all other people.
- I relax as deeply as I wish at any time I want.
- I am decisive in everything I do.
- I do everything now as it needs doing.

- I possess an endless supply of creativity, energy and tolerance for any work or project that I undertake.
- I am positive and prosperous in everything I do, every day.
- My universe is co-operating with me.
- Powerful tools for living successfully are mine to use.
- My talents are always with me.
- I take charge of my life.
- I take responsibility for who I am.
- I have the underlying power and creativity within me to solve any problem or situation that I may encounter.
- I feel loved every moment.
- I am healthy.
- I am happy.
- My eyes see clearly the world around me.
- I use wisdom in what I say.
- I am a spark of divine love.
- I am free to be who I am.
- I listen to my inner Self, every day.
- I am beautiful.
- I act with enthusiasm in all that I do.
- What I am doing is now moving me toward my goals.
- I believe that I can be what I want to be.
- I approach each task knowing to what greater good the task will contribute.
- I do everything mindfully.
- Do it right or do it wrong, just do it now!
- Explode inertia.
- Life is what I perceive it to be.
- I look at life as an adventure.
- I live in the now.
- I make each day count till it becomes the best day of the week.

- Criticism is useful only when it is constructive.
- I plan the future, but live in the present.
- I acknowledge my own progress.
- I reflect on who I am now and who I want to be.

Sources

Where the sources of the quotations which introduce each chapter of this book are known, they have been given. To those few authors whose identities are not known, I offer my sincere apologies for the omission, and gratitude for their wisdom. I also acknowledge the many other writers whose books are not listed below.

Books:

Appleton, William S. *Fathers And Daughters: A Father's Powerful Influence on a Woman's Life*, Macmillan, 1982

Barker, Hannah and Chalus, Elaine (Eds.) *Gender in Eighteenth Century England*, Longman, 1997

Bartley, Paula, *The Changing Role of Women, 1815–1914*, Hodder and Stoughton, 1996

Beddoe, Deirdre *Back To Home And Duty: Women between the Wars 1918–1939*, Pandora, 1980

Beer, Frances *Women and Mystical Experience in the Middle Ages*, Boydell Press, 1982

Branca, Patricia *Women in Europe since 1750*, Croom Helm, 1978

Elliot, Dyan *Spiritual Marriage: Sexual Abstinence in Medieval Wedlock*, Princeton University Press, 1993

Filbee, Marjorie *A Woman's Place; An Illustrated History of Women at Home from the Roman Villa to the Victorian Town House*, Ebury Press, 1980

Jalland, Patricia *Women, Marriage and Politics 1860–1914*, Clarendon, 1986

Jones, Vivien (Ed.) *Women in the Eighteenth Century; Constructions of Femininity*, Routledge, 1990

Laberge, Margaret Wade *Women in Medieval Life: A Small Sound of the Trumpet*, Hamilton, 1986

McLaren, Angus *Birth Control in Nineteenth-Century England*, Croom Helm, 1982

Pearsall, Judy and Trumble, Bill (Eds) *Oxford English Reference Dictionary*, 2nd edition, Oxford University Press, 1996

Rawson, Maud *Bess of Hardwick and her Circle*, Hutchinson, 1910

Reynolds, K. D. *Aristocratic Women and Political Society in Victorian Britain*, Oxford University Press, 1992

Rubinstein, David *Before the Suffragettes: Women's Emancipation in the 1890s*, Harvester, 1986

Schmitt Pantel, Pauline *A History of Women; from Ancient Goddesses to Christian Saints*, Harvard University Press, 1992

Trustram, Myna *Women of the Regiment: Marriage and the Victorian Army*, Cambridge University Press, 1984

Websites:

www.bbc.co.uk/history
www.britannica.com
www.labyrinth.org
www.nortononline.com
www.pantheon.org/mythica
www.spartacus.co.uk

Other:

Various pamphlets from National Union of Women's Suffrage Societies, Women's Social and Political Union and Liberal Women's Suffrage Group

Index

vision quest 183
Lilith 24, 25
Logos 101
love, falling into 103–104
Lytton, Constance 297

the maid 10–11, 27–32
  Brighid 18–20
  conflict within 29–30, 31–32
  dreams 29, 31–32, 108
  medieval times 27–28
  sexuality 30, 31
  spirituality 30–32
  today 28–32
Margaret I, Queen of Denmark, Norway
  and Sweden 293
Markiewicz, Constance 289
marriage, spiritual 249–250
Married Woman's Property Acts, 1870
  and 1882 273
Martineau, Harriet 285
Marx, Eleanor 285–286
Mary *see* Virgin Mary
masochism in dreams 109
mazes 57
  see also labyrinths
Mechthild of Magdeburg 251, 252
Meir, Golda 289
memories 218–220
men
  and relationship breakdown 113–114
  and women's liberation 279
  see also anima
menopause 78–82
  depression during 79–80
  diet during 79
  symptoms 78–79
menstruation 66, 154
mill workers 271–272
mine workers 270–271
mirror technique 225–226
mood swings at puberty 68
moon cycle
  and the Triple Goddess 17, 26
Moore, Henry 283
the mother 10–11, 32–34
  dreams 38–39
  historically 32–33
  sexuality 37
  today 33–34
  Virgin Mary 20–23

  see also Great Mother; menopause;
    pregnancy
mother figure 129–130
mother goddess
  universal concept of 23
  see also Great Mother
Mother Teresa of Calcutta 32, 280
motherhood 34–39
  each woman's self-assessment of 36–37
  women changed by 34–36
mothers
  and daughters 35–36
  giving up their children 37–38
multicursal 57
Murphy, Emily 286
mystics 251–253
myths 58–61
  analysing as an adult 60–61
  conflict within 58–59
  creating your own 61–63
  family myths 62–63
  identifying with characters in 60–61
  personal 61–63

negative behaviour 91
negative beliefs, overcoming 147–148,
  164–165
neopaganism 49
Nightingale, Florence 296

objectivity 240
observation, improving 238–239

Pankhurst, Christabel 298
Pankhurst, Emmeline 274, 298
Pankhurst, Sylvia 298
parents
  and children 128–134
  handing back baggage to 133–134
pay, equality of 271–272, 275
perception
  the Wise Woman 45–46
Peron, Evita 289–290
persona 104
personal freedom 46
personal undertaking 206–207
Pethick-Lawrence, Emmeline 298
post-natal depression 73, 77
power
  feminine 120, 122
  images of 51–58